A HOUSE IN GROSS DISORDER

A HOUSE
IN
GROSS DISORDER

❖❖❖

SEX, LAW,
AND THE
2ND EARL OF CASTLEHAVEN

❖❖❖

CYNTHIA B. HERRUP

NEW YORK   OXFORD

OXFORD UNIVERSITY
PRESS

M. DCCCC. LXXXX. IX

Oxford University Press

Oxford New York

Athens   Auckland   Bangkok   Bogotá   Buenos Aires   Calcutta
Cape Town   Chennai   Dar es Salaam   Delhi   Florence   Hong Kong   Istanbul
Karachi   Kuala Lumpur   Madrid   Melbourne   Mexico City   Mumbai
Nairobi   Paris   São Paulo   Singapore   Taipei   Tokyo   Toronto
Warsaw

and associated companies in
Berlin   Ibadan

Published by Oxford University Press, Inc.
198 Madison Avenue, New York, New York 10016

Oxford is a registered trademark of Oxford University Press

Library of Congress Cataloging-in-Publication Data
Herrup, Cynthia B.
A House in Gross Disorder : sex, law, and the 2nd Earl of
Castlehaven / Cynthia B. Herrup.
p.   cm.
Includes bibliographical references and index.
ISBN 0-19-512518-5
1. Castlehaven, Mervyn Touchet, Earl of, 1592?–1631—Trials,
litigation, etc.   2. Trials (Rape)—England.   3. Trials (Sodomy)—England.
4. Great Britain—History—Early Stuarts, 1603–1649—Sources.   I. Title.
KD372.C37H47   1999
345.42'02532—dc21   98-45382

1 3 5 7 9 8 6 4 2
Printed in the United States of America
on acid-free paper

CONTENTS

For JMB

ACKNOWLEDGMENTS

This book would have been impossible to write without the support and help of many people. The generosity of Duke University, the National Endowment for the Humanities, and the British Academy funded my research; the Folger Shakespeare Library and the NEH together underwrote the leave that allowed me to pull it all together. The Folger provided a wonderfully indulgent working environment for which the entire staff, and particularly reading room supervisor Betsy Walsh, have my gratitude.

I cannot individually thank the archivists at each of the more than two dozen repositories cited herein, but special mention must be made of the particular kindnesses of Anthony Malcolmson, Mary Robertson, Julie Springall, and Letitia Yeandle. For permission to cite papers in their possession, I am grateful to Lady Braye, whose manuscripts are on deposit in the Leicestershire Record Office; the Lamport Hall Trust whose manuscripts are on deposit in the Northamptonshire Record Office; the Henry E. Huntington Library; the Folger Shakespeare Library; and the James Marshall and Marie-Louise Osborn Collection, Beinecke Library, Yale University.

Sandra Bardsley, Scott Lucas, Philippe Rosenberg, and Jordan Sable have searched for answers to research questions, compiled genealogies and bibliographies, and successfully deciphered my cryptic writing, all with skill, tact, and patience.

Over the past decade, audiences at conferences, seminars, and colloquia on three continents have heard pieces of this work in progress. Their interest and their skepticism have been critical to its final shape. So, too, have been the contributions of those who shared with me their knowledge, sources, and unpublished work. I would particularly like to thank Susan Amussen, Barbara Baines, John Baker, Alastair Bellany, Ed Benson, Alan Bray, Peter Blayney, Esther Cope,

David Cressy, Richard Cust, Fran Dolan, Barbara Donagan, Elizabeth Eisenstein, Teresa Feroli, Richard Grassby, Paul Hardacre, Vanessa Harding, Barbara Harris, Clive Holmes, Lorna Hudson, Micaela Janan, Jeane Klene, Nigel Llewellyn, Scott Lucas, Dale Martin, Michael Mendle, Nancy Miller, Alan Nelson, Kristen Neuschel, Jane Ohlmeyer, Gail Kern Paster, Anabel Patterson, Linda Levy Peck, Linda Pollock, Wilf Prest, Bill Reddy, Lyndal Roper, Colleen Seguin, Susan Snyder, Alan Stewart, Christopher Thompson, Randy Trumbach, Garthine Walker, Rachel Weil, Susan Zimmerman, and Melinda Zook for their assistance. Judith Bennett, Anna Clark, Tom Cogswell, Jim Epstein, Henry Horwitz, Jean Howard, and Christopher Whittick read the penultimate version of the manuscript; their comments sharpened my arguments and my presentation. I am indebted to the gracefulness of their own work and to their support of mine. At Oxford University Press, Thomas LeBien and Susan Ferber have shown me how to produce a book that is scholarly and accessible. The errors and obscurities still remaining are my own, but there are fewer of them because of these nine readers.

In addition to my readers, Sue Porter Benson, Jan Ewald, Alice Yeager Kaplan, Temma Kaplan, and Steve Pincus shared my enthusiasm for this project. Leon Fink and Sue Levine have fed me, supported me, and made me laugh. Over the past two decades, I have come to rely upon Christopher Whittick's skill as an archivist, a reader, and a traveling companion. He and the late Margaret Whittick have saved me from more misjudgments than I can now count and taught me more things than I can now remember.

It may seem odd to dedicate to any person a story as indelicate as this one, but my retelling would not exist without Judith Bennett. She first encouraged me to explore the trial at length. Her confidence in it and in me is infectious. Together we have created a household that is the antithesis of the Earl's—safe, comfortable, and loving. This book is a partial appreciation for that gift.

ABBREVIATIONS
AND CONVENTIONS

Note: Unless stated, all books were published in London.

APC   *Acts of the Privy Council of England* (1890–1964), 46 vols.
BL   British Library, London
     BL Add. Additional Manuscripts
     BL Harl. Harleian Manuscripts
Bod.   Bodleian Library, Oxford
     Bod. Ashm. Ashmolean Manuscripts
CP   *Complete Peerage of England, Scotland, Ireland, Great Britain and the United Kingdom*, ed. G. E. C. Cokayne (1913), 13 vols.
CSPD   *Calendar of State Papers, Domestic*
CSPI   *Calendar of State Papers Relating to Ireland*
DNB   *Dictionary of National Biography*
DRO   Dorset Record Office
FSL   Folger Shakespeare Library, Washington, D. C.
HEH   Henry E. Huntington Library, San Marino, Calif.
     HEH EL Ellesmere Manuscripts
     HEH HA Hastings Manuscripts
HLRO   The House of Lords Record Office, London
HMC   Historical Manuscripts Commission Reports
LJ   *Journals of the House of Lords*
LRO   Leicestershire Record Office
PRO   Public Record Office, London
ST   *Cobbett's Complete Collection of State Trials . . .*, ed. W. Cobbett and T. B. Howell (1809–26), 33 vols.
VCH   *Victoria History of the Counties of England* (1900–present)
WRO   Wiltshire Record Office

Quotations have been modernized. Dates throughout are given in New Style, although the year has been taken to begin on 1 January.

TOUCHET FAMILY

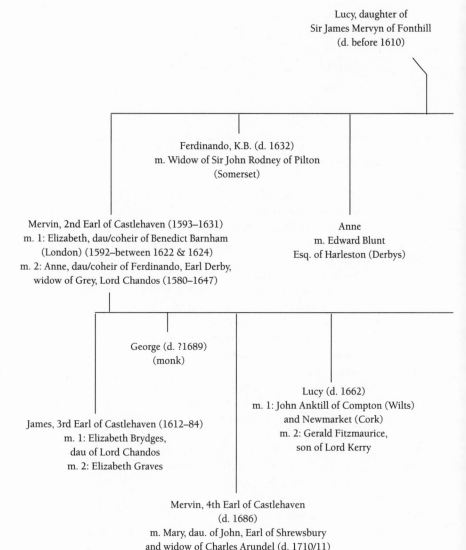

Lucy, daughter of
Sir James Mervyn of Fonthill
(d. before 1610)

Ferdinando, K.B. (d. 1632)
m. Widow of Sir John Rodney of Pilton
(Somerset)

Mervin, 2nd Earl of Castlehaven (1593–1631)
m. 1: Elizabeth, dau/coheir of Benedict Barnham
(London) (1592–between 1622 & 1624)
m. 2: Anne, dau/coheir of Ferdinando, Earl Derby,
widow of Grey, Lord Chandos (1580–1647)

Anne
m. Edward Blunt
Esq. of Harleston (Derbys)

George (d. ?1689)
(monk)

James, 3rd Earl of Castlehaven (1612–84)
m. 1: Elizabeth Brydges,
dau of Lord Chandos
m. 2: Elizabeth Graves

Lucy (d. 1662)
m. 1: John Anktill of Compton (Wilts)
and Newmarket (Cork)
m. 2: Gerald Fitzmaurice,
son of Lord Kerry

Mervin, 4th Earl of Castlehaven
(d. 1686)
m. Mary, dau. of John, Earl of Shrewsbury
and widow of Charles Arundel (d. 1710/11)

Sources: CP; PRO Prob 11; *Fasciculus Mervinensis*; Hutchens, *Dorset;*
Burke's *Extinct Peerage;* NLS Ms 2678; HA Legal Box 3 (1);
Collins Peerage by Sir Egerton Brydges, v.1 (1812).

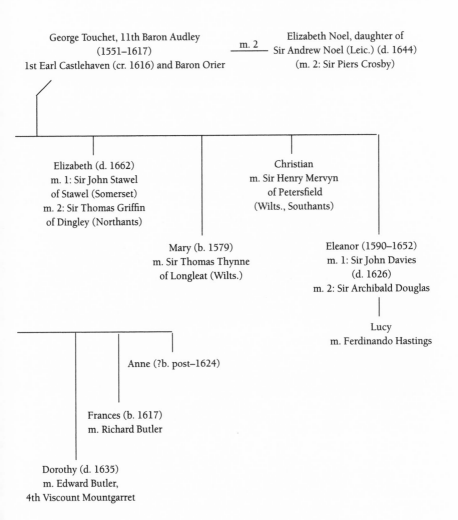

George Touchet, 11th Baron Audley
(1551–1617)
1st Earl Castlehaven (cr. 1616) and Baron Orier
—— m. 2 —— Elizabeth Noel, daughter of
Sir Andrew Noel (Leic.) (d. 1644)
(m. 2: Sir Piers Crosby)

Elizabeth (d. 1662)
m. 1: Sir John Stawel
of Stawel (Somerset)
m. 2: Sir Thomas Griffin
of Dingley (Northants)

Christian
m. Sir Henry Mervyn
of Petersfield
(Wilts., Southants)

Mary (b. 1579)
m. Sir Thomas Thynne
of Longleat (Wilts.)

Eleanor (1590–1652)
m. 1: Sir John Davies
(d. 1626)
m. 2: Sir Archibald Douglas

Lucy
m. Ferdinando Hastings

Anne (?b. post–1624)

Frances (b. 1617)
m. Richard Butler

Dorothy (d. 1635)
m. Edward Butler,
4th Viscount Mountgarret

The Castlehaven Earldom expired in 1777 with the
death of John Talbot Touchet, the 8th Earl. The Audley
Barony continues to the present via the female line.

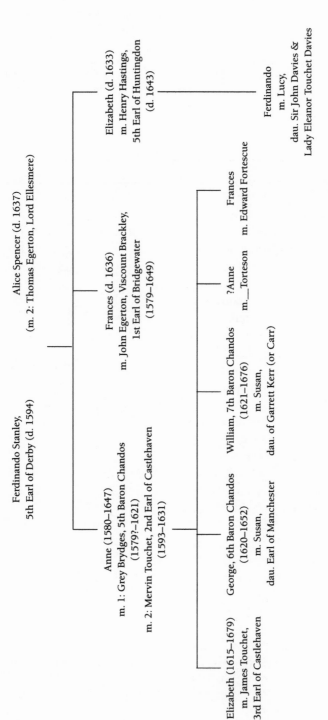

STANLEY FAMILY

Ferdinando Stanley,
5th Earl of Derby (d. 1594)

Alice Spencer (d. 1637)
(m. 2: Thomas Egerton, Lord Ellesmere)

Anne (1580–1647)
m. 1: Grey Brydges, 5th Baron Chandos
(1579?–1621)
m. 2: Mervin Touchet, 2nd Earl of Castlehaven
(1593–1631)

Frances (d. 1636)
m. John Egerton, Viscount Brackley,
1st Earl of Bridgewater
(1579–1649)

Elizabeth (d. 1633)
m. Henry Hastings,
5th Earl of Huntingdon
(d. 1643)

Elizabeth (1615–1679)
m. James Touchet,
3rd Earl of Castlehaven

George, 6th Baron Chandos
(1620–1652)
m. Susan,
dau. Earl of Manchester

William, 7th Baron Chandos
(1621–1676)
m. Susan,
dau. of Garrett Kerr (or Carr)

?Anne
m.__Torteson

Frances
m. Edward Fortescue

Ferdinando
m. Lucy,
dau. Sir John Davies &
Lady Eleanor Touchet Davies

Sources: CP; PRO Prob 11; *Fasciculus Mervinensis*; Hutchens, *Dorset*; Burke's *Extinct Peerage*; NLS Ms 2678; HA Legal Box 3
(1); *Collins Peerage* by Sir Egerton Brydges, v.1 (1812).

PREFACE

This book is about the 1631 trial of Mervin Touchet, the 2nd Earl of Castlehaven, for assisting in the rape of his own wife and for committing sodomy with his servants; it retells a vaguely familiar story with new material and new purpose. At first glance, this trial seems to speak only to the cruelty of humans to one another, and to the tragedies of unhappy families. But, in fact, the complex connections through which early modern prosecutors persuaded their listeners to condemn the Earl reflected quotidian struggles in more "normal" households over how to live within the accepted prescriptions of early modern English culture. In a world where the conventions of piety, inheritance, and patriarchal governance had greater purchase than those of individual self-expression, Castlehaven's trial spoke to fundamental questions about social organization. Sex and gender often provide the issues around which people learn about mastery and its abuse and about privileges and their obligations; what we see in Parliaments and in courts and in palaces as political behavior is typically learned in more intimate situations. The accusations here swiftly became discussions of obedience and rebellion; the trial became a test of the custodial obligations of the King as well as a constitutional struggle over the meaning of good paternal governance and good legal practice.

The following chapters examine the case from three discrete, but connected perspectives: biographical, legal, and literary. After a brief introduction, chapter 1 introduces the principals and explores the context of their involvements, stressing the striking intimacy of the trial. The defendant and accusers were related to each other. Aristocratic jurors could be expected to (and in this case did) know the men and women whom they judged. Trials such as this one were overtly tests of credit as much as they were tests of evidence; the conventions of character mattered as much or more than the conventions of the law. Many households fought over inheritance, marriage, fidelity, and favoritism; the liminality of this household lent credibility to the wilder accusations raised against any or all of its members. Castlehaven had lived a life of aggressive unimportance before 1631, and in 1631, he paid dearly for it.

Chapters 2 and 3 focus on the legal proceedings. Law is not the white noise of social confrontation; it is made as well as used in every application. These chapters are an exploration of that process—they ask what arguments each side believed would best persuade the jurors, how speakers associated acts with meanings, and why such combinations might seem both reasonable and dangerous to listeners. They assess the skill of prosecution and defense not in abstract terms, but in terms of the possibilities available within the distinctive conventions and limitations of both early modern English culture and early modern criminal law. The tropes through which prosecutors and defense worked will be familiar to anyone immersed in early modern English history. Both sides shared an understanding of the world around them; their differences were in interpretation, not in principles. The prosecution emphasized repeatedly the obligations of a head of household to teach by example the benefits of paternalism and deference. The Earl, even as he stressed what he saw as the legal anomalies that undermined the prosecution's case, also tied his situation to what it meant to be a patriarch. He presented himself as a living example of the risks faced by every head of household who governed strictly.

The King's attorneys said that Castlehaven was a man disordered in his understandings of male responsibility, genteel honor, and national identity, a danger to himself and to others. He had accepted the privileges of patriarchialism, but betrayed its duties; gloried in the status afforded to a peer, but upended the pillars of aristocratic honor; proclaimed his Englishness, but tainted it with Catholicism, Irishness, and sodomy. Charles I, the prosecutors told the peers, was relying upon the legal process to discredit such behavior. Condemning the Earl would rescue his dependents and the reputation of all patriarchs from disgrace. Castlehaven countered that he was a responsible man at the mercy of insubordinate inferiors; good governance had caused rebellion in his household. He contended that a vote for his acquittal was a vote for the integrity of the peerage and of the common law, a repudiation of social leveling and of procedural corruption. He, too, claimed that the jurors held the key to restoring harmony in home and state, but at least implicitly, he asked the jurors to reprimand the King for favoring inferiors against a nobleman. These contradictory presentations point to the unsettled meanings behind the law, to how the ideals of a regime could both prevail and fail in a single application.

Chapters 4 and 5 move from the rule-bound unreality of the law courts back to the unruliness of life. Chapter 4 looks at what happened to the story's principals after the trial. The men and women whose lives created the case were, in turn, in many ways created by it. Few of them escaped its shadow. These individual histories show how much clearer the ramifications of using the law are when we look beyond the discrete moments of trial and punishment. They reveal, too, the limits of simple historical distinctions between defendants and victims, punishment and exoneration. Chapter 5 takes a similar approach to the trial's textual remains. This case has had a resilience that belies its purported triviality. Despite often professed revulsion at its details, generations of writers have returned to the story with a voyeuristic fascination that make its characters more real than many of their more admirable contemporaries. In the 1630s the story spread both as legal text and as entertainment—in collections of manuscripts, in correspondence, and in libels. In the 1640s, a new dissemination began as the tale resurfaced in print—sometimes as a weapon for or against a King, sometimes as evidence of aristocratic decadence. In the 1650s, printed law reports began to include references to the trial's legal oddities, incorporating some and rejecting others. And the retellings have continued: in the eighteenth, nineteenth, and twentieth centuries, we can find the story of the 2nd Earl in popular amusements, historical discourses, and legal arguments.

The exceptional persistence of Castlehaven in different sorts of memories offers a rare opportunity to follow how meaning can shift and spin over time. Sodomy became the narrative's pivot in the 1690s, not the 1630s. The legal irregularities that worried commentators in the seventeenth century have become precedents in questions of spousal rights. Such changes are not random; they reflect the different needs for which the trial has been adapted. This functional malleability invites us to ask not which rendition of the trial is correct, but which was persuasive to whom, when, and why. It allows us to understand how a scandal embedded in one century has retained both its interest and its ability to shock in others.

CASTLEHAVEN REDUX

n the early 1940s, a historian of Wiltshire wrote of Mervin Touchet, the 2nd Earl of Castlehaven, that his was "a name at which the world grew pale."[1] For people interested in early modern England, Castlehaven's name, if not quite as shocking as it once was, is still very much alive. The focus of the greatest moral scandal of his day, Castlehaven has a bit part in our histories of the early Stuart age, a modest place in early modern literary studies, and a starring role in most histories of male homosexuality in England. The conventional explanation for the Earl's notoriety is simple: his story was one of the most shocking of its time. The outlines of the tale as traditionally told are these: (1) Castlehaven committed sodomy with several of his servants, he helped one of them to rape his wife the Countess and another to sleep with his adolescent daughter-in-law, and he intended to disinherit his son in deference to lowborn favorites. (2) In 1631, when his outraged heir reported this behavior, Castlehaven and two of his minions were tried, convicted, and executed for rape and sodomy. (3) Castlehaven was immoral, and/or mentally ill, and/or a victim of the prejudices of his time.

Castlehaven's history mystified and outraged contemporary observers, and has much the same impact today. Even to an age that had seen two of the favorites of James I accused of murder, Castlehaven's alleged transgressions seemed extraordinary. Castlehaven was one of the few aristocrats ever executed for sexual misbehavior; as such, his claim to a place in our historical consciousness would probably be secure. Because his trial took place in the decade before the authority of Charles I disintegrated into civil war, historians have woven his fate together with the fate of that Monarch, arguing that Castlehaven's execution illustrates both the probity of his King and a deepening aristocratic moral crisis.[2] Because Castlehaven's in-laws were important patrons of the arts, literary scholars have connected his history with John Milton's, exploring the possibility that the Earl's trial influenced the plot of Milton's only masque.[3] And because the scandal was the earliest secular English prosecution for sodomy for which we have extensive documentation, authors (particularly popular authors) interested in male homosexuality have used it to anchor their histories, seeing it as an important moment in the tortuous relationship between private individuals and the state.[4] The trial fits easily into a variety of moralizing narratives about the seventeenth century that have been popular in the twentieth century: tales of kingly prudence, aristocratic decadence, literary genius, and/or social prejudice.

Until a few years ago, I knew relatively little about the 2nd Earl of Castlehaven. I associated his name with a notoriety the origins of which seemed axiomatic. Then one day in the Public Record Office in London, while collecting information for an ongoing study of pardons in the seventeenth century, I came across two pardons, both issued late in 1631. One spared Anne, Dowager Countess of Castlehaven, of "all offenses of adulteries fornication and incontinency"; the other forgave Elizabeth, the then Countess of Castlehaven, for the same transgressions.[5] Although I knew that affluent individuals sometimes received pardons for crimes that they had committed involuntarily, I recalled only dimly that Castlehaven's case involved heterosexual as well as homosexual acts, and I did not remember anything about a second Countess.

The next day in the Institute of Historical Research, I pulled down volume 3 of *Cobbett's Complete Collection of State Trials* and read the case as reported there.[6] The Earl and two of his servants, it said, faced three indictments, each for felony. Two accusations were for sodomy; one was for rape. The alleged sodomies were between Castlehaven and a servant (Lawrence or Florence Fitzpatrick).[7] The alleged victim of the rape was Anne, the Countess of Castlehaven; the physical rapist was her footman Giles Broadway, but according to the indictment, the Earl had encouraged and assisted him. Since even assisting in a rape made one a principal, both the Earl and Giles Broadway were equally culpable before the law. The Earl's trial took place before a jury of his peers in April 1631; Broadway and Fitzpatrick faced their juries in the Court of King's Bench two months later. Eight members or former members of Castlehaven's household (including his co-defendants) testified against him. Yet the testimony, and the speeches of the King's attorneys as well as of the Earl himself, were not what I expected. Instead of focusing on rape and sodomy, they kept returning to issues of family and betrayal. There were long discussions about Castlehaven's relationship with his son and more talk of former servants (none of whom were ever indicted) than of Broadway or Fitzpatrick. There were insinuations that Castlehaven was a papist, if not an outright nonbeliever; that he was a voyeur and a whore master; that he hoped that one of his servants would adulterously impregnate the young wife of the future Earl. In contrast to what normally happened in criminal prosecutions, the trial of the alleged rapist, Broadway, took place after the trial of his alleged accessory, Castlehaven, in fact after Castlehaven's execution. In contrast to what normally occurred in the trials of aristocrats, Castlehaven refused to confess his crimes, and the verdicts against him were not unanimous (only a majority was needed to convict). The Earl made a vigorous attempt to defend himself, insisting that the case against him was legally flawed, and that he was the victim of a conspiracy by his avaricious wife and son. At his execution (in mid-May), he held to both those claims. And the dying speeches of Broadway and Fitzpatrick in July lent some support to his ideas. Intrigued by all this, I decided to write an essay exploring the disjunction in the trial between the accusations of rape and sodomy, and the persistent foregrounding of other issues, particularly issues concerning the organization of Castlehaven's household.[8]

As I began to talk about the case, I found that the story still generated considerable interest and enthusiastic questions, questions that were seldom easy to answer. What were the Earl's connections and who were the peers who condemned him? Why was such an embarrassing incident prosecuted publicly? Did the allegations against Castlehaven remind Charles I of the dissoluteness of his own father? And the first and last question always, everywhere, was Castlehaven guilty? As I searched for the answers, I discovered that, if much noticed, the trial had been relatively little studied. Scholars have used the case to show the problematic reputation of the English elite in the 1630s, but they have rarely examined the story on its own terms, and they have generally accepted the verdict without question. The scandal has been undervalued because of its peculiarity, its salaciousness, and (somewhat circularly) its apparent unimportance. Confident that a case alleging homosexual sex was about homosexual sex, scholars not primarily interested in that history have rarely looked beyond the scandal's surface. Even scholars of sexualities have begun with the assumption of Castlehaven's guilt and the belief that the case was primarily about sexual misbehavior.[9]

On the suggestion of a colleague, I wrote to every major archive in Great Britain and to the largest libraries in the United States asking for materials about the trials and their principal participants. Some archivists ignored my request, but from the ones who responded came a wealth of information. In addition to ample material in the British and the Bodleian Libraries, roughly contemporary texts of the trial and execution turned up in a wide variety of repositories: in the record offices of Wiltshire, Northamptonshire, and Lincolnshire, in the Public Record Office, in the libraries of Trinity College (Dublin) and the Inner Temple as well as in the National Libraries of Scotland, Ireland, and Wales; in the Folger Shakespeare Library and the Henry E. Huntington Library; at Harvard Law School, Yale, Chicago, and the University of Kansas. Many of these renditions include what purport to be the Earl's last letters, a confession of his faith, and an anonymously composed description of his character; some contain verses Castlehaven supposedly sent to his Countess; others append poems lampooning the Earl or his prosecution; still others boast versions of the trials of the Earl's confederates. The Bodleian has what appears to be a description of the trial by the senior justice present; the Huntington has notes apparently taken for the Countess of Castlehaven's brother-in-law. The National Library of Scotland has a copy of the survey of Castlehaven's estates drawn for the Crown after his death. The Braye manuscripts in the Leicestershire Record Office include many of the original pretrial depositions. The Record Office of the House of Lords holds documents from a hearing in the 1640s on the legitimacy of the verdict. Almost every scholarly audience to whom I have spoken about the trial has contained at least one person who generously offered up news of yet another buried reference. The deep entanglement of this trial with its surroundings is evident in the variety of records in which one finds it mentioned: genealogies, correspondence, newsletters, histories, pamphlets, drama, books of precedents, books of cases, account books, petitions, orders, writs, claims of property, and so on. I quickly moved from wondering how much information survived about the case to recognizing that more existed than I could possibly find or use.

But as I researched reasonably sure responses to many of my questions, a sound answer to the question I could always count on being asked—was he guilty?—became more rather than less elusive. I found evidence that might support the Earl's charge of procedural irregularities and of conspiracy. The case against him was technically flawed (and reexamined on those grounds within a decade). Castlehaven's heir (Lord Audley), whom scholars routinely believed to be a child in 1631, was in fact a married youth of nineteen, close to his majority, a precarious moment in the relationship between many propertied fathers and sons in early modern England. And it was Lord Audley, not his father, who was a staunch Roman Catholic. Rumors of prior adultery and even of infanticide circulated about Castlehaven's wife, the other alleged conspirator. There was evidence as well of contemporary scruples about the verdict, and the recyclings of the case—which date from 1631 into the 1990s—are better understood as functional re-imaginings than objective reportage. Each editor seems to have added, suppressed, embroidered, and, in some cases, created information to suit his or her own purposes. This is as true of *Cobbett's State Trials* as it is of penny pamphlets. None of these things persuaded me that the Earl was innocent, but they did lead me to ponder why almost no one in the past 370 years seemed to have seriously explored the possibility.

Yet the more that I explored it, the less comfortable I became. I wanted the story to have a moral, an appalling character rightfully punished or a hapless victim movingly redeemed. The ending was not clear to me, but I thought that it could be found. I was wrong. No amount of archival digging and no special slip of parchment will ever tell us whether the 2nd Earl of Castlehaven was monster or victim or both; but that is not, in fact, the historian's best question.[10] Once I asked not *if* Castlehaven was guilty, but why knowing if he was seemed so important, I realized the source of my discomfort: my audiences and I had been searching not for an ending, but for a beginning. Certainty about the verdict would offer us a way of seeing, a filter through which to assess all other information. Trials, after all, are supposed to provide closure or at least its illusion; if that closure remains elusive, later commentators are expected to provide it.

As my audiences grew impatient and sometimes even belligerent about my unwillingness to confirm Castlehaven's guilt or innocence, I came to see that this struggle was itself significant, part of an ongoing exploration into how we tell histories and the histories that we tell. A verdict is the clearest point of a trial's history, but the weakest focus for an historian. It is a filter built from artificial materials and one that obscures as much as it clarifies, reinforcing rather than upsetting the notion of a trial as a story with an objective ending.[11] Equating legal truth with actual truth hinders any meaningfully historical analysis of law enforcement because it offers answers where there should be questions. It sets the law above rather than within society and the textual remnants of the law above rather than within the demands of genre.[12] Agnosticism on the verdict allows us more easily to appreciate the mutual dependency of law and social forms. However many manuscripts are examined, observations collected, or references followed, there will always be clues outstanding—texts cited but now untraceable, references reported, but now unrecoverable—and clues left to be uncovered. Once we are willing to find a balance on less solid ground instead of trying to avoid it, we can better appreciate the multiple, but not infinite, influences that may have shaped a verdict; more freely explore contemporary understandings of terms such as "criminal" and "guilt" and "sodomite"; and see the enforcement of the law for what it is— a forum of cultural interaction. Law is a cultural dialect; in seventeenth-century England, it was, along with religion, the most ubiquitous and influential dialect.

So, if you have picked up this book to discover a whodunit, you might want to put it back down. The story of this trial is not recoverable; many of the stories about the trial, however, are. I emphatically do not want to turn a sexy movie of the week into a dry-as-dust academic monograph, but neither do I believe that the plot or the sexiness should be all that we can see. We should also see cultural presumptions and legal priorities, social concerns and forms of narrative, contingency and abuse and mischance and commercialism. And we should see strangeness. Castlehaven's case in many ways seems eerily familiar, as if it might appear tomorrow in the pages of the *Sun* or the *National Enquirer.* Like more modern scandals, this one rips through veils of privacy and privilege, leaving a haughty and rich family subjected to public scrutiny and ridicule. While many early modern accusations—for witchcraft, heresy, dueling—would seem exotic and unfamiliar today, the formal accusations leveled against Castlehaven—rape and sodomy—are live social issues for us. The case so fits our own preoccupations that colleagues have assured me (erroneously as far as I have been able to discover) that they have seen it retold on the BBC and in a Derek Jarman film. Moreover, the proceeding itself seems comfortably recognizable; even in a trial adapted for the special occasion of trying an aristocrat, there were indictments and verdicts, jurors and judges, prosecutors and witnesses.

Yet the similarities are deceptive, an artful facade of constancy that obscures the distance between ourselves and the past. Despite its continued resonance, the story is firmly grounded in the politics, law, and society of another place and time. Despite its superficial constancy, law draws its meaning from contemporary ideologies, not transhistorical categorizations. In early modern England, God, not the state, was the acknowledged power and the alleged presence behind the sovereign and the courts. The household rather than the individual was the bedrock of civilized organization. Criminal law aimed at exemplary rather than comprehensive justice. Few rules excluded evidence; jurors with prior knowledge of the defendant were welcomed rather than avoided. Lawyer's language struggled shakily against more popular vernaculars. Defendants usually had no right to counsel, no ability to call sworn witnesses, and no mechanism for appeal. Just where we feel most at home, then—in a visibly familiar legal landscape that claims and often seems to transcend both time and space, in an aristocratic scandal apparently about sexual adventurism—we need to feel like strangers.

The grammar of the law is as critical to understanding the content of a trial as are literary conventions to the understanding of literary texts or anatomical beliefs to an understanding of medical diagnoses. A trial was not and is not an occasion on which anything can happen or anything can be said and recorded; it was and is an occasion shaped by specific regulations. Long before the establishment of modern rules of evidence and procedure in the eighteenth century, informal conventions determined who appeared at a trial, what constituted legitimate testimony, and what defined legal culpability. The rules behind trial documents helped to determine their content, and, therefore, the story of the rules is integral to any story of any prosecution.

Authoritative speculation is the lifeblood of historians, the rationale for our claim to profession, but I have tried in the pages below to use that authority to do something different from that which is more commonly done. I have tried to retell a fascinating story with a greater richness than it has heretofore been told, but also to inspire a self-consciousness about our sources that too often we repress. I have attempted here to explain the verdict, not to test it; to contemplate the impact of a narrative, rather than surrender to it; to emphasize inconsistencies over time, instead of trying to reconcile them. I have tried to understand what the story meant in its time, without disclaiming its ability to speak to ours. Courts of law are places in which people win and lose—their fortunes, their reputations, and their lives—but they are also stages. This case offers a compelling story of sex, privilege, corruption, and revenge, and in each of those realms, it also offers a story about social tensions and the misappropriation of authority.

CHAPTER 1

A HOUSEHOLD KEPT UNTO ITSELF

othing remains of the mansion at Fonthill Gifford in which the Castlehaven household lived; even the church in which they worshiped is now gone.[1] When Castlehaven took possession of it in 1620, his maternal relatives had lived at Fonthill Gifford for almost seventy years; the manor itself dated from the eleventh century. The mansion stood at the heart of an estate of more than two thousand acres. Thick woodlands, gentle rises, and pacific glens surrounded it. Even the name suggested lushness: font hill referred to the springs that flowed abundantly from the sides of local hills. Like most great houses, Fonthill Gifford was built to be an embodiment of nobleness as well as the core of a working estate. The head of the household sat on the commission of the peace and appointed the local vicar. The mansion was the symbolic center of the parish, a place of business and of pleasure, of many adults, children, and servants, a magnet for some and a departure point for others. Shortly after Castlehaven brought his 2nd Countess to the house for the first time, a fire broke out, permanently damaging one wing of the mansion. In hindsight, the fire appeared to be an omen. While to the casual observer, Fonthill Gifford in the 1620s may have seemed unexceptional, in 1630, the gross disarray of the household became public. That year, grievous accusations would be made by the heir to the estate against his father, the lady of the estate against her husband, and the menials of the estate against their master. Within six

months following, the 2nd Earl of Castlehaven would be tried for rape and sodomy, convicted, and beheaded upon Tower Hill.[2]

We need some understanding of the biographies of the principals if we are even to begin to decipher this series of events because personal detail was the foundation of the prosecution's case against the Earl. The King's officials set the Earl's alleged perfidy against seemingly objective aristocratic qualities: nobility, Englishness, and loyalty to Protestantism. Arguments about what Castlehaven might have done started from and ultimately returned to a sense of who Castlehaven and his accusers were. The attorneys molded the defendant for their listeners through a selective recitation of his past. Castlehaven did the same; he created his accusers just as their agents had created him. Both creations, of course, were partial; they were the portrayals that their authors desired. But to be convincing, the word pictures had to be plausible. However good the evidence, however powerful the language, the images had to conform with those available from other sources.

The Touchets were a very old family—they traced their origins to Normandy, and at least one Touchet apparently arrived in England with the Conqueror. Yet until the seventeenth century, longevity without significant fortune was the family's principal distinction. The Audley barony came to them through a shrewd marriage in the early fifteenth century; they accrued land piecemeal through sales and legacies rather than through large purchases or rewards. Even as Barons, they were but poor cousins to the greater aristocracy. In the early sixteenth century, their Staffordshire estate, Heleigh, had "no house but an old ruinous castle"; at their Somerset manor, Stowey, the castle had been abandoned; at their Dorset property, Stalbridge, no manor house existed at all. Castlehaven's father, George Touchet, the 11th Baron Audley (and eventually the 1st Earl of Castlehaven), dedicated himself to ending that obscurity.[3]

George Touchet discovered, as did many other Elizabethans, that the surest path to wealth and status was a combination of service, supplication, and judicious marriage. Primarily a soldier, Touchet served the Queen and then King James I on the Continent and in Ireland. He commanded eight companies against the rebel Irish in 1599, and was wounded in the climactic English victory at Kinsale.

Touchet, like many of his colleagues, found James I to be a far more generous master than his predecessor; in 1605 the King granted Touchet Irish lands worth £100 per annum "in consideration of his good service to the late Queen." When the final defeat of the Earls of Tyrone and Tyrconnell in 1607 brought the King vast confiscated acreage in Ulster, Touchet and his sons received slightly more than half of the land on offer in County Tyrone as well as other scattered properties. Contemporary estimates set this grant at roughly eleven thousand acres, but the English were famously ignorant about Irish properties; modern experts assess the grant to have included more than two hundred thousand acres.[4] By 1612, Touchet had cast his lot firmly with Ireland. He sold or transferred his English properties; became a member of the Irish Privy Council; was summoned to the Irish House of Lords; and just three months before his death in 1617, was created an Irish Earl. He took his title from the place where the Spanish had landed their troops before the confrontation at Kinsale. It was Castlehaven, a small cove in County Cork.[5]

Disappointment with his English fortunes undoubtedly had some influence on Touchet's choice of residence. In the late 1570s or early 1580s, he had married Lucy Mervyn, the only child of Sir James Mervyn, perhaps the most prominent gentleman in Wiltshire and the owner of Fonthill Gifford. Sir James was devoted to his daughter, but was also determined that his estate remain associated with the Mervyn name. So although the Touchet/Mervyn marriage was exceptional for both its longevity and its fecundity, the couple never possessed Fonthill Gifford. Sir James instead adopted the son of a cousin, in effect begetting his own male heir. He betrothed that heir to one of his granddaughters, but to his daughter Lucy and her husband, Sir James left only the life use of his lesser properties. He bequeathed the reversion of these permanently to their heir, his "honored and well-beloved grandchild," Mervin Touchet, born in 1593.[6]

George Touchet's marriage assured the county grandeur of his family but little property; the two marriages of his heir, the 2nd Earl of Castlehaven, provided wealth as well as close ties to the City and royal court. Castlehaven's first marriage allied him with one of London's greatest fortunes; the second linked him with many of England's most prominent families. Around the same time that his father drew ever closer to permanent residence in Ireland, Castlehaven married Elizabeth Barnham, eldest of the four co-heirs of Benedict Barnham, a Master Draper who served London as alderman, sheriff, and member of Parliament. In early Stuart society, a city/noble marriage was still a "distinct mesalliance," but for the heir of the relatively impoverished Touchets such a match had obvious advantages. Elizabeth Barnham's inheritance included properties in Middlesex, Essex, Hampshire, and Kent as well as in London and its suburbs; she also received a portion of close to £2,250, an amount roughly equal to what one might expect for the daughter of a peer. If the marriage between Castlehaven and his 1st Countess was rancorous, no trace of that rancor has survived. They had six children who survived to adulthood, and a growing fortune. They held the Barnham properties, the estates in Somerset and Dorset that Castlehaven's father had rejected, and eventually Touchet's Irish lands and title. In 1620, despite the hopes of now-deceased Sir James, his appointed heir sold the couple Fonthill Gifford for £25,000. The estate embodied the family's claim to regional longevity and rising status.[7]

Elizabeth Barnham Touchet died sometime after October 1622. In 1624, the recently widowed Castlehaven remarried, this time wedding Anne Stanley Brydges, the recent widow of the 5th Baron Chandos. Lady Chandos was also an heiress, the eldest of the three daughters of Ferdinando Stanley, the 5th Earl of Derby. Derby was the sovereign ruler of the Isle of Man and held properties in almost half of England's shires. In addition to more routine aristocratic pastimes, he sponsored a company of actors, befriended playwrights, and even wrote poetry himself. He was lauded as "an apotheosis of the perfect country nobleman." When Derby died in 1594, his eldest daughter inherited the strongest English claim to the succession in addition to her portion of his lands and goods. Moreover, the 5th Earl's widow, Alice Spencer Stanley, was a force in her own right. For close to four decades, she was a redoubtable influence in the arts and in politics. Edmund Spenser, John Donne, and John Milton sang her praises in print. The Lord Chancellor became her second husband, the Earls of Huntingdon and Bridgewater her sons-in-law. Among her confidantes were several of the most important men at court.[8]

No one could doubt that the family of Lady Chandos was more

eminent than was Castlehaven's, but in 1624 she was not necessarily more prosperous. An extended battle over the 5th Earl's will had set the Stanley daughters against the 6th Earl (their uncle), and left both families with diminished resources. Life at the Chandos seat of Sudeley Castle, Gloucestershire, had been splendid enough that Lord Chandos had become known as the "king of the Cotswolds," but the Dowager Countess of Derby considered her daughter to be a spendthrift. When Lord Chandos died unexpectedly in 1621, he left his widow with four small children, and a less than princely income of £800 per year.[9] Castlehaven had grand estates, but little reputation; Lady Chandos little wealth, but considerable grandeur. Castlehaven's brother-in-law, Sir John Davies, was a long-standing client of the Lord Chancellor, and in 1623 Castlehaven's niece married Lady Chandos's nephew. Whatever their personal relationship became, in 1624 a second wedding between members of these two families seemed likely to confirm and augment the position of both; together they could claim ancient lineage, extensive property, and court connections.

THE HOUSEHOLD AT FONTHILL GIFFORD

An intricate hierarchy of gender, age, and status designed to inculcate obedience and self-discipline structured life within most genteel households in early modern England. The greatest of these households encompassed hundreds of people, but even a relatively minor aristocrat such as Castlehaven oversaw dozens of dependents. This involved more than simply administrative organization. The responsibility of a head of household encompassed the spiritual and civic as well as the economic well-being of every person in his care. Heads of household were expected to instruct their inferiors as well as to protect them. Superiors were to guide and to discipline their charges, but most important, to teach them by example. "As every man's house is his castle," explained the moralist Richard Braithwait, "so is his family a private commonwealth, wherein if due government be not observed, nothing but confusion is to be expected." A great house such as Fonthill was conceptualized as a public place, a private commonwealth that could teach a public lesson, a readable miniature to both teach and display the rudiments of order.[10]

Maintaining a well-ordered household (like maintaining a well-ordered society) could be a considerable challenge. At the heart of aristocratic households was a contradiction: they were intended as models of successful cooperation, but their essence was ambition. Families maintained them to display the power of their lineages; servants were drawn to them to find patrons; children and parents used them as platforms from which to arrange advantageous marriages and employment. Affection might soften, but it did not preclude, intense disagreements over favoritism toward servants, the choice of marital partners, and the disposition of property. Because the children of the elite often lived away from home from an early age—boarding at school, with future in-laws or with other relatives—relationships between masters or mistresses and servants, albeit temporary, could be more continuous, more dependent, and more intimate than those between parents and their offspring. Castlehaven and his 2nd Countess, for example, had eleven children between them, but in the late 1620s only two, Lord Audley and Elizabeth, the eldest daughter of Lady Chandos, lived at Fonthill Gifford. The three youngest Touchet children were at school in Salisbury, the three eldest girls were in Ireland, and the other Brydges children were with their maternal grandmother. In contrast, we can identify close to twenty servants who were in residence more regularly than these offspring. Several of the servants were youths who grew up in the shadow of properties held by either the Touchets or the Brydges, and they came to Fonthill intending to improve their fortunes.[11]

The 2nd Earl of Castlehaven was not a significant presence in the public life of either the nation or the locality. He was never a courtier, attended Parliaments only sporadically, and took no significant part in the governance of the shires where he held property.[12] Recognition of status apparently concerned him more than the rewards and obligations of public service. Castlehaven's father had refused to sit in the Irish Parliament unless he was given precedence over all Irish Barons; Castlehaven, when just an English Baron's son, had left Dublin rather than cede rank to the members of the Irish Privy Council. The Touchets (father and son) participated in coronations and investitures, but they seem to have had little interest either in the opportunities of the court and the capital or in the obligations of local governance and generosity. Castlehaven said little when he attended Parliaments. Like many other peers, he and his father were honorific rather than active justices of the peace, but in contrast to most peers, they had relatively little impact even in their home parishes. It was said that in Ireland Touchet did little to care for the buildings of either his family or his lessees and that he "love[d] not hospitality." Castlehaven was rarely in Ireland, and he raised the rents and reduced the size of the holdings of his father's tenants there. According to Castlehaven's steward, the Earl, after his second marriage, kept to himself, "drinking of wine and tobacco and hot waters." Whether from lack of ability, or lack of desire, or lack of resources, the roots that the Touchets set down in Ireland, London, and the West Country were all relatively shallow.[13]

Castlehaven's obscurity was also to weaken his ability to exonerate himself in 1631 because the superficial details of his personal history touched upon two sites of ongoing tension within the English polity: religion and nationality. In early Stuart England, there were few firmer prejudices than those against Catholics and the Irish. Like most prejudices, these were impervious to exceptions; one might live unremarkably beside a Catholic or an Irish neighbor until some discord (direct or indirect) collapsed individuals into categories. However comfortable specific relationships were, they detracted little from belief in the "known" dangers of The Catholics or The Irish. Castlehaven and his first wife flirted with Catholicism at least briefly after their move to Fonthill Gifford, but by the time of his second marriage, the Earl seems to have been at least outwardly conforming to the Church of England. The House of Commons included Castlehaven in the lists of Catholics they compiled in 1624 and again in 1626, but he took the Oath of Allegiance with no apparent qualms after the first accusation, and publicly insisted upon his conformity after the second.[14]

Like many aristocratic families, Castlehaven's had an ambiguous and hence easily suspected confessional history. Castlehaven's only brother was a Catholic; so were his children. Among his nearest neighbors in Wiltshire was the openly and avidly Catholic Lord Arundel of Wardour.[15] Not being a Catholic and not being suspected of being a Catholic, however, are two different things, and the difference exposes the dilemma of the Earl's position. Given the common Protestant understanding of Catholic duplicity, it was no easy matter to disavow an interest in Catholicism convincingly, and Castlehaven's openly Catholic relatives and lack of presence made it still harder. At his trial, prosecutors alleged that Castlehaven was religiously capricious, not a papist, but rumors that he adhered to Rome were so persistent that in the week before he was beheaded, he felt compelled to issue a confession of his resolute belief in the tenets of the Church of England. The position in which Castlehaven found himself was somewhat circular—he may have been marginal in part because he was believed to be a Catholic, but he was also believed to be a Catholic in part because he was already marginal.

When the English considered the nightmare that Catholic domination would present, their favorite examples were Spain and Ireland. The Spanish were the more important threat, but the Irish were nearer, and the long entanglement of England and Ireland made its threat seem that much greater. For many Englishmen and women, the Irish embodied the anarchic, traitorous, and infectious possibilities of the old faith. To English eyes, the Irish could properly order neither their households nor their governments. Their alleged savagery and the alleged savagery of popery were complementary. The English dismissed the Irish as barbaric and immoral at the same time that they portrayed them as boundlessly seductive. Writings on settlement contained repeated warnings against "going native"; English administrators lamented the intransigence of this problem. Generation after generation of English (and Scottish) settlers, it was said, married Irish women, converted to Catholicism, and fell into Irish customs of dress, morals, and politics. Such conversions mocked the very power of the "civilized" ideals that the settlers had been sent to Ireland to impose.[16]

Castlehaven was no more an Irishman than he was a Wiltshire man, but once again, what he was mattered less than what he could be made to seem. His family's embrace of Ireland was a means through which the King's attorneys might encourage people to question the Earl's loyalties. The Touchets traced their history as land-holders in Ireland back to the thirteenth century. Castlehaven's father and brother preferred Ireland to England. The Earl's eldest daughter lived in Cork; his second eldest with her Irish husband in Kilkenny. One of the Earl's early favorites was Irish, as was the foot-man with whom Castlehaven allegedly committed sodomy.[17] This was an English trial of an English peer for crimes allegedly committed in England, but Irishness, like Catholicism, seeped in around the edges. Castlehaven had an Irish earldom, Irish properties, Irish relatives, and Irish servants. In truth, Castlehaven's ties to any particular religion or cultural identity seem to have been tenuous. But assertive obscurity could have juridical implications. For many early modern English Protestants, Catholicism and Irishness were the negatives against which they defined their own integrity. The negative associations were there to be exploited, and the history of the Earl's life made them difficult, perhaps impossible, to contravene.

To the early modern English, the family and its head could be con-flated to a single entity: Castlehaven was his household. In the test of character that his trial became, that subsumption was even clearer: Castlehaven's credibility was a critical determination of his crimi-nality. Because in early modern England the head of a household was, in a sense, its only public adult, observers in the seventeenth cen-tury would have been less interested than are modern audiences in the trial's other participants. Even so, contemporaries would have known much more than we can now discover; an irremediable imbalance exists between the documentary remains of even this Earl and what can be found about his dependents. Their profiles remain patchy, filtered through testimony linked to the scandal, offering mere dots that must be connected by lines of educated speculation.

Castlehaven's initial accuser was his heir, Lord Audley. In 1631, Audley was an eager nineteen-year-old—avidly Catholic, unhappy in his three-year-old marriage, and anxious about his inheritance. His fifteen-year-old wife was his stepsister Elizabeth Brydges, about whose early life we know next to nothing. The wedding of stepsib-lings was a common way to consolidate alliances between great families, but it quickly became apparent that this couple loathed each other. Within a year of their marriage, Audley had left Fonthill. His wife, according to Castlehaven, wanted a divorce. Castlehaven claimed that he counseled patience, but either with his help or with his tacit consent (and perhaps that of her mother), Lady Audley was soon having a sexual relationship (which may or may not have been consensual) with the Earl's former favorite, Henry Skipwith. Before this point, the only evidence of tension between Audley and his father had concerned religion; an earlier betrothal (to a daughter of the Earl of Cork) had foundered over Audley's steadfast Catholicism. Now, Castlehaven's indulgence of Skipwith infuriated Audley. He maintained that the Earl refused to banish Skipwith from Fonthill, that Castlehaven encouraged the affair between Skipwith and Lady Audley, and that he even rewarded Skipwith's presumption with goods and property. Audley believed that Castlehaven hoped to make Skipwith his heir. The Earl, Skipwith later testified, was only too happy to make his son "look like a fool or like a simple fellow."[18]

However scandalous the Earl's treatment of his son and daughter-in-law might have been, in 1631 the most important voice against him would be not theirs, but his wife's. She was older, grander, and allegedly the victim of far worse crimes. The Earl and Countess of Castlehaven seem to have got on no better than did their children. Her past accustomed her to a world of luxury and access, to tournaments and masques and dramas, none of which seem to have appealed to Castlehaven. She was a dozen years her husband's senior and much his social better; their union had brought her neither great splendor nor great prominence. She later claimed that from the first week of their marriage, Castlehaven had shunned her in favor of prostitutes and male servants. Though several members of the household (including Lady Audley) believed that she was promiscuous and even murderous, the Countess steadfastly described her marriage as a war over her honor. Castlehaven, she said, humiliated her with lewd words and lewd suggestions, and tried to pair her with various of his favorites. Rape, she explained, was the price of her resistance.[19]

The intimacy of servants with their masters' families offered exceptional opportunities for both legitimate and illicit alliances, patronage, and frustrations. John Anktill, for example, was the younger son of "decayed" genteel stock from Dorsetshire. He came to Fonthill as Castlehaven's page, progressed to managing some of the estates, and, in 1621, represented the family interest as a member of Parliament. Allegedly without the Earl's consent, he married Castlehaven's eldest daughter. The rise of Henry Skipwith was even more dramatic. Born to a father of "no set occupation" and a mother who distilled "hot waters," within a few years of his arrival at Fonthill he sat at the Earl's table and was called "Mister." Castlehaven said that he considered Skipwith more a "companion" than a servant and lavished him with gifts even before Skipwith began his affair with Lady Audley. Giles Broadway, on his way to a life at sea, arrived at Fonthill, heard Skipwith's story of success, and decided to stay. Broadway later claimed that Castlehaven had convinced him that a relationship with the Countess could be his path to fortune.[20] But the mutual dependence of servants and masters provided endless occasions for jealousy and grumbling and revenge as well. Castlehaven said that all the servants who testified against him were men whom he had dismissed for disobedience. Skipwith admitted that there had been tension between Anktill and himself, complaining as well that his wife had been slighted by the Earl. Florence Fitzpatrick confessed to "a little malice" toward both the Earl and Skipwith. Giles Broadway reserved his animosity for the Countess, whom he admitted "he hated of all women living."[21]

The tensions at Fonthill in the late 1620s were extraordinary; if one believes the later evidence, this was a house in which neither spouses, nor parents and children, nor servants and masters, nor servants among themselves saw eye to eye. Yet the strains behind such tensions were unexceptional. Particularly in a society where custom and law made it virtually impossible for aristocratic families to separate, the distresses revealed here were fairly common. However unique their expression in this case, frustration between spouses and impatience between generations were certainly not unusual. That jealousy, lust, and rebelliousness existed at Fonthill would have shocked no one; that the head of the household allegedly reveled in rather than restrained such passions should have shocked everyone. Women, children, and men of inferior position were believed to be innately susceptible to emotion and distraction; this was why male heads of households needed unequivocal authority. It was necessary in order to constrain subordinates from their "natural" vulnerabilities; to allow heads of household to act as bulwarks against the excesses of humanity's post-Fall vulnerability to corruption. Fonthill may have been superficially like other aristocratic households, but if the stories told about life within its grounds were true, then it was rotting from within.

THE VIEW FROM WHITEHALL

Perhaps no King in England's history was less likely to be sympathetic to Castlehaven's situation than King Charles I. He was the most conventionally familial of Monarchs, publicly devoted to his wife and children, with no sign of the sexual enthusiasm of his father or his sons. His children seemed relatively free of familial intrigues and jealousies. He seems to have admired his father intellectually, but temperamentally they were near opposites. Whatever the strengths of James I as a King, decorousness was not among them. The Jacobean court had contained Scots notorious for their greed, and courtiers notorious for their drunkenness, adultery, and corruption. Rumors of promiscuity, incest, and even murder touched both sexes. The late King had done little to inspire dignity; he was unkempt, emotional, and, frequently, as concerned with hunting as with governing. He was famously captive to his favorites, his relationship with his Queen was distant, and he clearly preferred his minions to his natal family. Through lavish gifts and advantageous marriages, James I figuratively and then literally ennobled the men closest to him. Robert Carr (later Earl of Somerset) and then George Villiers (later Duke of Buckingham) governed access to the King, handled his business, and controlled his patronage. He called them his sons and his spouses, and people wondered openly if the attachments were merely maudlin or actively sexual. An admittedly unfriendly source in the 1650s remembered how these "golden calves . . . were daily interposed between him and the subject," and how they allegedly cost England more than Elizabeth I had spent together in all her wars.[22]

For Charles I, who was determined that his court would be as ceremonious and upright as his father's had been raucous and incorrigible, Castlehaven was not only a bad exemplar, but also an unwelcome reminder of the weaknesses of the King's own father. The household at Fonthill recalled (at least superficially) many of the old King's excesses. Here was another husband estranged from his wife, and more underlings taking advantage of a smitten master. Here, too, was a household putrid with sexual impropriety and drunken excess, controlled not by its proper head, but by greedy foreigners and upstarts.

Such reminders were particularly offensive to the King because he believed deeply in the power of personal example. Lacking any talent or interest for the personal appearances that marked the Tudor style of ruling, Charles I wanted to rule through representation. In the regulation of his court, in the entertainments that he favored, in his public references to his own relationships, Charles hoped to show how a realm of happiness and order rested upon families of happiness and order. He considered kingship as a species of domestic stewardship and understood the keys to that stewardship to be piety, order, and obedience to hierarchy. He took it as his personal responsibility to be the public conscience (albeit conscience as he, not necessarily as his people, might define it).[23]

The years immediately preceding 1631 had put this philosophy under considerable strain. Lawsuits were still pending from the King's attempt to collect a forced loan in 1626. The last two sessions of Parliament (in 1628 and 1629) had been fractious. Since then, there had been deeply wounding arguments over religion, foreign policy, and constitutional prerogatives, and while some of them had been quieted, none of them had been settled. Skirmishes broke out over theology, liturgy, and conformity. Charles had first agreed to and then renounced the Petition of Right. Against its strictures, he continued to collect taxes on authority of precedent rather than specific parliamentary sanction, to impress men into armed service, and to quarter them on unwilling residents. He had imprisoned several prominent members of the last Parliament, setting off a judicial battle over parliamentary privilege. Ongoing disagreements festered over the penal laws, foreign policy, finance, and what many saw as the King's unwillingness to rely on proper councilors. The assassination of the Duke of Buckingham in 1629 enraged and frightened Charles; the raucous opposition to Buckingham before his death and the celebrations following it reinforced the King's convictions about the fragility of order. Persistent rumors circulated that Charles would never call another Parliament.[24]

Although Castlehaven's behavior may have reminded Charles I of his late father, disturbing parallels could also be drawn between the Earl's understanding of patriarchal authority and the King's. The Earl justified himself, as did the King, through an appeal to order, arguing that he had organized his household as best he could given the unruliness of those beneath him. Castlehaven and Charles I both attributed many of their troubles to undue license taken by inferiors; each saw themselves as a victim of a misperception of the right relationship between superiors and subordinates. The early 1630s were a time when it was particularly important that both the King's commitment to conscience and the power of his personal example be seen to be effective.

ANNUS HORRENDUS

The Earl, too, would have understood his position to be an amalgam of his past and present, albeit with a different emphasis. In addition to stressing the unreliability of unruly dependents, paramount in his story would have been a series of recent encounters between his family and the Crown, encounters that had made the King's distaste for the Touchets unmistakable. To a man who believed himself wrongfully accused, as Castlehaven did, that dislike seemed fatal. It encouraged the discontent of his son, wife, and former servants. It predisposed others to distrust him. It left him vulnerable to those who might hope to appropriate his property. A sense of persecution could have easily encouraged the Earl's claim that he was the victim of a conspiracy.

The year 1630 began with the imprisonment of Castlehaven's recusant brother, Sir Ferdinando. In February, port officers at Dover arrested him traveling with foreign servants, in disguise and under a false name. The commander of Dover Castle considered the group likely to be "practical enemies to this church and state." Although never charged with a specific crime, Sir Ferdinando was imprisoned until late April; he claimed that the experience permanently destroyed his health. In May, Castlehaven's youngest sister, the

Protestant prophet Lady Eleanor Touchet Davies Douglas, found herself called before the Privy Council. Lady Eleanor had been a prominent and eventually troublesome presence at Whitehall since the late
1620s. She had established her prophetic authority there by making
specific, often eerily accurate predictions, beginning with a premo-
nition of her first husband's death. She outraged Charles I when she
correctly foretold the deaths of, among others, the Duke of Buckingham and an infant prince. By the spring of 1630, she was also deep
into an escalating property dispute with her daughter's in-laws,
none other than the Stanleys. The disagreement seems to have
turned violent, and by the end of the year, the King had banned Lady
Eleanor from his court.[25]

Property was the primary issue in the next blow against the family. Castlehaven's stepmother had married a minor courtier named
Sir Piers Crosby; her jointure was the Touchet land in County
Tyrone. The Duke of Buckingham thought highly of Sir Piers; the
knight traded on that and minor military successes to become a gentleman of the Privy Chamber in England and an Irish privy councilor. Richer rewards were to follow, at the expense of the Touchets.
Exploiting the fact that like many other landholders in Ulster, neither Castlehaven nor his father had fulfilled the original Articles of
Plantation, in 1628, Crosby asked the King to order an investigation
of the Earl's properties in Armagh as well as in Tyrone. Few planters
had accomplished what the rules intended, the replacement of
"unruly" Irish tenants with allegedly more industrious English and
Scottish leaseholders; Castlehaven was no exception. In September
1630, Charles I granted Crosby full custody of the jointure property
as well as of all the Touchet manors in Armagh. The Touchets still
held properties throughout the south, but at one stroke, they had lost
their largest and most prestigious holdings.[26] Castlehaven may not
have been very fond of Ireland, but this was still a shocking reduction in the size of his estate.

Recent history, then, supported at least two very different explanations for the charges that surfaced in the fall of 1630. On the one
hand, Fonthill Gifford was riven with domestic fractiousness, two
of Castlehaven's five siblings had been cited as publicly disruptive,
and the Earl had done little to curb the "natural" disruptiveness
of his Irish tenants; if one wanted evidence beyond the Earl's own

person for a propensity to misbehavior, this provided it.[27] On the other hand, spring had seen Castlehaven's brother suspected of treason; the summer his sister displaced from the court; and the fall himself dispossessed of his properties in Ulster. To the Earl and anyone sympathetic to him, the new accusations appeared preternaturally convenient. Lord Audley, Piers Crosby, and presumably many others stood to profit if Castlehaven died a felon and his estate fell to the Crown.

The exact impact of personality on legal decisions is irrecoverable; the mix of character and style that governed such interactions was ephemeral as well as individual. But in a legal structure where prior experience with, and preconceived views of, defendants were valuable parts of the evidentiary process, biographical impressions were influential. Castlehaven was a peer who stood apart from many of the conventions of the peerage: he had no ancient seat, no friends at court, no political involvement. His siblings were refractory; his subordinates dissatisfied; his spouse's relations distrustful. He was associated with the bugbears of both Catholicism and Irishness. Since neither as an individual nor as a nobleman had he demonstrated unblemished honor, the accusations against Castlehaven seemed far from preposterous. His reputation did not condemn him, but had it been otherwise, it might have helped to save him. Had Castlehaven been someone different, the self-interest of his son and others, the multifaceted tensions between the Touchets and the Stanleys, and the strained relations between the Touchets and the Crown might have given his contemporaries more pause.

In a case where no witness was disinterested, and where divergent testimonies offered little common ground, reputation was a logical means to mark the line between the credible and the incredible. The Earl's adamant denial of the allegations against him, whether it was sincere or merely tactical, focused the proceedings exactly on this demarcation. The public face of the Touchets was an unfortunate mixture of detachment, arrogance, irresponsibility, and ambition. As a private man, the Earl seemed simply unremarkable, but once accused of public crimes, that mediocrity seemed ominous. In 1631, the 2nd Earl of Castlehaven was not so much abandoned as revealed to be the outsider that he had always been.

CHAPTER 2

A DEBAUCHED SON
OF A NOBLE FAMILY

n Monday," John Pory wrote to Sir Thomas
Puckering on 21 April 1631, "the Sheriff of Lon-
don began to build scaffolds in Westminster
Hall against Monday next, for the trial of the Earl
of Castlehaven, there being twenty-seven lords
summoned by writs to be his judges (whereof all
the lords of the Privy Council except the Earls
of Exeter and Bridgewater, are part), and my Lord Keeper to sit Lord
High Steward for the day. His sentence, as I am told by an active
Justice of the Peace, is like to undergo some difficult questions of
the law."[1]

News traveled fast and far in early-seventeenth-century England;
in addition to information conveyed in person and through private
correspondence, a network of newswriters kept patrons in the coun-
tryside informed of international and domestic politics, court gossip, and legal affairs. By the spring of 1631, rumors had been circulating about Castlehaven's alleged offenses for at least six months,
and Pory's comments capture the anticipation. They also suggest an
awareness that this would be no simple prosecution, that the allegations against the Earl might encounter legal difficulties or even outright resistance.[2] Pory's expectations reflected the novelty of the trial
as well as its particulars; no English peer had been tried for felony
in a generation. No peer in memory had been tried for rape or
sodomy. And while prosecutions for homicide or assault involving

members of the same household were not uncommon, no previous criminal trial had exposed such thorough and ongoing familial dysfunction.[3]

RAPE AND SODOMY IN CASTLEHAVEN'S TIME

However unusual the allegations against the Earl, and however important his background was to the outcome of his trial, to understand what happened, we must begin with the two crimes for which he was indicted: rape and sodomy. The evidence through which to contextualize charges of either crime is elliptical. The terms and the difficulties inherent in subjecting sexual activity to public scrutiny are familiar, but the meaning of rape and sodomy, and our appreciation of their origins today is completely different from what it would have been in the seventeenth century.

Rape and sodomy were crimes of both great and little importance in sixteenth- and seventeenth-century England. Scriptural and classical history offered examples of their dire public consequences; sermons and literature rehearsed the dangers for contemporaries. The stories of Lucretia's rape (among others) and of Sodom's destruction were graphic reminders that such behavior had forbidding communal, as well as individual, repercussions. The legal commentator Sir Anthony Fitzherbert called rape "the most great offense next to murder." King James I wrote that sodomy was among the handful of crimes that Kings were "bound in conscience never to forgive."[4] Many felonies restrained desires that in their proper place were legitimate—thefts masked industry, treason suggested counsel— but rape and sodomy concerned the most troubling of appetites within the Christian world—corporeality turned to lust. Legislation and judicial opinion defined culpability broadly for both crimes: all parties were to be tried as principals; none could plead benefit of clergy (the most common means by which convicted felons avoided execution).

The King's attorneys in Castlehaven's case would claim that neither rape nor sodomy was a familiar crime in England, but many commentators disagreed. The most comprehensive contemporary guide to legal matters concerning women (*Lawes Resolution of Wom-*

ens Rights), introduced the discussion of rape by lamenting men's proclivity to the crime—"if the rampier [rampart] of laws were not between women and their harms," the anonymous author claimed, "I verily think none of them [women], being above twelve years of age, and under a hundred, being either fair or rich, should be able to escape ravishment." And despite the status of sodomy as a crime not to be named among Christians, contemporaries certainly did not find it unmentionable—far from it. Augustine Baker was an English Benedictine monk, yet many early modern Englishmen and women would have seconded his lament that in the late sixteenth century, sodomy was "the greatest corruption in our land." Oxford and Cambridge, Baker warned parents, were rife with sodomy, fornication, and drunkenness. London was no better. Sir Simonds D'Ewes wrote ominously in 1622 of "how frequent it [sodomy] was in this wicked city." The theaters were notorious for allegedly encouraging transgressive behavior. Speculations about sodomy among aristocrats and at the royal court were plentiful. Among those suspected during Elizabeth I's reign were the Earls of Oxford and of Southampton, and during the reign of James I, suspicion fell upon the Earl of Bath, the Viscount St. Albans (Francis Bacon), Lord Stanhope, and Lord Roos, as well as upon the King himself.[5]

Yet rape and sodomy seem to have perplexed as much as dismayed early modern people; the crimes were much maligned in prescriptive literature, but more ambivalently received in daily life. Both felonies were much denounced, but little prosecuted, often vilified, but rarely punished. Formal accusations of either crime were unusual. Men charged with rape rarely confessed or fled, suggesting a certain confidence in their ability to triumph over a charge that, if successful, carried an almost invariable penalty of death. The confidence was well founded; rape was among the least likely of crimes to earn indictments from grand juries or convictions from trial juries. The pattern for sodomy was similar.[6]

Opinion about these acts was cut through with contradiction and ambiguity outside the courts as well. Nicholas Udall, dismissed in 1541 as headmaster of Eton for transgressions including sodomy, went on to become an important literary figure, a Master of Revels at the court of Edward VI, and the schoolmaster in Bishop Stephen Gardiner's household. Augustine Baker and Thomas Shepard, clerics of

different generations and opposing religious complexions, acknowledged good in men whom they denounced as sodomites, com-
mending them respectively as "a great sermon listener" and "an eminent preacher." General pardons before 1609 did not commonly
exclude sodomy from their largesse. Modern critics such as Suzanne
Gossett, Jonathan Goldberg, and Bruce Smith have shown us that
the literature of the day contained manifold examples of positive or
at least morally neutral models for both rape and male sodomitical
relationships.[7] Such apparent equivocation about rape and sodomy
reflects many things—the limitations of legal categories, the incomplete survival of documents, the invariably skewed fit between crime
and prosecution—but it additionally reveals deep incongruities in
the early modern conceptions of these behaviors.

The contemporary legal definitions of rape and of sodomy seem
clear. Rape, a felony by both common and statute law, was defined
as "an unlawful and carnal knowledge of a woman by force and
against her will." To convict a man of rape, his complainant had to
prove sexual intercourse and force; penetration and emission distinguished rape from the lesser crime of assault, and compulsion distinguished it from consensual sexual relations. Consent meant free
and specific acquiescence; except in the case of one's spouse or con-
cubine, it could not be inferred. Children under ten were not capable of consent, so intercourse with girls younger than ten was always
rape.[8] Sodomy, in contrast, was a statutory offense with roots in ecclesiastical rather than in common law. It was defined as carnal knowledge between two men, between human and animal, or "unnaturally" between man and woman. Unless one participant was under
the age of discretion, both partakers were equally culpable. The
threshold of proof was even simpler than in rape: penetration alone
determined the felony.[9]

Yet rape and sodomy were each exceptionally difficult felonies to
prove. Even in a society so much less private than our own, disinterested witnesses to sexual acts were uncommon and in any case,
carnal knowledge and consent (the critical matters at law) were
issues rarely provable by the testimony of nonparticipants. According to the Attorney-General in 1631, Sir Robert Heath, the fact that
there were alleged eyewitnesses against Castlehaven was further
proof of the Earl's depravity. Obtaining evidence from participants

or victims was also difficult for other reasons. The line between vindication and humiliation, always thin in accusations of sexual impropriety, made public testimony dangerous for complainants as well as for defendants. To convict a defendant of rape, a victim publicly had to acknowledge illicit sexual experience; to convict a defendant of sodomy, a complainant (unless he was a child) had to be willing also to incriminate himself (since the law defined all adult participants in sodomitical acts as agents). And as Castlehaven's alleged partners in sodomy discovered, promises of immunity in return for testimony could always be rescinded.

Alleged victims willing to bear these burdens faced additional ones. Rape and sodomy were the felonies in which imbalances in credibility between complainant and defendant were likely to be the starkest. Both crimes tended to match relatively privileged defendants against less privileged and youthful victims; no other felonies involved so many defendants identified as gentlemen, yeomen, or clerics or so many victims identified as females, preadolescents, or servants.[10] Convention taught that women and children were congenitally unreliable and servants always vulnerable to bribery or malice, yet believing complainants in accusations of rape or sodomy often meant preferring the testimony of a woman over that of a man and/or the testimony of a youth or servant over that of a head of household.[11] Except in cases involving children too young to give consent or where physical evidence was incontrovertible, contemporary common sense made trusting such testimony above the word of an adult male implausible, if not ridiculous.

Ambiguities about the crimes themselves made the issue of reliability still more troublesome. The established attributes of rape—carnal knowledge and consent—begged more questions than they answered. Often, as in Castlehaven's case, defendants simply denied that there had been carnal intercourse.[12] However, things were no easier when intercourse was conceded, and the issue was consent. The law in the early seventeenth century recognized only pregnancy as a sure proof of consent; it demanded none of the standards of resistance later enshrined by Sir Matthew Hale (e.g., crying out, complaining quickly). But that is not to say that a woman's behavior after being raped and her prior reputation did not matter. Even while arguing the legal insignificance of such standards, the author

of *Lawes Resolution* acknowledged their importance. "Outward lasciviousness," he protested, seemed to some "an infallible argument
of sensuality, whereby some men have been emboldened to offer
force, because they thought it was expected." Castlehaven certainly
felt justified in raising questions about his wife's initial silence and
her past life. Hale would later approvingly declare that jurors were
inevitably "triers of the credit of the witnesses as well as the truth
of the fact."[13] We do not have to share his pride to recognize the
inescapable veracity of his statement.

Interpretative issues confused the category of sodomy as well.
Alan Bray and Alan Stewart have deftly shown us how (and why) in
a society that valorized male intimacy, the behavior of most men provided the raw materials from which to construct an accusation of
sodomy. Early modern society was a world of ubiquitous homoso-
ciability, where male companionship was the expected preference,
male friendship the standard path of social mobility, and shared beds
and chambers the normal practice.[14] The ordinariness of such intimacies could ground either a complaint of sodomy or a defense
against such an accusation. Without a stereotyped homosexual identity to use as a foil, accusations of sodomy, like those of rape, were
left to rise or fall on more general issues of credibility. Finding both
transgressions in one man, odd in a modern prosecution, would have
seemed less unlikely to the Earl's contemporaries. Both felonies
were believed to stem from an imbalance of which lust was just a
symptom. More than one Jacobean dramatist presented rape as a
crime of undisciplined masculinity; Sir Edward Coke was only
repeating a commonplace when he located the seeds of sodomy in
arrogance, idleness, and gluttony. Rape and sodomy, contemporaries argued, were by-products of greed and egoism.[15]

Since rape and sodomy were felonies difficult to identify, difficult
to define, and difficult to prove, it is not surprising that the law most
readily "saw" them as they disrupted the social order rather than
individual lives. Official concern about rape had focused traditionally on the crime's repercussions for inheritance. The distinct, but
often associated, practice of kidnapping heiresses or widows for their
fortunes and then sealing the bargain with forced intercourse, made
rape a crime that seemed to assume a breach of both body and
estate, of the individual within the context of the family. By the

1630s, rape and abduction were technically distinct, but legal and cultural memory drew from a pond fed indiscriminately by both streams.[16] This legacy had mixed consequences. The ancient tie of rape and property probably reinforced the standing of rape as a crime worthy of sustained attention. But the connection also associated rape with virginity, realty, and family rather than with bodily integrity, and thereby influenced which sorts of victims male jurors would find most persuasive. Avarice was a language that made rape comprehensible even in cases as peculiar as Castlehaven's: he allegedly used the promise of property, not carnal satisfaction, to persuade the servant Broadway to commit the crime. But this conceptualization also made it harder to convince jurors that women without property or married women could be raped, and it invited skepticism when a modestly placed woman suggested that the attentions of a gentleman were unwelcome.

Literary images of rape strengthened the assumption that its ramifications were more than personal, but also augmented its image as a crime linked to property and reputation. Attorney-General Heath reminded Castlehaven's jury of the story of the Benjaminites, whom God had destroyed when they failed to surrender a rapist.[17] Retellings of the classical stories of Helen, Lucretia, and Philomela—popular in print as well as in performance—encouraged the belief that violence against women was a public issue, that the disorder of rape disturbed more than even the family of the assaulted. Of these tales, Lucretia's was the most familiar; it was a narrative as powerful in its public resonances as it was distant from the reality of rape in early modern life. In the thirty years before the Castlehaven trial, Thomas Middleton, Thomas Heywood, and William Shakespeare had all produced versions of Lucretia's story. The most recent edition of Shakespeare's *The Rape of Lucrece* had appeared in 1624; Heywood's play of the same name had appeared in 1630.

Whatever the artistic variations, the drama's central plot remained straightforward. It began with a boasting contest between Lucretia's husband and his friends. Tarquin, the son of the reigning King, took the confidence which Lucretia's husband had expressed about her chastity as a challenge. Having exploited Lucretia's hospitality, Tarquin threatened her first with death, then with dishonor, and finally, he raped her. The next morning Lucretia told her story to her husband, father, and other witnesses. She urged them to avenge her shame and plunged a dagger into her heart. She so inspired first her relatives and then the Roman populace that they deposed Tarquin's tyrannous father and overturned the monarchy. From Lucretia's humiliation (according to tradition) was born the Roman Republic. Lucretia could represent a blameless rape victim, culpable only because her virtue aroused envy. She was a wife abused because of her generosity, a woman who placed honor above life, and a female citizen whose private shame gave rise to a public good.[18]

Early modern English versions of the story (not surprisingly for a tale that ended in rebellion) focused on the narrative's moral rather than its political consequences, implying that rape soiled the victim as well as the perpetrator, that it was a crime from which there was no full recovery. Some contemporary replottings echoed St. Augustine by questioning Lucretia's purity; her suicide became a paradox rather than a triumph. Did Lucretia resist Tarquin as fully as she might have, these narratives asked? Was her death an expiation for some measure of—if not moral, then at least physical—consent? Stories such as Lucretia's told audiences that rape was evil, but also that it was a test of an inherently fragile female will. And the view that rape was tyrannical as well as deplorable brought the crime yet again into the public realm, configuring it once more as a problem between men. Lucretia's story was less about lust or violence than about greed and jealousy, less about her violation than about the ultimate rejection of immoderate power.

Rape, it seems, was a crime that everyone deplored, but one that was difficult to recognize. The struggle of avenging a crime for which women were always the primary witnesses, that might so easily be confused with abduction, and that turned upon the vexed issue of consent, narrowed the cultural capacity of men to acknowledge rape and the cultural capacity of women effectively to describe it. Rape was a crime whose prosecution exposed the engendered nature of perception—the surest way to make rape visible was to explain it in conjoint rather than in singular terms. It was most serious when it touched upon a danger to something larger than one female body.

Early modern legal and religious authors understood sodomy in social terms that made it similarly difficult to "see."[19] Sodomy represented weakness before temptations that were universal; it had little to do with either sexual or gender identity. The prosecutions for sodomy about which we have information before the late seventeenth century rarely condemned defendants for effeminate behavior; conversely, reproaches for effeminacy rarely included sexual examples.[20] The danger of the sodomite was not that the focus of his attention was a man, but that his desires had no focus; they ran in indiscriminate streams that undermined allegedly categorical boundaries between men and women, humans and animals, nobles and commoners. Hence, the logic behind conflating sodomy and bestiality under a single legal category: buggery. Sodomy, in the words used to prosecute it, was "against the order of nature." Yet the order concerned here was not heterosexuality; it was organization born of moderation. Sodomy represented desire unfettered, appetite ruling the mind rather than ruled by it. Sodomy was less about desiring men than about desiring everything.

This understanding of sodomy contained an unresolved tension between two distinct myths of origins, one that emphasized an individual's failure of self-governance, the other that focused on contagion. Unlike rape, which was about control of property and women, sodomy was about control of self. Because the crime involved only men, there could be no excuse of female wiles; because it was consensual, there could be no alibi of force. Sodomy became a synonym for intemperance. In the fevered writing of the antitheatrical moralists, for example, sodomy meant excessiveness, excessiveness meant instability, and so all destabilizing moments became sodomitical. Drunkenness, the most common alibi (for Castlehaven as well as others) for behavior seen as sodomitical, was an excuse that said nothing about sex, but confirmed a self-inflicted breakdown of control.[21]

Like rape, sodomy threatened not only the individual, but also those around him; it was an act of corruption as well as of desire. Whether or not actually pederastic, the sodomitical relationships described in the legal records invariably paired authority and dependency—men and boys, masters and servants, teachers and pupils, patrons and clients. The most openly secret sodomitical example of the age, King James I, was but an extreme case of the same principle.[22] And sodomy was seen as an invading force; born not in English hearts, but carried to English shores to be left as a corrosive legacy. Coke believed that it arrived in England with the immigration of the Lombards; John Marston wrote that it had entered the country with the Jesuits. And in a wonderful inversion of such prejudices, Father Augustine Baker blamed the growth of sodomy on the influx of Protestantism from the Continent.[23] Sodomy, like rape, seemed the perversion of the most sacred of positive relationships; the one a cruel parody of marriage, the other a crude degeneration of mastery and male friendship. But rape undermined a trust between men and women that most people saw as intrinsically delicate; sodomy, by weakening homosocial bonds in a society where so much of public life relied on male clientage and male patronage, more directly attacked the sinews of community.

Sodomy was not a crime in common law, nor was it a secular crime at all until legislation against it was passed in the parliamentary session of 1533–34. The "Act for the Punishment of the Vice of Buggery" remains the basis for antisodomy laws in several Anglo-American societies, but it was born of needs quite specific to its place and time.[24] Although the law fitted easily among the legislative accomplishments of a reign that produced more new felonies and excluded more extant crimes from benefit of clergy than any other before the eighteenth century, it is best understood as part of the Henrician government's assault on the authority of the Catholic Church. By exploiting a long-held belief that priests were particularly dissolute and depriving the ecclesiastical courts of their authority over sodomy and bestiality, the act laid the ground for the expropriation of both the Church's monastic properties and its moral jurisdiction. Buggery was the first crime explicitly to be taken away from the church courts. The fact that the law was not made perpetual until seven years after its first passage illustrates its connection to the government's incremental, but unsuccessful, campaign to win cooperation from the Pope.[25]

Edward VI's first Parliament modified the Henrician act, Mary I's repealed it, and Elizabeth I's restored it to its original (and then lasting) form. Although the statutes describe buggery as "detestable," "abominable," and a "most horrible vice," none save the Elizabethan bill discussed it in any but mundanely civic terms. None of the legislation seems to have inspired extended discussion in the Parliaments. The Edwardian statute invalidated accusations not made promptly, disallowed witnesses who might gain materially from convictions, and restored inheritance rights to a convict's heirs. The changes typified the initially tolerant approach of Lord Protector Somerset, but also implied that secular as well as clerical men of property had found themselves vulnerable to hard-to-answer sexual accusations. The Marian revocation encompassed all recently created felonies and treasons; it was intended to undo the legislative redefinitions of religious conformity passed by the Queen's father and brother. In a parliamentary session focused on more directly confessional offenses, the failure to except buggery from the revocation was most likely an oversight.[26]

The Elizabethan reinstatement of Henry VIII's legislation was deliberate, but it appears to have originated outside of the Privy Council. The bill's preamble declared that under the Catholic Mary I "diverse evil disposed persons have been the more bold to commit the said most horrible and detestable vice." Even here, though, the government's acquiescence fit a broader purpose. In Elizabeth's first decades, legislation barring only three felonies reemerged; all three (sodomy, witchcraft, and embezzlement by servants) subverted the imagined natural order. Sir Simonds D'Ewes, who (as we have seen) had quite impassioned views on the prevalence of sodomy in Jacobean London, considered the Elizabethan legislation to be an act "of no great moment," but the Queen and her councilors may have believed that she could reassure those skeptical of female rule by proclaiming that she would allow no other inversions of what was understood as "natural."[27]

Extensive information survives about only a handful of charges involving sodomy; the documents in the records of the Assizes are sparse, rumors almost by definition are terse and unexplorable. Even more than categories of nonsexual crime, sodomy "existed" only when someone chose to see it. Like everything else in early modern life, sexual transgressiveness shifted shape with social position and public reputation. What was sodomy in a commoner could be high spirits in a peer, and what was sodomy in a peer could remain eccentricity for a commoner. In the parish or the shire, sodomy "appeared" when drunkenness, aggression, or pederasty disturbed the peace. While any generalization is dangerous with such sketchy evidence, the handful of documented provincial cases suggests that most prosecutions were a response to persistent disruption. In the labyrinthine worlds of Whitehall and Westminster, however, charges of sodomy were often preemptive, emerging where a disruption of civic calm was threatened, but not yet realized. Most prominent men against whom there were public complaints of sodomy were never indicted for the crime; most accusations emerged alongside suspicions of other species of corruption. The two best-documented charges of sodomy before 1631, those leveled against the first Lord Hungerford in 1540 and the 17th Earl of Oxford in the 1580s, fit this pattern; both incorporated charges of apostasy, foreign allegiance, and spousal abuse.[28]

Walter, Lord Hungerford, was condemned in July 1540 for committing sodomy with his servants, for knowingly harboring a supporter of the Pilgrimage of Grace (whom he retained as his chaplain instead of handing him over to the Privy Council), and for procuring a prediction of the time of King Henry VIII's death. A client of the recently disgraced Thomas Cromwell, Hungerford's attainder began its legislative journey two days after the condemnation of his patron had been concluded. The two men died together on the scaffold, Hungerford caught in the wake of the Secretary of State's destruction. In a plea to Cromwell written sometime between 1532 and the early months of 1540, Lady Hungerford had charged her husband with incontinence, alleging that there were "many strange things" to discover about his behavior. She also said that after keeping her a virtual prisoner for several years, he now intended to poison her. Only the charity of local, humble women, she contended, had kept her alive. Lady Hungerford's allegations, if truthful, revealed a man who kept a traitor out of a prison, while keeping his own wife within one; who fed a heretic, while starving his own spouse; who made his household the focus of charity rather than of alms. Hungerford did not die because he was a sodomite or because he mistreated his wife, but the allegations in her petition helped to make his other behavior and his link to Cromwell seem more ominous.[29]

In contrast to Hungerford, the 17th Earl of Oxford was of a long-ennobled family, beholden to no contemporary for either prominence or favor.[30] Oxford was, however, perpetually in debt, notorious for brawling and dueling, and indefatigably ready to imagine himself slighted. Infamous for the mistreatment of his wife, the daughter of

William Cecil, Oxford had abandoned her entirely for a time in the 1570s and later challenged the paternity of their son. The Earl was never prosecuted for sodomy, but in the early 1580s, his enemies depicted him as a sodomite, as well as a compulsive liar, a drunkard, a blasphemer, and a murderer. They also accused him of both Catholicism and of treason. The Council took the accusations against Oxford seriously enough to imprison him for several months in 1581.

Despite the differences of status, what happened to Oxford both echoes what happened to Hungerford and foreshadows what would happen to the 2nd Earl of Castlehaven. The association of Hungerford, Oxford, and Castlehaven with Roman Catholicism, and therefore Italianisms tapped into the long-imagined association among the Roman Church, Italy, and sodomy. The allegations that each failed at husbandry—that their inability to restrain themselves extended to an inability to manage their wives with moderation—reinforced the message that all asymmetric relationships within the social hierarchy depended for integrity upon each another. And the pairing of sodomy in each case with some other, more established, felony, reinforces the contention that sodomy was a charge more potent as an organizing principle for other fears than as a focus for solitary prosecution. Intuiting whether sodomitical acts inspired these accusations or were convenient, even disingenuous, afterthoughts to other suspicions is less important than recognizing the social utility of sodomy as an accusation. It was a nearly impossible-to-disprove slander and it made other accusations seem more credible. Sodomitical behavior never appeared alone in charges against elite defendants. On occasion, sodomitical acts may have raised suspicions, but like a quark, sodomy was known primarily by its effusions. What justified its prosecution lay not in any physical act, but in concomitant disruptions; sodomy began in its social ramifications. Disloyalty to one's self was part and parcel of other, more iniquitous, disloyalties. Through this door, religious recalcitrance, a lack of favor, or a disruptive household could exit transformed into sodomy, and sodomy could transmogrify into treason.

Despite their apparently private nature, rape and sodomy were felonies with dramatic public implications. They threatened inheritance and loyalty, familial order and individual sobriety. Both categories encompassed, but were not defined by, sexual behavior;

physical acts became felonious only when they accompanied other disorders. Rapists and buggers were overconsumers; they lusted after property and luxury as well as men and women. They embodied an immoderation that was as destructive as it was enticing, and it was that excess, not specific acts, that so endangered society. To prosecute someone successfully for rape or sodomy meant proving not only a particular form of carnal knowledge, but also the insidious infection for which these acts were but a symptom.

PREPARATIONS: BUILDING A CASE

The legal difficulties of the 2nd Earl of Castlehaven began late in October 1630, when Lord Audley complained about his father to the Privy Council. According to Audley, Castlehaven intended to disinherit him; the proof was the Earl's inappropriate generosity to Henry Skipwith, a servant to whom, Lord Audley said, the Earl had given gifts worth at least £12,000: a furnished townhouse, a farm, and significant personal property. Castlehaven, his son alleged, had also encouraged Skipwith and other servants to cuckold Audley. And the common fame of the household, he maintained, was that Skipwith was "overfamiliar" with the Countess of Castlehaven. Audley claimed to have confronted his father, only to find his protests "slighted" and himself accused of disloyalty. As the younger man reported it, his father's dismissiveness and an inconclusive personal confrontation between Skipwith and Audley at Fonthill Gifford forced him to ask the Council to intervene. He later told his father:

> Though I had advice and perhaps a spirit to have set a sword in the entry, yet my better thoughts chose rather to refer my course to God than to be my own executioner. That Reverend name of father sounded in my ears and charmed me to quietness . . . although virulent passion has canceled in you the tenderness of a father . . . I never went about to abridge your bounty to a well deserving follower. Yet [I] desire your courtesy may keep a method, and [not take] out the difference between a servant and a son.[31]

Audley's complaint appears to have only inferentially concerned sodomy; unmentioned, it was, however, a logical explanation for a father's obscuring the "difference between a servant and a son."

No record survives of the Privy Council's initial response to Audley; no formal investigation appears to have begun until late November. In the interim, most likely, councilors informally tried to reconcile Lord Audley and the Earl. If the heir's central concern was his inheritance, he had every reason to prefer a settlement to a criminal prosecution. According to Castlehaven's steward, whatever the Earl might give away, lands worth an annual income of about £2,200 had been set aside for Lord Audley "without the power of revocation."[32] Were Castlehaven to be convicted of felony, that property would fall to the Crown. Because English laws of forfeiture did not apply in Ireland, Audley would retain his Irish estates and title were his father to be condemned, but that would be small recompense for what he would lose in England. Private intervention, then, best served Audley's financial interests. If moral outrage alone inspired Audley (an explanation favored by some Victorian commentators, but one with little contemporary support), protecting the Touchet name would still have been important. Considering the embarrassment of a public challenge, negotiation served the Earl's best interests as well as his son's. And given the fragile moral reputation of the regal court, it also suited the King and Council. If reconciliatory efforts were made, however, they failed; the Council proceeded with formal criminal inquiries.

Between 30 November and late April, councilors scrutinized the Castlehaven household; they secured and examined suspects and witnesses, confiscated and protected properties, broadened and focused the shape of accusations.[33] Working both in Wiltshire and in London, they questioned and requestioned family, servants, and former servants, relying largely on lists provided by Lord Audley and his attorney, William Wroughton. Five councilors were particularly assiduous in the inquiry: the Earls of Manchester and of Arundel and Surrey (the Lord Privy Seal and the Earl Marshal), Lords Coventry and Weston (the Lord Keeper and the Lord High Treasurer), and William Laud, Bishop of London. Laud was one of the King's few confidantes; the other men occupied four of the most important offices of state. They were joined at the beginning and the conclusion of the investigation by Sir Nicholas Hyde, the Lord Chief Justice. Probably none of these men were strangers to either the Stanley or the Touchet families, and the prior connections that we can document would not have reassured the Earl. Manchester and Coventry were allies of the Countess of Castlehaven's mother, the Dowager Countess of Derby. Weston and Laud had witnessed the expulsion from court of Castlehaven's sister, Lady Eleanor. Hyde had grown up almost in the shadow of Fonthill Gifford, in the same parish as Sir John Davies, Lady Eleanor's estranged (and, by 1630, dead) husband. Castlehaven would later object to the presence of Manchester and Arundel as jurors, saying that he "deemed [both] his enemies."[34]

As suggested above, Lord Audley's complaint was much more modest than the eventual outlines of the prosecution. He had not explicitly accused his father of rape or of sodomy. He had said that his stepmother, the Countess of Castlehaven, was promiscuous, not that she was a victim of assault. In October 1630, the rancor between Audley and Castlehaven was about possessions—realty, goods, and wives. By April 1631, however, the Earl's "virulent passion" was understood as quite specifically physical. Yet Henry Skipwith, the leading man in Audley's story, faced no indictment, or, to the best of my knowledge, even formal accusation. Two men never mentioned by Audley (Giles Broadway and Florence Fitzpatrick) appeared as Castlehaven's co-defendants. In short, a critical reorientation occurred over the intervening months. New accusations, new names, and new faces dominated the Earl's trial.

Based upon information from both Audley and Wroughton, Chief Justice Hyde began this phase of the investigation on 1 December by questioning three of Castlehaven's male servants who were already in London; the investigation ignored (then and later) the maidservants whom Audley and Wroughton had also named as important witnesses.[35] The questioning centered on Audley's charges of his father's dissipation and on the position of Henry Skipwith. All three men confirmed that Skipwith, who by his own admission had come to Fonthill "almost naked and very poor," was Castlehaven's special favorite, that Skipwith slept regularly with Lady Audley, and that he did "often lie in bed with the Earl."[36] Castlehaven, the deponents noted, arranged his young daughter-in-law/stepdaughter's adulterous relationship and rejoiced in it. He openly hoped the result would be a son whose birth would humiliate Lord Audley and make Skipwith's progeny Castlehaven's heir. One servant swore that the

Earl had stationed him at the Lady Audley's chamber door to "see when Skipwith should get up to perform" so that the Earl might watch. Castlehaven, the servant said, enjoyed observing not only the coupling of Skipwith and Lady Audley, but also intercourse between other servants and a "whore" named Blandina.

Having heard this testimony, during the next week, investigators called back William Wroughton and asked for fuller details about Henry Skipwith. Wroughton emphasized the servant's poverty, the precipitous speed of his rise to favor, and the lavish gifts that Castlehaven had bestowed upon him. According to Wroughton, Skipwith was effectively in charge of the Earl's finances. The attorney reported a rumor that Skipwith's endowments from the Earl amounted to more than fifty times his testamentary bequest to his youngest daughter. Within days of Wroughton's testimony, the Council ordered the arrest and imprisonment of Castlehaven and of Skipwith.[37]

On 7 December came the first of at least five formal interrogations of the Earl. The Attorney-General and members of the Council joined Hyde in the examination. Castlehaven's relationships with Skipwith and Lady Audley were the focus of the questioning, but somewhere in the five days since their meeting with Wroughton, the councilors had become interested as well in Castlehaven's dealings with an earlier favorite, John Anktill, who had eventually married Lucy, the Earl's eldest daughter. Anktill, like Skipwith, had apparently found it exceptionally lucrative to be in the Earl's employment. Castlehaven denied anything untoward about his generosity to either Skipwith or Anktill. He said that he seldom slept with fewer than four servants in his chamber, and that he and Skipwith lay together only when rooms were scarce (a practice so universal that in a later letter Lord Audley jested about his own similar situation). Castlehaven initially denied knowing anything about an affair between Skipwith and Lady Audley, but soon confessed that, over his opposition, Skipwith and Anktill had become the intimates of, respectively, his adolescent daughter-in-law/stepdaughter and his eldest daughter. He was, he insisted, powerless to prevent either relationship. Anktill and Lucy, he said, contracted to one another "without [his] privity or foreknowledge." Skipwith and Lady Audley united out of her despair over her husband's neglect; to reproach them in such circumstances "was to no purpose." Since he could have a definitive impact on neither situation, Castlehaven alleged, liberality on his part made good sense.[38]

When he was examined the next day, Henry Skipwith told a similar, yet not identical story, to the Earl's. Skipwith admitted to sharing the Earl's bed regularly, and he insisted that the Earl's largesse to him came not from illicit infatuation, but from a desire to "bridle" Lord Audley. Animus between the Earl and his heir underlay both Castlehaven's generosity and his lassitude. Skipwith's explanation for the enmity was "some jealousy the young lord had of his wife and with this examinate." The servant at first tried to avoid discussing his intimacy with Lady Audley, asserting that "he [was] not bound to accuse himself." On further questioning, he claimed that there was long-standing affection between himself and Lady Audley, affection rekindled by marital unhappiness. Skipwith insisted that despite their mutual attraction, they had not slept together until more than six months after Lady Audley's marriage. For at least a year, he said, not only the Earl, but also Lord Audley had known of their "love and familiarity." At least four servants had seen them in bed together at Fonthill Gifford or at the Earl's townhouse in Salisbury; Castlehaven had visited them together frequently. Asked what they discussed on such occasions, Skipwith said that the Earl talked of his estate, of the lands and the £15,000 or £16,000 that he hoped to leave to a son born of the illicit union.[39]

To this point, Lord Audley's imputations of favoritism and incontinence had held center stage. The confidence that Castlehaven had once rested in John Anktill seemed to parallel the intimacy he now had with Henry Skipwith. The corruption of Castlehaven and his servants with Blandina seemed to complement his tolerance of adultery. His daughter-in-law/stepdaughter's alleged distaste for her husband seemed to supplement the Earl's own estrangement from his son. All the deponents agreed that Lady Audley and Skipwith had committed adultery; all agreed that Castlehaven had shown considerable favor toward Skipwith. The truly shocking element in what the councilors had heard thus far was the allegation that Castlehaven would allow, much less invite, the disparagement of his blood in the next generation. To encourage the very thing that so much law and custom was intended to avoid was almost unthinkable. Whatever his hostility to Lord Audley, Castlehaven's willingness to have a bastard heir, if true, demeaned both his lineage and the integrity of the nobility. Sodomitical affection would explain such perversity, but the perversity itself could not legally prove buggery. Castlehaven could expect the King and Council to demand vehemently that he change his ways, but on the evidence collected by midday on 8 December, the persons most likely to find themselves in a court were Henry Skipwith and Lady Audley, both of whom were clearly culpable for the ecclesiastical offense of adultery. That sort of prosecution, even if successful, would neither have loosened Skipwith's hold on his gifts from Castlehaven, nor have freed Lord Audley from the embarrassment of cuckoldry or his marriage, nor have constrained the Earl.

When the Council examined Skipwith a second time on 8 December, he reasserted the "ancient" love between himself and Lady Audley, and suggested that Lord Audley and he might have happily exchanged spouses. But he also added a new allegation, one that shifted the attention of the councilors from adultery to rape, from Lady Audley to the Countess of Castlehaven, and from Skipwith more directly to the Earl. We do not know what inspired the new revelations; perhaps the councilors were just slow in getting to Lord Audley's earlier aside about his stepmother; perhaps some now lost clue redirected their interest. In the new examination, Skipwith said that while in Ireland Castlehaven had ordered him to bed the Countess and on one occasion, had even held her down for him to do so. Skipwith and the Countess never had intercourse (a point confirmed by the Countess), but the servant had let the Earl think otherwise. Castlehaven flatly denied the new accusation; both men held to their stories when the councilors brought them together two days later.[40]

The examination of Lady Audley the next day made things worse still for her father-in-law/stepfather. Having been discovered in hiding by the Council's messengers (a concealment made necessary, she claimed, by the Earl's desire to spirit her out of the country), Lady Audley's particulars diverted attention still further away from Skipwith and herself and onto the Earl. She called Skipwith "that villain," but dismissed the idea that he had had illicit relations with anyone but her. The evil at Fonthill Gifford originated with the Earl, she insisted, not Henry Skipwith. Castlehaven, Lady Audley said, had tried to entice her to sleep with various of his servants. He had wheedled, manipulated, and finally blackmailed her into adultery with Skipwith by putting him in charge of her allowance and telling her that

> her husband loved her not, that if she did it [adultery] not, he would
> turn her out of doors and allow her nothing, and that if she did not
> consent, yet he would tell her husband, that she had done it; and
> when she did consent, then the Earl let her have anything.

According to Lady Audley, her father-in-law/stepfather was not only a voyeur, but also a felon. He had staged the rape of his own wife, but by John Anktill, his former favorite and current son-in-law, not by Henry Skipwith. Lady Audley had heard that Castlehaven also "used himself like a beast" but with his footman Florence Fitzpatrick, not with Skipwith. And none of this, she claimed, was particularly secret: several servants knew of her affair; her mother had seen her with Skipwith and "never persuaded her against it"; she heard that the parson of the parish spoke of Castlehaven's sodomy.[41]

Here was unequivocal, although certainly not incontestable, evidence of felony. Unlike Skipwith's accusations, Lady Audley's concerned a rape consummated rather than just encouraged and one within English, not Irish jurisdiction. Here was a categorical account of sodomy rather than an inference. If the earlier examinations had suggested gross irresponsibility, these realized the worst consequences of that failing, things more startling and sinister and unrestrained. Lady Audley was hardly an ideal witness: she was young and female; her story clearly served her interests (and Skipwith's); initially, she had fled rather than come forward. But her testimony could not be disregarded as motivated by a menial's enviousness; she had nothing directly to gain from her father-in-law/stepfather's demise. Moreover, her accusations were explicit; having spared Skipwith, she offered up others in his stead. If true, these were accusations of public rather than only familial consequence. Although they effectively demonstrated the truth of Lord Audley's grievances, his concerns necessarily now become the background rather than the focus of the inquiry.

On 10 December, the councilors questioned Castlehaven for a

third time. The fact that five privy councilors signed this examination (more signatures than on any deposition before or after) suggests the solemnity of the occasion. Telling the Earl that he had been accused of "diverse things" by Skipwith, Lady Audley, and unnamed others, the councilors suggested that he reconsider his earlier "reservedness." "Neither law nor conscience," he protested, required him to accuse himself, but upon their further urging, he agreed to seek advice from his attorneys. After this meeting, the Council had Castlehaven moved from the Gatehouse prison to the grimmer Tower of London. Within the next five days, they issued warrants for the appearances of John Anktill (currently in Ireland) and of the Countess of Castlehaven's page, Giles Broadway (currently in Gloucestershire). The Bishop of Winchester (another privy councilor) was asked to keep the Countess of Castlehaven "some few days"; Sir William Slingsby was asked to take in Lady Audley. The Council moved to protect Castlehaven's property, both for and from the Earl. They ordered a stop on the sale of any Touchet realty, took the Earl's estates under their supervision, and ordered an inventory made of the current contents of Castlehaven's Salisbury townhouse.[42]

The Council did not examine Anktill until early February, but almost immediately, someone (most probably the Countess) redirected their inquiry into the allegations about rape yet again. Now vanished depositions in late December and early January established the circumstances of the Countess's rape as later presented in court. The Earl, she maintained, had tried from the beginning of their marriage in 1624 to corrupt her with various of his favorites, including both Anktill and Skipwith. She confirmed Skipwith's denial of any intimacy between them. Her relationship with Anktill was less clear, but it apparently contained no direct use of force. According to the Countess, however, in June 1630, Castlehaven did successfully incite her page Broadway to rape her. The Earl allegedly had promised his wife an annuity of £200 if she would sleep willingly with Broadway, and he promised Broadway the same amount to have intercourse with her if she refused. Broadway had forced himself upon her, and although she did not immediately report the crime, the Countess claimed that his success had driven her to the brink of suicide.[43]

Like Skipwith, Anktill adamantly denied any charge of rape.

When questioned, he declared "with many exertions" that he had not slept with the Countess "and wished that God would never have mercy upon his soul if it were otherwise."[44] Broadway was more ambivalent. On 20 December, he was seen drinking in the cellar of the house where the Countess was staying, apparently with at least one privy councilor. By the time that he formally presented himself to the Council two days later, his fellow servants knew that "if he were taken [he] would be like to lose his life" for "some things" concerning his relations with the Countess. In January, he confessed to an attempted rape of the Countess but in at least one examination he insisted, as he would again at his own trial and execution, that his assault upon her had been unsuccessful. He also admitted to mutual masturbation with the Earl. When brought to confront Castlehaven, a chastened Broadway affirmed "every part of the former questions to be true, directly contrary to the Earl's denial."[45] Castlehaven "utterly" denied the claims of both his wife and Broadway. When the interrogators said that the Countess herself would confirm her page's confession, the Earl answered firmly that she "was no competent witness against him."[46]

The probing of Lady Audley's allegations about Castlehaven and sodomy proceeded in these months as well, although little of the documentation that must have existed about it remains. There were intimations of buggery in private reports as early as 6 December, but it is hard to know what, if anything, the Council made of them. Both Castlehaven and Skipwith denied any impropriety between them. The Countess apparently told investigators that "there went a rumor in all the house" of intimacy between Castlehaven and Anktill, but Anktill (like Skipwith before him) vaguely acknowledged only that he had "lain" with his former master. Broadway conceded that Castlehaven had on occasion "used his body as a woman," but disavowed any penetration. Sometime in the spring, Castlehaven's footman Florence Fitzpatrick, who in December had been treated only as an informant and asked nothing about his own dealings with Castlehaven, also acknowledged an intimate relationship with the Earl. The footman's confession was damagingly graphic, but since he too insisted that the Earl "did not penetrate his body," legally even Fitzpatrick gave no proof of felony.[47]

In a month or two of investigation, the councilors had moved considerably beyond Lord Audley's original accusation. They had heard explicit allegations that suggested a household of gross immorality, orchestrated rather than foiled by its aristocratic head. Castlehaven seemed to dote upon his favorites physically and emotionally, as well as financially. He apparently committed sodomy with them, used them to humiliate his wife and daughter-in-law, and schemed to make them permanent members of the family. He allegedly arranged myriad scandalous heterosexual couplings, applauded them, and on his orders insisted that they occur before the eyes of various household servants. The local parson as well as all the members of the household, it was claimed, were well aware of his behavior. As the Attorney-General declared in court, "in so dark a business a clearer [evidence] cannot be, for let a man be never so wicked, he will not call witnesses to see it"; public gossip compounded an already sobering situation.[48]

But if by early February too much was known not to consider a trial, the difficulties of such a hearing must also have been apparent. In December, Joseph Mead had informed Sir Martin Stuteville that Charles I was determined that the Earl "should be hanged or howsoever for his villanies"; the comment fits the King's sense of his obligations, but the conclusion was too simple. First, although a trial might serve the King's sense of self and even abstract justice, it would frustrate Lord Audley's desire to secure his inheritance with minimal public humiliation. The investigation, Audley himself would later argue, had already given greedy courtiers a weapon with which to enrich themselves at his expense. Castlehaven was defiant. The men who could best testify to the largesse that implied sodomy (Skipwith and Anktill) refused to implicate themselves. The more cooperative Broadway and Fitzpatrick had received nothing that Audley might claim or want. A successful trial for felony would stop Castlehaven's dispersal of his estate, but not necessarily maintain it for the family.

Second, as Mead also recognized, "whether the judges can find law enough for it, it is not yet resolved": circumstantial evidence of felony was plentiful, but technically sound evidence was thin.[49] Castlehaven and Skipwith may have intimidated Lady Audley into sexual intercourse, but intimidation was not physical force. The depositions of the Countess of Castlehaven and Broadway conceded the issue of force, but directly contradicted one another about whether or not there had been carnal knowledge. Skipwith and Anktill denied physical relationships with Castlehaven; Fitzpatrick and Broadway denied that their intimacies with the Earl crossed the threshold into sodomy.

Third, legal and cultural flaws undermined the integrity of virtually all of the likely witnesses: they were either servants (envious) or women (hysterical) or dependents (impatient). As a rape victim, the Countess was unusual because her status was so much higher than the alleged attacker's, but she had let six months elapse between her alleged rape and its report, and she had never spoken publicly of the abuse that she now dated to 1624. Furthermore, "for modesty's sake," she would not appear in court to face the defendants or to answer questions. Fitzpatrick was unusual in putting his own life at risk to testify (an oddity he later explained by claiming that he had been promised immunity from prosecution in exchange for his cooperation), but in addition to the legal difficulties of his testimony, Fitzpatrick was not only a servant, but also an Irish Catholic. His credibility before English jurors, therefore, would have been dubious in the best of circumstances, and these were circumstances in which he could be accused of testifying in order to save himself. Public knowledge and the sheer implausibility of this case made official action necessary: the alleged transgressions were fantastical, the cast of characters was even more so, the investigations hard to explain without some formal closure. Yet in addition to the other complications, trying an Earl who refused to cooperate with his investigation, as Castlehaven had so far, was always a dangerous and unpredictable endeavor.

PREPARATIONS: GETTING TO COURT

No evidence exists that any depositions were taken between Anktill's interrogation and late April; perhaps there were none. Investigators could have tried to entice recalcitrant witnesses, but the gathered evidence already laid out clearly the outlines of the case and its difficulties. What remained were the innumerable administrative matters relevant to producing a successful trial. The Council tried to ensure Castlehaven's relative comfort in the Tower, allowing him furnishings and household goods brought from his various residences, servants to attend him during his detention, and, under the watchful eyes of the Lieutenant of the Tower, access to his medical, legal, and business advisers. The councilors similarly oversaw the maintenance (at a more modest level) of the Countess and of Lady Audley. Settlements regarding the direct and indirect costs of keeping Skipwith in the King's Bench prison, Anktill in the Gatehouse prison, and Broadway and Fitzpatrick in the custody of various royal messengers demanded attention, as did questions about the payment of Castlehaven's servants and the oversight of his estates.[50]

By mid-March, the formal process of indicting and trying the Earl had begun. The King appointed a commission headed by Edward, Lord Gorges and the chief judges of the three courts of common law to preside in Salisbury over a grand jury's hearing of the Crown's evidence. Thirty men from throughout Wiltshire were summoned to be jurors; twenty-one appeared and seventeen of these sat as the grand jury. About half of the jurors came from parishes near Salisbury; although some were called, none at all came from the quadrant of the shire that included Fonthill Gifford. The only bailiff to fail to summon potential jurors was from the district adjacent to the Earl's estate. More than half of the seventeen men who were impaneled had had some previous acquaintance with Castlehaven—as fellow commissioners of the peace, students at the Middle Temple, or neighbors in Salisbury. On 6 April, they indicted Castlehaven for three felonies: two sodomies allegedly committed on 1 June and 10 June of the previous year with Florence Fitzpatrick, and the rape of the Countess of Castlehaven allegedly committed ten days later by Giles Broadway with the Earl's assistance. Since the Earl could hardly be accused of abetting a crime if there was no principal criminal, the grand jurors also indicted Broadway; they did not, however, indict Fitzpatrick, lending credence to his later claim that he had been promised some form of immunity. After the indictments were returned, Broadway was imprisoned; Fitzpatrick remained in the looser custody of the

Council. Ten days later, John Flower wrote to Viscount Scudamore that "it is thought that [Castlehaven] will be found guilty, for they say that the evidence is very full and clear."[51]

The indictments paved the way for further preparations. The space needed for the trial of a peer, much less the trial of a peer for sexual misconduct, was more than what was routinely available. There would be more than twice as many jurors, councilors, and officers of the court than in routine criminal cases, and they all would need room. So, too, would the general public, whose right to observe the law in action was a point of national pride. Westminster Hall, the venue of the common law tribunals since the eleventh century, was an unpartitioned expanse in which the courts had enclaves, but they normally conducted business in sight and hearing of one another. Their proceedings competed as well with the conversations of roving shopkeepers, spectators, and attorneys. For Castlehaven's trial, held during the recess between legal terms, a gallery was built so that the Lord High Steward, peers, judges, officers of the court, and the defendant would sit above the normal working space for the courts of King's Bench and Common Pleas. Scaffolds for observers were constructed along each side of the Hall "for people to stand and hear the trial." Added construction was standard practice in important trials; so many observers had crowded into the Hall in 1616 during the trial of the Earl of Somerset that a scaffold had collapsed. Despite the recognition of public interest, Charles I hoped for a restricted audience. "Understanding that some great ladies intended to be spectatrices of that obscene tragedy," he ordered a proclamation cried at the court gate that women of whatever status who appeared did so "upon pain of ever after being reputed to have forfeited their modesty." If his order was followed, there is no sign that it had any impact.[52]

Since no Parliament was sitting in 1631, there was no House of Lords to act as Castlehaven's judges and jurors; the alternative was to commission a Court of the Lord High Steward specifically for the occasion. Because it was the vacation between law terms, not only jurors, but also judges would have to be selected and called to London. The man named as Lord Steward would manage the proceedings; individually summoned peers would adjudicate in place of the full House. The common law judges would act as legal advisers to the peers. On 16 April, Charles I appointed Thomas Coventry to be Lord High Steward, a logical choice since Coventry was the Lord Keeper of the Great Seal. He was respected both as a lawyer and as a man of moderation. Like many successful barristers his age, however, it is more likely than not that one of Coventry's early patrons had been Thomas Egerton, himself an earlier Lord Keeper, and the Countess of Castlehaven's stepfather. When the Countess's mother died in 1637, she remembered her "noble friend" Coventry with a silver gilded cup worth £20.[53]

The week before 25 April, the day of the trial, was particularly busy, as the King's men worked through difficulties with both the material preparations and legal presentations. On Wednesday, the King ordered a full dress rehearsal of the ceremony of the trial, but he canceled it when no precedent for such a proceeding could be found. Attorney-General Heath and Chief Justice Hyde checked and rechecked testimony, the one reexamining Castlehaven's steward, the other Skipwith and Lady Audley, and probably several others. Castlehaven's steward, Walter Tyte, was the prosecution's most disinterested witness. Heath asked Tyte to rehearse once more the social rise of Anktill and Skipwith; Tyte added nothing new. Heath probed for Tyte's opinion of the accusations. Tyte, insisting that he "never lived in the Earl's house and therefore can say little of knowledge what passed there," refused to verify anything beyond rumors of "disorders." Castlehaven, the steward insisted, had lived "honorably and prospered" until he had bought Fonthill Gifford. Since then, however, the Earl had "turned in his religion . . . all went backward." The Chief Justice had Skipwith, Lady Audley, and probably other witnesses confirm under oath their earlier depositions.[54]

Until quite late, neither the exact number nor names of the jurors was secure. Juries of peers did not need to return unanimous verdicts, but no conviction with less than twelve votes of support was legitimate. The more jurors, therefore, the better the assurance of condemnation. Charles I wanted a jury of at least twenty-five men, although peers had in other reigns been condemned by smaller panels. Two days before the trial only twenty-three of the twenty-seven men summoned had agreed to serve. The Earl of Hertford, one

of Wiltshire's two most important peers, stayed in the country with
the King's permission; the Earl of Suffolk was lame; Lords Hervey
and Powys were not expected "upon any certainty."[55] And the
twenty-three willing jurors were not without their detractors. John
Pory understood that "my Lord of D." intended to acquit the Earl,
whatever the evidence.[56] Castlehaven petitioned the King to exclude
the Earls of Arundel and of Manchester, both of whom had been
active in the investigation, from the jury on grounds of prejudice.
Castlehaven said that Arundel "showed himself above all others most
officiously and severely inquisitive into his crimes" and Manchester, the temporary receiver of his accounts, "would never send him
a penny." A jury roster made the day after this complaint listed the
Earl of Lindsey rather than the Earl of Arundel, but that seems an
error, not a change. Arundel and Manchester stayed on the jury, and
substitutes for the absentees were found among the peers already in
the capital.[57]

Despite the absences, the jury as impaneled was forbidding. It
included almost every active privy councilor, and all the great officers of state: the Lord High Treasurer, the Lord Privy Seal, the Earl
Marshal, and both the King's and the Queen's Lord Chamberlains.
There were no noticeable efforts to produce a jury of one religion or
political complexion: there were men in their twenties and men in
their sixties, the godly sort and the popish sort, enthusiastic supporters of Charles I and those who would eventually oppose him.
However, virtually half of the jurymen had been ennobled relatively
recently; they were men who owed their titles to the Stuarts. The
Chief Justice's nephew Edward Hyde told his father that Castlehaven
was tried by "peers such a number that had he been arraigned at the
coming in of King James, he could not have been tried by." Whether
Hyde meant only that a larger jury made an acquittal less likely or
something more slighting about those who had profited from the
recent inflation of honors, the jury clearly struck him as more than
ordinarily unbalanced.[58]

Most of the jurors knew each other well; most of them also knew
the Touchets and the Stanleys. The fathers of Castlehaven, Leicester, and Essex had fought together in the days of Queen Elizabeth.
Pembroke, Danby, and Berkshire had seats in Wiltshire; Conway and

Howard were married to Wiltshire women. Berkshire, Clifford, Holland, Kent, Leicester, Manchester, Warwick, Weston, and Wentworth sat, as Castlehaven did, in the 1614 House of Commons. But the closest connections were familial rather than incidental and most of these favored the Countess. Manchester's close relationship to the Countess of Castlehaven's mother has already been noted; in addition, among the jurors were Lord Strange (the Countess of Castlehaven's first cousin), the Earl of Bedford (married to her first husband's first cousin), the Earl of Pembroke (whose first wife had been the Countess's aunt), Lord Petre (whose wife was related by marriage to the Countess's sister), and Lord Goring (for whose brother-in-law the Countess had stood as godparent). Viscount Wimbledon, moreover, was the brother-in-law of Sir Piers Crosby's estranged wife, the Dowager Countess of Castlehaven.[59]

As we have already seen, the laws regarding rape and buggery were ambiguous. The procedures for trying a peer when no Parliament was in session were also uncertain. And the privileges due a peer on trial for a crime that was neither treason nor murder were no clearer. On the weekend before the trial, Heath met twice with a group of common law judges at Serjeants' Inn Hall in Fleet Street to ask for guidance. Such meetings were not unique, but some believed that they "preengaged" judges against defendants, further adding to the Crown's already substantial legal advantages. Most of the questions that Heath posed involved the special treatment due a peer. Heath wanted to know the legal options if the Earl refused to plead, refused to be tried by his equals, refused to give evidence, or in any other way denied the authority of the court. The judges equated such contempts with a nonaristocrat standing mute; any peer who attempted them, they concluded, could be punished accordingly and the evidence against him might still be publicly presented. Heath posed specific questions about process: what was the threshold of votes necessary for a guilty verdict in the trial of a peer (a majority, but never less than twelve); could a peer who refused to plead still claim benefit of clergy on the grounds that by not pleading, he had never been convicted (no, in the statutory crime buggery, but yes, in the common law crime of rape). And he asked more directly substantial questions: could a wife testify against her husband (yes, if she was his

victim); did a rape necessitate proof of penetration (yes); could a prisoner demand to confront the witnesses directly (the answer is now
lost, but was probably yes, since such confrontations in court were
routine). Castlehaven pleaded not guilty without apparent reluctance, and accepted trial by his peers. It is impossible to say whether
this willingness meant that Heath's concerns had been unfounded
or that Castlehaven knew of the judges' opinions, but in either case,
the discussions suggest the range of technical concerns associated
with the trial, as well as official anxiety that Castlehaven intended
to remain recalcitrant.[60]

In contrast to this visible activity, we know little about how
Castlehaven prepared to defend himself. He certainly claimed no particular legal skill or talent; at the trial, he said that he was "but of
weak speech, when I am at the best," that he had been "without
friend, without counsel" during the five months of his imprisonment.
As a young man, the Earl had spent some time at the Middle Temple; since managing an estate and protecting one's dynastic interests
in early modern England invariably meant going to law, he had had
at least indirect experience with the world of civil litigation. And
although they were both dead by 1631, two of the most successful
attorneys of the age—Sir Francis Bacon and Sir John Davies—had
been part of his extended family.

In fact, the Earl had talked with attorneys during his imprisonment (albeit only in the presence of the Lieutenant of the Tower).
He had been allowed to question his accusers, thereby, as the Lord
High Steward said, was "better enabled to make defense." He knew
enough to ask for bail and the privilege of having counsel at his trial
and to complain to Charles I that not only some of the jurors, but
also the three chief judges, were predisposed against him. Castlehaven was in the Tower at the time of his indictment, but he was still
able to follow the progress of his case quite closely. He complained
to the King that in Salisbury three of the judges had "expressed more
passion against him then became other judges or commissioners."
Dorchester thought that the Earl even knew of "the difference of the
judges opinions." Castlehaven's factual knowledge impressed the
King more than the Earl's legal claims did. Secretary Dorchester
rejected the Earl's complaints; Heath asked for and received reas-
surance from the judges that requests for bail, counsel, and the

right to challenge jurors or judges were inappropriate. The King dispatched one of the clerks of the Council to discover how Castlehaven stayed so well-informed. He answered that an anonymous benefactor had written out the news, had wrapped it around a stone, and had tossed the stone through the window of his cell in the Tower.[61]

THE TRIAL

We like to think of trials as structured quests for facts. But adversarial law is as much about style as about fact, about obfuscating as much as clarifying, about self-interest as much as objectivity. Fact and process constrain the possibilities for persuasion, but they alone neither assure nor achieve a specific outcome. Trials are confrontations, rhetorical swordplay within set rules. Like the swordplay of the theater, trials are constructed to persuade their audiences. The purpose of a prosecution is to convict its defendant, and the purpose of a defense is to avoid conviction. Regardless of fact and even law, the best performance is the most convincing one. And the most convincing performance is usually the one most strategically attuned to the fears and ideals of the judge and jury. Despite proprietary discussions of the law's reliance upon "artificial reason," even in court, attorneys worked within the world. Contemporary conventions of rhetoric and logic conceded this, linking style to action and persuasiveness to practical results.[62]

Criminal trials in early modern England were quite different from their modern counterparts; in far too many cases, "nasty, brutish, and short" was an apt description. Except on points of law (which rarely arose), counsel was not allowed. Defendants in felony trials had no right to warning of the evidence against them and only a restricted right to call witnesses. There were few formal rules of evidence or restraints upon judicial questioning. The defendant had a virtually unrestricted freedom spontaneously to challenge those speaking against him or her, but this was matched by the equally unrestrained power of those opposing the accused. Few defendants probably had the nerve or the ability to do more than stand silent or deny the charges against them. As James Fitzjames Stephen put it, "A criminal trial in those days was not unlike a race between the

King and the prisoner, in which the King had a long start and the prisoner was heavily weighted."[63] Early modern trials were the prosecution's to lose; the King's men had the advantage in legal knowledge, in evidentiary resources, and in witnesses.

However, the trial of a peer was a little different.[64] On the one hand, the odds of acquittal were even slighter than in other hearings. The Crown's case was presented by highly skilled attorneys; the jurors were hand-picked; the division among investigators, judges, and jurors was exceptionally blurred. Acquittals for aristocratic defendants were so rare that the verdict itself could justify the inclusion of a case in collections of state trials. The situation was too politically charged for it to be otherwise; when, as in Castlehaven's situation, the King's antipathy for the defendant was already clear, no result but conviction could reasonably be expected. On the other hand, the trial of a peer was more complicated than most other hearings. Castlehaven's trial had two opening statements, eight witnesses for the prosecution (some of whom were examined twice in court), and innumerable small wrangles between the Lord Steward and the defendant over questions of procedure. Most early modern criminal trials took minutes; the trial of a peer routinely took several hours or even days. There were likely to be set speeches instead of simply stated accusations, technical defenses instead of just denials. The legal issues were often muddier, the defendants better prepared, and official interest keener than in more ordinary cases. Because the crimes at issue were more complex and less familiar than the thefts and homicides that stocked the standard criminal courts, a better chance existed to exploit and to explore legal ambiguities. Gentle defendants had no more rights than any other prisoner, yet high status often translated into discretionary privileges—visitors, books, and prosecutorial information that enabled prisoners with or without formal counsel to construct detailed defenses. In court, some aristocratic defendants (but not Castlehaven) were allowed pen and ink to help them follow the case against them; in the same spirit, others (but not Castlehaven) were permitted to answer each specific accusation when it was presented.[65]

If the accused was a peer, the King's attorneys had to be concerned about not only a loquacious defendant, but also an exceptionally demanding jury. Aristocrats acting as jurors had extraordinary freedoms: they had often been investigators in the case they now heard; they sometimes questioned the witnesses themselves; they used the judges only when they chose and only as advisers concerning technical points of law. In most ways, they were both judge and jury. And given the education of many English gentlemen, the audience they comprised was a special challenge to any speaker; they shared with many attorneys a classical education in both logic and in rhetoric.

With the possible exception of the Bishops of the Church of England, probably no group was more attentive to the King's desires than was the aristocracy, but the jurors were not the only ones who mattered. The trial of a peer was a public spectacle, likely to be well-attended, widely reported, and repeatedly discussed. Like all trials, it was, therefore, valuable as a didactic opportunity; properly controlled, it could be a vehicle through which to tutor the public about the King's views of the law, hierarchy, and the bond between monarch and people. Because it was the trial of a peer, it had lessons to offer as well about the obligations of privilege and about the Monarch's particular loyalties. These possibilities made the performances in the trial almost as important as the verdict. A prosecution that allowed a defendant to assuage the insult to his honor or to besmirch the reputation of the King was a failure even if it resulted in a conviction. If the lessons of the prosecutors did not prevail, something was lost regardless of the verdict.

The trial of the 2nd Earl of Castlehaven opened early on Monday, 25 April, and was completed in a single day. The twenty-seven peers chosen to act as judge and jury filed into the Hall shortly after eight o'clock in the morning, ascended twelve steps to the top of the gallery, and seated themselves according to rank on benches arranged on either side of a long table. At the head of the table was a chair draped with a cloth of state. Next, the seven judges who would act as legal advisers to the peers entered in order of precedence and sat at a table arranged for them at the lower end of the gallery. The four prosecuting lawyers (Attorney-General, Solicitor-General, the Queen's Attorney-General, and a King's Sergeant-at-Law) and the two clerical officers of the court (the Clerk of the Crown and his assistant) followed, settling into their own assigned places near the chair of state. Castlehaven waited under guard in a small room nearby.

About nine o'clock, seven sergeants-at-arms carrying seven maces entered. Behind them, in "greater state than ever I saw before" one witness claimed, came Coventry, Keeper of the Great Seal, and for this occasion, Lord High Steward of England. Resplendent in black velvet laced with gold, Coventry saluted the peers; they saluted him; he mounted the gallery to sit in the chair of state. The Clerk of the Crown in Chancery presented him with the royal commission empowering the court. After a sergeant-at-arms called for silence, the commission was read aloud. The Usher of the Black Rod, kneeling, presented Coventry with a white rod of state. A second sergeant-at-arms took the staff and held it upright throughout the trial. The jurors answered as their names were read aloud. The Lord High Steward asked that the indictments be brought in. The Lieutenant of the Tower was called to produce the prisoner, and Castlehaven, accompanied by guards, was brought to the bar. He bowed to Coventry and to his peers. The first trial of an aristocrat for felony in the reign of Charles I had begun.[66]

Castlehaven's trial was an uncharted challenge; the public threat was obvious enough when a charge of sodomy was linked to treason, but was it clear when sodomy was linked to rape and property? These were serious accusations, but were they serious enough to cost a peer his life? The inquiry had gone too far for the Council not to act, and the Earl's recalcitrance limited their options. But was there a greater threat in allowing the testimony of such vulnerable witnesses to condemn an Earl? In presenting a case where the fit between the evidence and the legal requirements was so insecure? And in offering Castlehaven a public forum for his own complaints?

Three legal officers shared the responsibility of presenting the case against the Earl: Sir Robert Heath (the Attorney-General), Sir Richard Sheldon (the Solicitor-General), and Sir Thomas Crew (King's Sergeant).[67] Heath, the senior attorney, had a well-deserved reputation for his piety, his seriousness, and his support of royal prerogatives. It was primarily his responsibility to persuade, while the more junior men reenforced his contentions with the relevant legal histories. Crew and Sheldon opened and closed the case; Heath controlled the proceedings in between. Trials of peers were rare enough that to some extent each was sui generis, but in most instances, the King's attorneys focused their speeches upon a defendant's alleged acts rather than upon his life more generally. In deference to the social position of an aristocrat, the lawyers assailed the improbability of a defendant's guilt with scrupulously detailed discussions of the evidence against him. In Castlehaven's case, however, the attorneys reversed the trajectory of deduction; they presented the defendant's prior life as the central proof against him. Ultimately, the prosecution implied, the Earl was guilty not because of what he had done with Broadway and Fitzpatrick, but because of what he had once done with Skipwith and Anktill. He was guilty not because there was clear evidence of rape and sodomy (although royal officials would insist that there was), but because his history showed him to be capable of such behavior. As one rendition of the case has Heath explain:

> if your lordships could be persuaded, that this wicked Lord at bar, has heretofore led a virtuous life . . . then it is probable and likely that these so heinous crimes now laid to his charge, proceed from malice . . . but if all his actions (as by evidence it will plainly appear) have been beyond imagination brutish and beastly . . . then have your lordships just cause to judge of the present by that which is formerly past and esteem of him as an all-mischief-daring offender.[68]

The prosecution built its argument upon three contentions: rape and sodomy had long been reviled; these were no ordinary rapes or sodomies; Castlehaven was dishonorable and so likely culpable. Each attorney rehearsed the Biblical and legal history of the crimes, stressing a long and constant pattern of condemnation. Rape, Heath said, had been a crime in England since "time immemorial," and a felony since the time of the Anglo-Saxons.[69] Crew reminded his audience about Sodom and Gomorrah; Heath brought Leviticus, Genesis, Judges, Romans, and Thomas Aquinas to his aid in order to suggest that sodomy could be a crime of intention as well as of consummation. Sheldon tried to turn a potential liability (that sodomy had not been a secular crime in England before the 1530s) into an asset, arguing that there had been no need since sodomy was "not known in England in ancient time." Heath and Sheldon also tried to deflect potential objections to the narrative that they were orchestrating. They assured listeners that rape required carnal knowledge, but not prior chastity, nor crying out, nor prompt prosecution. They told their audience that justice demanded that an injured wife be allowed to testify against her husband. And contending that "where the law does not distinguish, neither must we," Heath (in contradiction to the tradition of construing capital offenses narrowly) maintained that the general words of the antisodomy statute provided a definition of carnal knowledge that emission, not only penetration, could fulfill.[70]

Once the history of rape and sodomy generally had been demonstrated, the attorneys turned to the particulars of Castlehaven's case, specifics that Heath said surpassed even the imagination of pagan rulers, poets, and historians. Sodomy or rape, Heath told the audience, had been "scarce" heard of among the English. And until Castlehaven, the Attorney-General lamented, Charles I's reign had been free of aristocratic scandal. For a husband to procure the ravishment of his wife, Crew said, turned a horrible crime into one "in the highest degree against the bond of nature." Heath marveled that a man would sully his partner "which the wickedest man that ever I heard of before would have [wished] virtuous and good, how bad so ever himself be."[71] "It has been reputed one of the miseries of war [for] men to see their wives and daughters ravished and deflowered before their faces," Sheldon elaborated, "yet he [Castlehaven] esteems this a happiness and a pleasure, he desires it, procures it, enjoys it and delights in it."

Typically, the King's attorneys would have followed such speeches by previewing the evidence for the jurors, but in this instance, saying that it was "so full and so obscene," they left the witnesses themselves to introduce the details. The witnesses essentially repeated the contents of their depositions. In other trials with aristocratic defendants, jurors questioned the men and women giving testimony, but there is no evidence that they did so here. Nor is there evidence that Castlehaven spoke to the witnesses, although at several points he did address the Lord High Steward and the King's attorneys. The Earl spoke at length only after the last witness against him had testified. The first witness to speak was Walter Tyte, Castlehaven's steward. His evidence was not a discussion of the alleged felonies, but a recitation of how poor Skipwith and Anktill had been before coming to Fonthill Gifford, and how prosperous they had since become. The Countess's written testimony was read next; she, too, began her story well before 1630, with the first week of her marriage. Telling her that "her body was his body and what he commanded her do she ought not but to perform," Castlehaven, she testified, ordered her first to sleep with John Anktill, then with Henry Skipwith, and finally, with Giles Broadway. Since she was unwilling, he had held her down while Broadway raped her. Broadway "had the use of her body"; but, she insisted, she never surrendered to him in her heart.

Then came Fitzpatrick and Skipwith, still focusing upon Skipwith's background and Castlehaven's generosity. They described Skipwith's affair with Lady Audley as a consensual relationship that the Earl hoped would produce a son. The two men testified as well to group sex among the Earl, his men, and the woman named Blandina. Two other servants told similar stories. Fitzpatrick's admission that the Earl had "spent his seed but did not penetrate his body" appeared almost as an afterthought, even in the one version that portrayed Castlehaven as not only the footman's active, but also (and still more shamefully) as his passive, partner.[72]

The last three witnesses contradicted what had come before. Lady Audley's written testimony denied anything but coercion in her relationship with Skipwith. As her mother had, the younger woman detailed not one, but a series of humiliations from the Earl. Giles Broadway claimed that despite the involuntary actions of his body, he had done his best to resist the Earl's exhortations. Broadway admitted that he had been convinced to assault the Countess, but insisted that in the attack, he had "spent seed but entered not."[73] Castlehaven denied both felonies. As we will see in more detail in the next chapter, he attacked the competency of the witnesses and the evidence, pointed to the discrepancies between various testimonies, and accused his son and wife of plotting to murder him.

Rape and sodomy are not, of course, merely symbols of disorder—they are acts with real consequences for real people. If such crimes figuratively threatened the family and the state, they also actually harmed unwilling participants. But what makes acts into crimes is not intrinsic qualities, but the circumstances of their occurrences. So intimately do the circumstances attend the result, that in a sense, they themselves become the crime. All acts of rape and sodomy had the potential to be seen as threats to individuals, families, and the state, but in early modern England not all such acts were seen that way. Heath, Crew, and Sheldon built upon the premise that a man who violated his protective responsibilities as a father and a husband, and his social responsibilities as a peer, was a man who could commit rape and sodomy in circumstances with palpable repercussions for the jurors, the Monarch, and the broader social fabric. By linking the fate of Castlehaven and the nation, Heath, Crew, and Sheldon reintroduced, albeit obliquely, the link between sodomy and treason. They framed the evidence so that listeners troubled by its technical proficiencies had to weigh that danger against the danger of acquitting someone whose betrayal was more insidious than most, but no less treacherous for that. Castlehaven, prosecutors argued, was profligate with property that belonged to him only in trust for future generations, he encouraged sin where he was expected to teach rectitude, he betrayed the safety of those whose protection should have been dearest to him. He was so impious in his soul that he was capable of unbelievable impieties in his actions. He betrayed male honor through his weakness as a father, master, and spouse, and aristocratic purity through his attempt to corrupt his lineage. His behavior, the attorneys reminded people, showed how without proper vigilance, even the cornerstones of society—hierarchy, family, authoritarianism—might prove a mask for tyrants.

The true por-
traiture of

the Earle of
Castlehaven.

The Lords that were his Peeres fate on each fide of a great Table
covered with greene, whofe names are as followeth.

1. The Lord Wefton, Lord Treafurer. 2. Earle of Manchefter,
Lord Privy Seale. 3. Earle of Arundel and Surrey, Marfhall. 4. Earle
of Pembroke and Montgomery, Lord Chamberleyn. 5. Earle of Kent.
6. Earle of Worcefter. 7. Earle of Bedford. 8. Earle of Effex. 9. Earle
of Dorfet. 10. Earle of Leicefter. 11. Earle of Salifbury. 12. Earle
of Warwicke. 13. Earle of Carlifle. 14. Earle of Holland. 15. Earle
of Danby. 16 Vifcount Wimbleton. 17. Vifcount Conaway. 18. Vifcount Wentworth. 19. Vifcount Dorchefter. 20. Lord Piercy. 21. L:
Strange. 22. Lord Clifford. 23. Lord Peter. 24. Lord North. 25. L:
Howard. 26. Lord Craven.

This "true portraiture of the Earle of Castlehaven" served as the frontispiece of
the first pamphlet devoted to the Earl's trial (1643). Appearing in London about
six months after the beginning of the English Civil War, *The Arraignment and
Conviction of Mervin Lord Audley, Earle of Castlehaven...* did its best to draw parallels between the disgraced 2nd Earl and Charles I. By permission of the Folger
Shakespeare Library, Washington, D.C.

Elizabeth Barnham, Countess of Castlehaven, 1st wife of Mervin, 2nd Earl of Castlehaven. The co-heiress of a prominent London alderman, Elizabeth Barnham married Castlehaven (then Lord Audley) sometime before 1612. Her inheritance helped finance the purchase of Fonthill Gifford, a lavish Wiltshire estate that became the family's primary home in England. When she died (sometime between 1622 and 1624), the Countess left the Earl with six children. Engraving by Lombart after a portrait by Anthony van Dyck. By courtesy of the National Portrait Gallery, London.

Called James Touchet, 3rd Earl of Castlehaven. The son and heir of Mervin and Elizabeth, it was James's complaint to the Privy Council that prompted the investigation of his father. The complaint alleged that the 2nd Earl wasted the family's estate on servants and had even encouraged one servant to sleep with James's adolescent wife. Portrait by Peter Lely. By courtesy of the National Portrait Gallery, London.

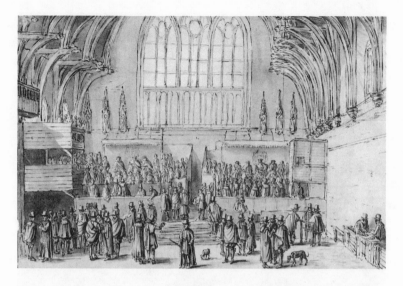

The Courts of the King's Bench and Chancery in Westminster Hall, where in 1631 a special "theater" was constructed for the trial of the 2nd Earl of Castlehaven. © The British Museum, London.

A detail from *The Life and Death of Mr. Edmund Gennings, 1614*. In early modern England, status mattered even in disgrace: while aristocratic criminals were usually beheaded, common felons died more slowly and painfully by hanging. In this scene, the condemned felon prays, standing in the cart that will soon pull away to leave him hanging. Giles Broadway and Florence Fitzpatrick, the servants accused along with Castlehaven, died in this way; six weeks earlier, Castlehaven had been publicly beheaded on Tower Hill. By permission of the Folger Shakespeare Library, Washington, D.C.

Alice Spencer, Dowager Countess of Derby, by an anonymous engraver. Renowned for her formidable will, the Countess (shown here in a widow's veil) was the mother of Anne Stanley Brydges, the 2nd wife of the 2nd Earl of Castlehaven. In this engraving, Alice Spencer sits above a genealogical tree that depicts her marriage to Ferdinando Stanley, 5th Earl of Derby, and the subsequent unions of their daughters with the Earls of Castlehaven, Bridgewater, and Huntingdon. © The British Museum, London.

MONUMENT OF ALICE COUNTESS OF DERBY.

Funeral Monument of Alice, Dowager Countess of Derby, built to her speci-
fications shortly before her death in 1637. Engraving by W.P. Sherlock. The
Countess's eldest daughter, Anne Stanley Brydges, who had married the 2nd
Earl of Castlehaven in 1624, survived him by sixteen years. But in this mon-
ument, still standing in St. Mary's Church, Harefield, that marriage is effaced.
Anne, the first daughter kneeling beneath her mother's tomb, is identified not
as the Countess of Castlehaven, but instead as the wife of her first husband,
Grey Brydges, 5th Baron Chandos. By courtesy of the National Portrait
Gallery, London.

A satirical depiction of Edmund Curll, from "The Art and Mystery of Printing," the *Grub Street Journal*, 1732. Curll, one of Grub Street's most infamous and prolific printers, is shown here drying the ink on copies of his best-selling collection, *Cases of Impotency*. This anthology of aristocratic scandals included a version of the Castlehaven trial. © The British Museum, London.

CHAPTER 3

A VERDICT, BUT NO RESOLUTION

ike most societies, Tudor and Stuart England was a civilization rife with anxieties—about physical and spiritual security, about geographical and economic mobility, about masculine identity and authority, to name just a few. The public articulations of these concerns (often embodied in the imagined mannerisms of Catholics, foreigners, women, and the poor) revealed a series of shared assumptions. People assumed that there was a clear and constant distinction between good and evil; that evil was not only easier but also more guileful than good; that despite its superiority, good did not routinely triumph; that sinning often became addictive because small sins inured one's sensitivity and led to ever larger and less reversible transgressions. Temptation was never merely individual; the commonwealth was understood to be an integrated community in which collective responsibility implicated people legally, financially, and spiritually for one another. The battle against sin was constant, and the strong in that battle were both obligated to the weak and endangered by them. In a fallen world, even predestinarian salvation had a social element—how could one defend oneself and one's dependents against the onslaughts of the demonic?

This was the question around which the King's attorneys built their explanations of Castlehaven's danger to the country. They used concepts that were both familiar and reliable, extracted from the specific fears of the surrounding society. Good prosecutors—then as now—sever the bond between jurors and accused that is implicit in the notion of a jury of peers. They replace it with sympathy between jurors and accusers, melding what most distresses the prosecutor about the charges with what he or she believes will most distress the jurors. The images invoked may seem formulaic, but conventionality lends them strength. Prosecutorial recitations are lessons in applied social theory, not speculative exercises. Whether done cynically or sincerely, the simplest way to communicate effectively with jurors is to remind them of what they already believe. Today jurors choose between tales told by competing attorneys; in early modern England, where defendants almost never had attorneys, prosecutors sparred with a more difficult and shadowy opponent. Despite their greater control over courtroom speechifying, they had to contend with jurors who might know the defendant and/or the accusers. In most instances, mobility, population growth, and growing social differentiation had vitiated the tie between jurors and defendants, but in the close world of the peerage, prior knowledge remained a safe assumption.[1]

What is most striking about the prosecution against the 2nd Earl of Castlehaven is the diversity of fears that the attorneys invoked in their presentations. The crimes of which the Earl was accused were capital, but not unpardonable, and, as we have already seen, the case against him was not invulnerable. Yet, embedding the specific charges into a broader edifice of sin, the prosecutors found the means to argue that the accusations signaled not only a specific danger, but also the lurking dangers behind all hierarchical relationships. The aggregation of sins which the Earl committed suggested both his incorrigibility and evil's ubiquity. The accusations against Castlehaven touched upon so many different fears that regardless of which legal audience we consider—grand jury, trial jury, or King—each had likely reasons to judge the defendant as beyond redemption. Equally as important, by framing the case as they did, the prosecutors implicitly asked jurors to transcend the imperative to punish a particular defendant and instead to accept a more general responsibility. Every conscientious householder heard at least one thing that could chill the heart, and at least one that might suggest a worrisome association between the Earl's life and his or her own.

This was a brilliant approach to the evidence gathered in the investigation. It not only obscured the fact that the technical evidence for both rape and sodomy was imperfect, but also concealed the narrative weaknesses of the case. Castlehaven's co-defendants in a coherent story would have been Anktill and Skipwith: they were the ones enriched by Castlehaven's favor, they were the ones allegedly forced upon the Countess and Lady Audley, they were the Earl's admitted favorites. The substitution of Fitzpatrick and Broadway for Anktill and Skipwith, in fact, remains mysterious. Whether Anktill and Skipwith were spared by ongoing relationships with Castlehaven's daughter and stepdaughter/daughter-in-law, by a refusal to be drawn into confessions by intimidation or promises of immunity, by greater loyalty to the Earl or still some other consideration, their impunity left the prosecution's story hopelessly disjointed. The prosecutorial strategy created continuity by grafting one tale onto another. The histories of Anktill and Skipwith became the background to the indictment of Fitzpatrick and Broadway rather than unfinished and unattended business.

Regardless of the verity or falsity of the capital charges against Castlehaven, the case was a catalog of behaviors and attitudes that contemporaries feared as both base and powerful.[2] Instead of controlling his household, the Earl, it would be said, was effectively a servant to his servants; they controlled his purse as well as his emotions. He gave them money, he gave them land, and he gave them the use of his female relatives. He quite happily tried to disinherit his son and in encouraging the "pollution" of his own lineage, seemed quite happy to corrupt the peerage. He equivocated in religion, and his family had more intimate ties to Ireland than to any English shire. So Castlehaven appeared unreliable in his will and masculinity, unfaithful to the peerage, and unstable in his Englishness. These failings were not felonies, but their inclusion in the case was critical to its success; it was through these misbehaviors that the prosecutors deflected the question of specific guilt onto a broader, more diffused plane of vulnerability. These characteristics appeared as both cause and effect of the two felonies.

Every common law trial began with an arraignment, a formal charging of the defendant in which the Crown officially entered its complaints, and the accused publicly declared innocence or admitted guilt. The arraignment of any prisoner, even an Earl, was usually routine. The indictments were read aloud, the defendant pleaded guilty or not guilty, and, if not guilty, accepted the conventions of a jury trial. Ritualistic as this exchange might be, it had considerable symbolic as well as practical importance. The ceremony affirmed before all observers that the defendant was the person named in the accusations, and more important, that he or she accepted as legitimate the power of the legal forum. The authority of the law relied upon such affirmations; it was difficult legitimately to shame someone through procedures that he or she had publicly rejected.

As Lord High Steward, Coventry oversaw Castlehaven's arraignment, instructed the jurors in their duties, acted as a go-between for the jurors and the judges on points of law, and pronounced the final sentence. He also opened and closed the proceedings. Coventry used these opportunities to speak, through Castlehaven, to a wider audience. His themes were the uprightness of the King, the purity of English justice, and the intimacy of both with the Divine. Coventry was presiding rather than prosecuting, but he reinforced the messages of the King's attorneys; his speeches strengthened the notion of the trial as a contest between not simply good and evil, but good stewardship and bad. Lord Audley had told his father that he had turned to Charles I because, "that hope to find him a father when my own forsakes me is now under God my only comfort." Coventry made sure that his listeners knew how willingly the King had embraced that role without repudiating his custodial obligation to the Earl. The King's interest, Coventry explained, was only in truth and fairness. Charles I did not establish the court to orchestrate a mindless condemnation of Castlehaven; the Earl deserved a chance (if he was innocent) publicly to redeem his reputation. Coventry assured his listeners that, despite the seriousness of the charges, the King had instructed him to give the Earl every possible legal advantage. Having been indicted by "gentlemen of quality" in Wiltshire, the Earl would now be tried by his social brethren, men "whose heads and hearts are as full of integrity as their veins are of blood," men whom Coventry would instruct to ground their verdict in reason rather than emotion.[3]

Coventry likened Charles I's response to the suspicions about Castlehaven to God's response to the stories of iniquity at Sodom and Gomorrah (surely not an accidental example). Like God, the King had sent men to investigate the rumors; like God, he would have preferred repentance to the need for punishment. The trial, Coventry said, showed the desires of both God and King to bring sinners to redemption. "He [God] has formerly by lighter afflictions sought to draw you to him," the Lord High Steward told Castlehaven, "but they not prevailing, now he forces you to come to him and implore his mercy." And as God was the model for the process, so, too, He would be a participant in the proceedings. Coventry held that the peers were incorruptible, but he warned Castlehaven that, in any case, dissembling would be useless. If he were innocent, he should "speak boldly and not be daunted," but if he were guilty, the only course was to

> use no subterfuge to conceal truth for that is *concilium adversus Dominum*. And if you have a guilty conscience that is more than a thousand witnesses. And if God knows that you are guilty, he will put it into the hearts of the said peers to find you so.[4]

Emphasizing the great concern of both God and Charles for their "children" drew attention to the Earl's apparent unconcern for his. Coventry's invocation of Sodom indirectly introduced one of the crimes at issue, although since God had promised to spare that city if it contained even ten righteous men, the reference also alluded to the power of even last-minute repentance.

The Lord High Steward's next speech, a charge to the peers, combined praise of their nobility with uneasiness about their potential independence. Coventry vested the privileges of a jury of peers in their integrity; they took no jurors' oath nor could they be challenged. Yet the Lord High Steward spent considerable time as well cautioning the men who sat before him. He warned them to fight against their respect for Castlehaven's family and against their hatred of the crimes alleged; "the head must sway the heart," he said. In questions of law, he urged them to rely upon the expertise of the judges rather than upon their own opinions. Once again, his words implicitly contrasted the jurors and the defendant—the integrity that was supposed to separate peers from more humble men, and the judgment that allowed reason to "rule the affections" were exactly what the prosecutors would contend that the Earl had failed to manage.[5]

Coventry's addresses were important, but the crux of the official presentation against Castlehaven was the performance of Attorney-General Heath. While his juniors Sheldon and Crew told the jurors what the Earl had done, Heath told them why it mattered. In his first, and longest oration, given before the jury heard the witnesses, Heath explored the roots of Castlehaven's alleged degeneracy. The Earl, Heath explained, had betrayed four different sets of obligations—to God, to his gender, to his status, and to his country. The most important of his sins was impiety, the root, Heath insisted, of all of the rest. Castlehaven had lost his own way, and he had endangered the sanctity of others. Instead of protecting his inferiors for God, he turned them from God, and he did so in a manner that undermined the very distinctions that guaranteed the social order.

Heath's accusations invoked something still darker than rumors of Catholicism: atheism. "I shall be bold," he said, "to give your Grace a reason why he [Castlehaven] became so ill; he believed not God." He reproached the Earl not for popery, but for "being constant in no religion." Heath's comments made a sin out of what in other circumstances might have been a virtue: that the Earl, tempted by Catholicism, had returned to the rites of the English Church. To the Attorney-General, this was evidence of irresolution, not enlightenment, a cloak for the "sin of all sins." By making devotion rather than theology the issue, Heath could condemn Castlehaven without impugning either the jurors (several of whom were either Catholics or had Catholics in their immediate families), the spectators, or the Earl's accusers (two of whom, Lord Audley and Fitzpatrick, were Catholics). Allegations of atheism were also more damning; they meant disloyalty not only to Christianity or to the national church, but also to a moral way of life.[6]

Castlehaven, Heath elaborated, treated religion as a fashion, changing it to suit his desire of the moment. Such wavering implied a lack of control, a vulnerability to influence, an effeminate vacillation. The Earl was faithful to no religion, Heath said, but "in the morning would be a papist, and in the afternoon a Protestant." The witnesses offered details that appeared to support Heath's view. According to one rendition of the trial, Castlehaven's steward testified that the Earl and his first wife "turned" in religion after moving to Fonthill Gifford; in another, the steward associated the conversion with the time when Castlehaven "went into Ireland and entertained this Skipwith." Either version offered the same message; here was yet another example of Castlehaven's weakness before the influence of others. In her deposition, the Earl's stepdaughter/daughter-in-law told the jurors that she had been married both "by a Romish priest in the morning and at night by a prebend of Kilkenny." In fact, such arrangements undoubtedly reflected accommodation to the Catholicism of Lord Audley and the Protestantism of his young wife, not to Castlehaven, but the episode appeared to support Heath's portrait of the Earl as a religious Janus, born a Protestant, become a Catholic, untrue to both. Castlehaven's fault, then, was hypocrisy, adhering outwardly to two religions, but respecting none. While this stance might have had certain tactical advantages for an Englishman with an Irish title, it suggested someone who took not even the most momentous commitments seriously. If a man scoffed at the promises of hell and heaven, what respect could he have for human relationships? The Earl's hardness toward God inured him, the argument went, to all sin, eventually blinding him from even recognizing sin. Heath concluded that "there never observed to be such a concurrence and confluence of vices in the person of any one man as in the prisoner at the bar." Both Catholics and Protestants, then, had ample reason to distrust the Earl.[7]

By grounding the indictment of Castlehaven in a religious problem that had been the focus of public concern in England for more than half a century, the Attorney-General reminded his listeners that while Castlehaven's crimes might be unusual, the enticements that led to them were not. Religious inconsistency and occasional conformity were not rare in early-seventeenth-century England; the civil restrictions on nonconformists inescapably encouraged religious opportunism.[8] The temptation was one that many people could recognize. Heath's speech was a challenge to his audience; their reactions were to be a gauge of their own ongoing struggles with sin and with religious constancy. Castlehaven was brought to them for punishment, but also to be made a palpable example. No man could turn from God without endangering himself, his family, and his nation.

CASTLEHAVEN AND THE
RESPONSIBILITIES OF MANHOOD

To the authors of conduct books and hortatory sermons, the responsibilities of a head of household were clear and constant.[9] As noted earlier, the position meant accepting not only material but also spiritual responsibility for one's dependents (wife, children, servants). It meant offering them an ongoing school for the body and the soul, a place where subordinates could learn to make their ways in life. It meant caring for the immediate physical welfare of those within one's supervision, guiding them toward productive futures, and preparing them for their appropriate places in church and nation. Well-ordered households meant hierarchies that produced order through social harmony, families that produced stability through dynastic tenacity, and leaders who produced authority through self-control and moderation. Being a subordinate within such a household meant accepting the benefits and the constraints of one's position, appreciating the former and recognizing the importance of the latter.

Anarchic households were particularly abhorrent because the household was the emulative structure that at once illustrated and legitimated the benefits of monarchy. Analogies between family and kingdom were ubiquitous in early modern England. Many commentators saw in fatherhood the figurative if not the literal origins of kingship; many saw in kingship the rationale for a particular kind of fatherhood. The family was depicted as a little commonwealth, the kingdom as a family writ large. Good kings offered their subjects fatherly protection, help, and comfort; good subjects offered their kings familial obedience, loyalty, and aid. Claims of political importance strengthened the case for patriarchal fatherhood; claims of biological inevitability the case for paternal monarchy. In both family and nation, the best government was the simplest; authority vested in a single, male, ruler. Anything less opened the door to the anarchy to which fallen humanity so easily inclined.[10]

The proper head of a proper household (or kingdom), by definition, was an adult male. The superiority that devolved "naturally" to men made them the legitimate rulers of both women and inferiors. Their supremacy was quite literally written into their bodies. The predominant medical construct of the day, the humoral system, dictated that gender, health, and disposition depended upon an always fragile balance of bodily fluids. This balance depended itself upon each body's internal thermostat. Although the structure was more continuum than polarity, women generally were colder and moister than men. This lack of heat and dryness translated into female weaknesses of not only the mind, but also self-control and moral constancy. Physiological frailty made women constitutionally unsuited for authority. The anarchic propensities of male children and servants were less indelible; with time and proper influence, they could grow into proper men. Without a steadying adult male hand, however, unruly, ineffectual, and ultimately riotous households were inevitable. In what everyone acknowledged was neither an easy nor a simple nor an ever completed task, adult males were expected to restrain the intrinsic inclinations of wives, children, and servants for extravagance, willfulness, and idleness. Wise superiors, like judicious monarchs, used persuasion rather than punishment to get their way, but they never forgot the didactic value of physical chastisement. Adroit heads of household, like adept rulers, knew the value of careful delegation and good counsel, but they also understood the difference between consultation and dependency. Men were expected to be violent, but they were also expected to control their violence. Self-mastery was the characteristic that distinguished a responsible adult male. It was so critical to resisting the temptations that would foment disorder that it came virtually to define respectable manhood. Outside of the aristocracy, the surest indication of self-mastery was moderation; within the peerage, a caste for whom performance and display were considered necessary attributes, self-mastery meant emotional restraint, probity more than moderation.[11]

In theory, wives were first among the household's subsidiary members, the immediate authority for most matters concerning children, servants, and the daily routines of domestic management. In their husbands' absences, wives acted in their stead; they were partners (albeit inferior partners) to their husbands. Although under no obligation to do so, successful husbands used their wives as advisers and as deputies. Similarly, although the ideal offspring listened more than spoke, wise parents consulted with their children on matters that would affect them and whenever possible, took account of their opinions. And while good servants and apprentices were obedient, they, too, might properly have some influence with their masters. They were never to usurp the places of wives or children, but they could earn trust and even limited authority if they proved themselves to be reliable and responsible. In large households, hierarchies as clear as those within the family also developed among the servants. Theoretically, life within a household was a mix of absolute and graduated structures of authority. Different authors of prescriptive literature emphasized different elements of this formula, each stressing what attracted him or her in the ideal and what alarmed him or her in contemporary practice. Allowing for such differences, convictions about roles within the household were relatively impervious to the fundamental religious and political upheavals of English life between about 1450 and 1650.[12]

Yet not even in prescriptive literature could authors ignore the fact that their tidy images rarely encompassed the untidiness of life. Structurally and individually, households and kingdoms routinely deviated from the ideal, inadvertently testing cultural beliefs about what was necessary for social harmony. First, a society built of nuclear families was a hopeful fantasy in a country where as many as 25 percent of adults never married, and an even larger percentage of those who did found themselves widowed within fifteen years. Households without male heads were not common (or welcomed), but neither were they rare.[13] Second, even in households where nuclear families were unbroken or had been reconstituted, the realities of war, business, and patronage meant that husbands and masters were often absent. In such situations, subservience was often of necessity more titular than tangible, and direct supervision by a household's head necessarily sporadic.[14] Third, biology both was and was not destiny; the divisions so fundamental to social organization were also recognized as dangerously porous. Men and women had different humoral constitutions, but within each individual, the humoral balance was perpetually in flux. Some men were cold and effeminate, some women were hot and masculine, any person might on occasion diverge from his or her own norm. The usual barrier between the sexes could all too easily be transversed.

Personal idiosyncrasies invariably added to these structural anomalies. Legal records, state papers, literature, and even prescriptive works bristle with stories of unruly wives, oppressive husbands, ungrateful children, and deceitful servants. Separation agreements (de jure and de facto), dismissals, disappearances, disciplinary codicils to bequests, complaints of adultery, bigamy, theft, and various forms of domestic violence testify to the innumerable disjunctions between ideal and application.[15] Husbands and wives, parents and children, masters and servants spontaneously modified the rules for households to suit their own capacities and preferences. But variations were not necessarily dysfunctional; as long as the conflicts and compromises remained personal, the system could absorb them. Incidental diversity affirmed the durability of the broader model. And egregious individual irregularities were the abnormalities that proved the rule. Like most paradigmatic structures, patriarchal ideology was largely self-confirming.

And yet conundrums remained. What were the acceptable limits of obedience, discipline, or incongruity? What recourse was allowable if heads of household or their dependents breached those limits? If inferiors were like subjects, did allowing a spouse or servant actively to disobey an ungodly order mean that a subject could do the same with an unjust command from the Monarch? If a King could impose corporal punishment for the greater good, could a master legitimately use similarly bloody forms of discipline? No consensus existed about the practical answers to these questions. Anxieties about the uncontrollability of women and servants were quite open; they suffused contemporary treatises, ballads, plays, and pamphlets.[16] Anxieties about the political implications of interdependence were more difficult to articulate; their implicit repercussions constrained all but the most general discussions of legitimate domestic disobedience. The solutions offered for repressive situations—to defy one's secular lord only should he defy God, to take oppression as a test of spirit, to love one's spouse and household so wisely and so well that serious discord was impossible—evaded rather than confronted the tensions that produced them.

Castlehaven's case starkly exposed such difficulties. An aristocratic household that failed as dramatically as did the one at Fonthill Gifford endangered its inhabitants and the broader logic of analogical didacticism. For the King's attorneys, Castlehaven's household revealed both the horror of his crimes and an explanation for his behavior. Only an immoral man could have contemplated acts such as those alleged against the Earl; only an ineffectual man would have been unable to restrain himself if presented with such temptations. The Castlehaven portrayed by the prosecutors was helpless before the dependents whom he was entrusted to command. As the attorneys presented the story, rape and sodomy were merely the latest in a series of offenses affirming that long before 1630, the Earl had been unmanned. The prosecution's emphasis upon how much worse Castlehaven's crimes became when he chose his wife, son, and stepdaughter/daughter-in-law as his victims set the stage for what one commentator called "inducements to believe this indictment" from the witnesses.[17] The inducements illustrated not the specifics of felony, but the specifics of Castlehaven's abnegation of authority. Of the witnesses who spoke against the Earl in court (or whose written answers spoke for them), only the three without whom there could have been no case (the Countess, Fitzpatrick, and Broadway) directly mentioned rape or sodomy; of the ten deponents whose pretrial evidence helped to frame the prosecution, only these three plus Lady Audley specifically discussed the felonies. The information offered by the witnesses showed how completely Castlehaven's was a household turned upside down; how a weak head, sly servants, and unruly women fomented disorder at Fonthill Gifford.

The testimonies provided two complementary stories, each of which virtually ignored Fitzpatrick and Broadway in favor of other members of the household. One was the general tale of carnal debauchery—adultery, group sex, voyeurism, and exhibitionism—already detailed. The second molded those details into a story of obsession and humiliation: the Earl's obsession with his servants and his willingness to humiliate his family for their benefit. Castlehaven had doted upon favorites long before his current troubles, the witnesses contended. Anktill earned £1,000 in service; Skipwith the freedom to spend £500 per year from the Earl's resources, and each considerable single gifts of money and property. The Countess deposed that the Earl had told her that "he loved Anktill above all the world"; several witnesses testified that Castlehaven told Skipwith that "he had rather have a son of his [Skipwith's] begetting than by any man in England."

The power of these infatuations overwhelmed for the Earl any sense of patriarchal responsibility. Castlehaven campaigned to convince both his wife and his stepdaughter/daughter-in-law to sleep with Anktill and Skipwith (as well as others), assuring the Countess that "it was no sin for her to lie with a man by his desire or appointment" and Lady Audley that if she did not obey his injunctions, he would "turn her out of doors." He made the women dependent upon the favorites for spending money, and offered both his wife and stepdaughter/daughter-in-law cash in exchange for sexual cooperation. The testimony of Giles Broadway offered evidence that, left unrestrained, this pattern would have continued. Broadway had received neither gifts nor special privileges from the Earl, but, according to the page's testimony, Castlehaven had assured him that lying with the Countess "might be his [Broadway's] making."

These details chillingly corroborated the results of misrule. The evidence exposed the Earl as deeply impressionable, ready to betray his soul, his fortune, and his family to please a favorite. Here, apparently, was a household in which the master fomented disorder, a commonwealth in which obedience brought physical abuse and deference brought dishonor. Here servants governed with the master's blessing, and their rule illustrated the horrific consequences of such a transposition: they made sexual partners of aristocratic women, both matronly and young; they spent lavishly on themselves while refusing necessary monies to their superiors; they humiliated their social betters and were cruel to their inferiors. Castlehaven had humiliated those whom he was to protect, indulged those whom he was to restrain. In place of hierarchy, lineage, and order, his household followed principles of opportunism, dispossession, and endless strife. As the prescriptive literature cautioned, when the feet directed the head, chaos was inescapable. The condemnation of the Earl would not only right the inversion of his household, but affirm the integrity of both the jurors and the broader social structure. Coventry, in his exhortation to Castlehaven before his sentencing, singled out the Earl's affronts to his Countess, his stepdaughter/daughter-in-law, and his son as those that were "too much for me to speak . . . too much for you with shame to hear."[18]

The Earl tried to defend himself by drawing a different picture from the same materials, one emphasizing the qualities that made all servants and all women suspect. Denying anything improper in his relationships with his attendants, he insisted that neither his wife nor daughter needed coaxing from him to be unchaste. Of the Countess, he said, "tis too well known my wife has been naught." He alleged that she had had numerous affairs with servants without his encouragement or consent. Her sexual voraciousness (and his inability to satisfy it) was, according to Castlehaven, her motive for plotting his judicial murder. As for Lady Audley, the Earl concurred with what Henry Skipwith had alleged in court, that "there was love" between the two. Somewhat contradictorily, one text supplements that statement with a claim that Lady Audley, too, slept with "divers of the Earl's servants." Either way, according to Castlehaven, Lady Audley refused to accept the finality of her marriage or to suffer its shortcomings quietly; he "would gladly have [had] his daughter in law leave his house." The Earl had no better to say about his male inferiors: his son was manipulative, impatient, and a bad husband; his servants were duplicitous, disruptive, and vengeful.[19] In its ramifications, the Earl's depiction of Fonthill Gifford was less different than he might have hoped from the prosecution's. If (as he argued) his intimates now schemed against him, then in proving their conspiracy he proved as well his inability to keep order. If (as he argued) his wife was adulterous and sexually gluttonous, then in proving her betrayal he proved as well his incapacity to control her. If (as he argued) his servants wanted revenge for earlier attempts at discipline, then in proving their insubordination he proved as well his ineffectuality.

Castlehaven's claim that his son "would have his lands" and the Countess "a younger husband" invoked tensions surrounding gender and generation that would have been both familiar and ominous to his jurors.[20] If in the prosecution's narrative, patriarchal nonfeasance ended in chaos, in Castlehaven's, it ended in patricide and petty treason. Neither ending likely quieted the concerns of listeners. Castlehaven's account was less sensational than the story presented by the Crown, but both explanations suggested that he could not govern. Both depictions of the household at Fonthill Gifford disclosed how fragile, how critical, and how vulnerable to personal idiosyncrasies were the foundations of every household. Both led to the same conclusion. Without self-mastery, there was no manliness; without manliness, no hierarchy; and without hierarchy, no harmony and no order. Whether victimizer or victim, Castlehaven was an example that could not be allowed to stand unanswered.

CASTLEHAVEN AND THE HONOR
OF THE PEERAGE

Castlehaven's failure as a head of household affected the image of every male head of household; his failure to be honorable spoke more specifically to his fellow peers. The aristocracy considered itself to be *the* community of honor; if the Earl was guilty, the shame touched the entire group. But what exactly constituted honor? Like other concepts intended to secure precarious social truths, the notion of aristocratic honor was conveniently vague.[21] Peers were born to honor, yet lineage created a propensity for honor, not the thing itself. A growing sentiment argued that honor came by doing as well as by being; that it belonged to those who provided their King with advice, arms, cash, and continual parochial illustrations of the advantages of paternal governance, not merely to those born of a certain rank. This more meritocratic definition joined rather than replaced the old equivalency between honor and blood. The two were not always easy companions. Could any man, however lowly born, be raised to honor through good service? Did any peer, regardless of his behavior, retain some honor? Was honor ultimately a matter of internal conviction or of external affirmation? And if the latter, confirmation by whom? Such questions were of course unanswerable. Yet the Castlehaven case made their contemplation unavoidable as well as raising yet again sharp questions about gender. What constituted female honor among aristocrats? Could an adulterous woman be honorable if her adultery was involuntary? Could adultery ever be truly involuntary?

The spokesmen for the King during Castlehaven's trial repeatedly reiterated the aristocracy's special claim to honor. As we have already seen, the Lord High Steward opened his charge to the jury by praising the peerage's particular integrity. Peers, Coventry said, were men whose probity was absolute; they were so accountable that the law did not need oaths from them as it did from more ordinary jurors. Peers would "do that for justice, which others do for oaths."

Heath praised the jurors as "honorable peers, such as of whose wisdom and sincerity there can be no questions, but to have an honorable hearing."[22] Extravagant flattery was in the Crown's interest, to be sure, but the acclaim here was quite specific. Peers might be peers by blood, but what ennobled them, the language suggested, was their reason and their responsibility, exactly the two forces which the prosecution was about to argue that Castlehaven had abandoned. "The offenses whereof the delinquent at the bar stands now charged are much aggravated in respect of the quality of the person indicted . . . ," Heath explained, "as he is great in his birth so should he have been good in his example." It was not, of course, a crime to behave ignobly, but if Castlehaven lacked the benign virtues of other peers, claims of his degeneracy became not only more credible but also more serious. His sins, the prosecution implied, betrayed his rank as well as his gender. Coventry, in condemning the Earl to death, did so with special grief, he said, because Castlehaven was "of an ancient noble family within the kingdom."[23]

Having defined the peerage as a community of honor based in virtue, the prosecutors then worked to separate the defendant from that community and to settle the victims within it. The charge to the jury, the prosecution's primary arguments, and the Lord High Steward's sentencing each contrasted the Earl's status and his actions. His plans struck, the speeches maintained, at the sanctity of land and lineage, the two defining substances of nobility. Castlehaven seemed willing to squander what had been entrusted to him to preserve. The Lord High Steward found the idea that the Earl would debase his lineage by encouraging Skipwith and Lady Audley to produce a son of polluted stock particularly appalling. He could not fathom how "having honor and fortune to leave behind, you would have had the spurious seed of a varlet to inherit both." That the Earl entertained fantasies of encouraging the Countess to take a page as her third husband made things (if possible) still worse. The purity of aristocratic blood was a fiction, but the concept of its inviolability was sacrosanct. Castlehaven's "gentling" of Skipwith and Anktill through patronage, gifts, and marital ties could be read as a parody of the standard path for promotion in early Stuart society, a process particularly strained by the ambitions of recent favorites such as the Duke of Buckingham. That any nobleman could tolerate, much less arrange, liaisons such as those arranged by Castlehaven seemed incredible. For a jury upon which sat so many newly ennobled men not to punish such aberrations was unthinkable.[24]

The King's attorneys presented the behavior of the Earl's victims in a stark contrast to Castlehaven's conduct. As already noted, the Countess and Lady Audley both absented themselves from court in the name of modesty; each reaffirmed her written deposition privately in nearby chambers rather than expose herself unnecessarily to public view. Their testimonies suggested a view of honor as conventional as Castlehaven's was eccentric. The Countess, Heath noted, obeyed her husband even when it made "a shipwreck of her honor"; Lady Audley did her stepfather/father-in-law's bidding to the same effect. Encouraged to commit adultery, both women (according to some accounts) initially hid from their attackers. When raped, the Countess had tried to kill herself "for grief of her misfortune" even though her sin had been involuntary. The attorneys portrayed her as a woman striving, like Lucretia, for honor in an impossible situation. Lady Audley's compliance sat less easily, but by emphasizing that her corruption had occurred when she had barely passed the age of legitimate consent, the prosecutors encouraged doubts about her culpability. The contrast with the Earl, who talked of honor, but seemed incapable of embodying it, was obvious. The Countess accepted responsibility for acts that had been forced upon her; Castlehaven forced dishonor upon others and denied responsibility for his own actions. The Countess and Lady Audley were willing to make their victimization public, even when it hurt their reputations; the Earl thought so little of "degenerating from nobleness and humanity" that he refused to acknowledge guilt even when it was incontestable. "Nothing," Coventry told Castlehaven, "does more trouble me than that deep and great protestation which you made against so clear and apparent an evidence."[25]

The Earl countered these claims by associating himself with the nearest immediate embodiment of honor (his jury) and attacking the honor of the witnesses upon whose stories the prosecution had relied. He had been undone, he told the jury, by the malice of those whom he commanded, and what had happened to him could happen to them as well. His difficulties were not random afflictions; his tribulations, he claimed, were the direct consequence of his concern for, not his neglect of, honor and public respectability. His wife was a "common whore"; she had borne a bastard soon after they were married, and "for her honor," Castlehaven said, "it was my ill fortune to wear the horns, though I put them in my pocket." His son and daughter-in-law despised each other, yet, according to evidence deposed but not repeated in court, Castlehaven had begged Lady Audley "not [to] make herself and her husband an open shame and scandal to the world." The servants rebelled against the strictness of his discipline; his son against the strictness of his control. Honorable men deserved protection from dishonorable inferiors—lewd women, avaricious heirs, and spiteful menials. Castlehaven asked his jurors to put the "condition" of the accusers against his own in deciding whom to trust, their "parentage" next to his "condition and state." "No man," he concluded, "ought to be condemned but [by] sufficient witnesses." Neither servants nor wives, Castlehaven argued, could be sufficient to condemn an English peer; to decide otherwise was to make him a martyr to the honorable support of lineage, public decorum, and hierarchy.[26]

Castlehaven's belief in conspiracy would not have seemed fantastical to any of his jurors. Everyone knew that only fifteen years before, when the then Countess of Essex had wanted a new husband, she had managed both the sexual liaison and the murder of a courtier who had opposed it. If a reminder were necessary, her discarded husband now sat on Castlehaven's jury. Castlehaven's depiction of his own Countess fit the view of women generally, but more particularly it fit the view of women who, as both the former Countess of Essex and the current Countess of Castlehaven had done, frequented the Jacobean court. The jurymen knew as well that sons nearing their majority did sometimes grow impatient with long-lived parents. Bitter quarrels within aristocratic families were hardly rare. In addition to any number of less esteemed examples, Charles I had rather unceremoniously ignored his father's wishes as the old King aged. The Prince's behavior in his father's last years had made very clear his unwillingness to wait quietly for his inheritance. Successful plots by servants had no recent public history, but they were a staple of the theater, and less than three years after the murder of the Duke of Buckingham, his career was still a powerful example of how influential an ambitious favorite could become. In a society where strained relationships between husbands and wives, or fathers and sons, or masters and servants were common, the court's unwillingness to support him, Castlehaven argued, could only threaten the security of every peer.[27]

The Earl hoped to use the dishonor of his household to prove his virtue, but it was extremely difficult for him to establish himself both as an honorable patriarch and as someone whose family and servants were disreputable. The prosecution depicted a lineage polluted by Castlehaven's treachery; the Earl, by blaming those closest to him, depicted one polluted by his weakness. Either way, there was infidelity, betrayal, and debasement. Only an honorable man, the prosecution contended, could lead an honorable household, and a household in chaos was in itself evidence of dishonor. Peers, moreover, had a special duty to be honorable because they influenced not only their households, but also the wider community. A peer who treated honor as the prosecution claimed Castlehaven did, soiled the characters of his wife, children, and servants; unless the jurors acted firmly, his very presence would condemn the peerage to disparagement by association. The words of the moralist Owen Feltham, written in 1620, could have summarized the prosecution's argument: "Earth has not any thing more glorious than ancient nobility, when it is found with virtue. [But] a debauched son of a noble family, is one of the intolerable burdens of the earth, and as hateful a thing as hell."[28]

CASTLEHAVEN AND THE DUTIES OF AN ENGLISH SUBJECT

The dissipation of authority within Castlehaven's household impugned the Earl's manliness, and the dishonor of his actions undermined the honor of his station, but the prosecution tied these difficulties to questions about a further site of potential disorder: the Earl's political obedience. They saw in Castlehaven's behavior confirmation for anxieties about the degrading results of Catholic and Irish seductiveness. The prosecutors had to do relatively little to exploit fears about the Earl's Englishness; as we have already seen, he had ties to Catholics and ties to Ireland, and he was accused of sodomy, a crime whose origins the Solicitor-General firmly placed abroad. The gravest political treacheries in recent memory had had Catholic origins and in 1630, the Earl's Catholic brother had been imprisoned upon suspicion of treason. The bloodiest rebellions in recent memory had come from the Irish, and in 1630, Castlehaven had been punished for being more tolerant of Irish tenants than the Articles of Plantation allowed.

Castlehaven's contrariness, moreover, undermined the credibility of Charles I as an exemplar, a peacemaker, and a just judge. Few Englishmen or women would have doubted the sincerity with which the King presented himself as a personal model to his subjects. And as the patriarch of secular patriarchs, he was expected to be a resource for his people in times of trouble. He was to resolve conflicts large and small, not only conflicts in matters chargeable at law, but also discord between husbands and wives, parents and children, near and distant neighbors. A good King ensured peace among his subjects by acting as a mediating parent, combining concern, fairness, discipline, and mercy to dissolve animosities before they became too destructive or too public. This was not an empty obligation, particularly for the early-seventeenth-century aristocracy; royal intervention (usually via the Council; sometimes, but not always, in combination with more formal legal avenues) was perhaps the most common and most effective means of dispute resolution for the nobility. Castlehaven's son drew upon this expectation when he first complained about his father, telling the Earl that "on this monstrous change of a father into an enemy, I stand upon my guard, and from you appeal to the father of our country, the king's majesty."[29] Good kings reconciled their subjects to one another, and accepted responsibility for their people's sins. In return, subjects were expected to listen, to be grateful, and to obey.

Charles I's personal interest in this case was public months before the trial. Despite rumors that suggested that he was determined to see Castlehaven punished, in court, the King's spokesmen emphasized the Monarch's determination to find the truth, his desire "to free his sacred person from the cries of his people if he should leave unpunished such matchless crimes." The King, his attorneys said, understood punishing Castlehaven (were he guilty) as a matter of spiritual as well as of secular importance; crimes as grievous as his could justifiably expose England to Divine retribution if left uncastigated. "If these offenses be not punished," Attorney-General Heath assured the court, "certainly a heavy judgment must fall upon the land." God had destroyed the tribe of Benjamin for refusing to surrender a brutal rapist; he had annihilated Sodom and Gomorrah when they had failed him. For the health of England, Charles I could neither spare the rod nor use it carelessly.[30]

Associating Charles I with successful peacemaking was an unexceptional, but somewhat generous, characterization, since the King had already failed first to influence Castlehaven's behavior by example and then to convince his family to reconcile.[31] Castlehaven's household defied the personal values dearest to the King: order, sobriety, and uxoriousness. Such blatant disregard of the royal example made a mockery of Charles I's belief that his behavior could will loving families into existence. The King's attorneys elided such conclusions by drawing attention to the contrasting characters of the two men. The King, Heath told the court, was "the pattern of virtue, not only as king, but in his person also." The Earl, he continued, did more "foul things" than any man ever before him. The Earl was a legitimate ruler who had not ruled legitimately; the King was a governor punctilious in his devotion to proper process. Hence, his refusal to proceed against Castlehaven merely upon rumor; hence, his instructions that this trial be "as equal as equity itself." "You shall demand nothing that the law can allow you," Coventry told the prisoner at the King's command, "but you shall have it."[32]

The Earl responded to what the prosecution saw as royal beneficence with neither submission nor gratitude. He insisted upon his innocence despite the repeated admonitions of the King's attorneys. He claimed that the prosecution was manipulating the legal process, and that they, not he, threatened order in society. As the King's attorneys busily tried to paint a picture that overwhelmed the legal problems of their case, the Earl posed question after question that reintroduced them. He answered Coventry's paean for the legal system with a complaint about the conditions of his imprisonment and a request for counsel; he interrupted Heath's oration about impiety with the demand that the Attorney-General leave off discussions of religion and "hold himself to the points of the indictments"; he stopped Fitzpatrick's testimony of buggery with the claim that evidence was inadmissible from any person (much less from an Irishman) who had not taken the Oath of Allegiance.

As we have already noted, he questioned the acceptability of a wife's testimony against her husband and of a base man's against a peer. He challenged the ability of an unchaste woman (as he said the Countess was) to complain of rape, and the validity of any such complaint not tendered immediately after the incident. He asked how evidence that did not confirm sexual penetration could meet the legal definition of either rape or sodomy. Castlehaven tried to cast the specter of treason that hovered around discussions of apostasy or Irishness back upon the prosecution through an assault upon the image of the King as just and upright. The case against him, the Earl argued, relied upon deficient witnesses offering defective testimony. Its persuasiveness was illusory, the product of bad faith, bad law, and corruption.[33]

The Earl's objections look like what in modern law would be a defense grounded on individual rights, but in the early modern context, they were more likely to have been intended as proofs of conspiracy. Castlehaven's complaints were not frivolous: counsel was permissible where the interpretation of the law was at issue; wives were not usually allowed to testify against their husbands; normal practice was to construe capital felonies narrowly, not broadly. Castlehaven was suggesting that justice in this case was being used instead of served, that interpretations of an ill-defined and unfamiliar process were really justifications for stratagems intended to advance the King's prerogatives and the conspirators' agenda. The Earl could only lose this confrontation, but his defense was still potentially damaging for the King. No aspersion against Charles I or his legal representatives by a peer in a public forum could just be left to stand. And in 1631, popular memory would not have forgotten that the agitation surrounding the King's imprisonment of recalcitrant members of the 1629 House of Commons had been (among other things) about his indifference to the niceties of legal process.[34]

Making the trial rather than himself the focus of attention, Castlehaven gave the jurors an alternative way of understanding his position. In effect, he was demanding that the law protect subjects not only from each other, but also when necessary, from the King and his deputies. The prosecution had argued for the Earl's unique corruptness; he countered with insistence upon his ordinariness. Legal irregularities and corrupt individuals, he said, explained how a man of good character, beset by the sorts of problems found in many households, could find himself convincingly attacked in a court of law. Were he convicted, he warned his listeners, "no foreman might lie with his mistress but his master should be accused as accessory to it . . . no man should be secure for his life, when his son came of age . . . none should strike his footman, but he might accuse him of buggery."[35]

By his alleged crimes, the prosecution said, Castlehaven had defiled the image of the head of household. Now, by his defiance and his counteraccusations, he frustrated the display of beneficent paternalism so cherished by the King. Castlehaven's defense was in many ways a transposition of the prosecution's own arguments. Both announced how critical dynastic continuity was to stability, and how fragile, how vital, and yet how tenuous were the bonds of mutual accountability that sustained it. Both portrayed fathers like kings in their own kingdoms; families like little commonwealths; and households as places of special dangers as well as special pleasures. Both drew attention to one of the most unremitting constitutional problems of the day: the proper limits of prerogative. The King's counsel emphasized the responsibilities of patriarchs; Castlehaven stressed the reciprocal obligations of dependents. The attorneys spoke of a subject's duties; Castlehaven spoke about their vulnerabilities. Both prosecution and defense claimed to speak in support of the paternalistic household; both implied that a victory for the opposition held considerable political as well as personal danger.

Castlehaven answered the prosecution's portrait of a patriarch turned miscreant with one of a patriarch turned victim. If this was a tale of impiety, it was one of impiety fueling the case against Castlehaven, not the actions by him. In contrast to Heath, the Earl spoke less of character and more of proximate causation, but in a manner similar to the Attorney-General's, he had a single explanation for the case. In the Earl's view, greed, not impiety, accounted for his predicament, the greed of his son, his wife, and his servants. The Earl believed that the necessary machinations of a conspiracy could explain many of the oddities of the prosecution: why he was imprisoned so rapidly; why six months elapsed between the alleged rape and the complaint; why, if he had colluded with a servant in a felony, he had allegedly chosen his wife's page rather than one of his own menials. Castlehaven told the jurors that he was a victim not of irreverence, but of the dangers intrinsic to the exercise of rulership. As a slightly later text had him tell the peers, "It is my estate, my Lords, that does accuse me this day, and nothing else."[36]

Rape, sodomy, besottedness, dissipation, weakness, and ingratitude on the one hand; conspiracy, lust, greed, and corruption on the other; both represented disorder and dishonor in particularly insidious varieties. Heath asserted that the Earl's impiety vitiated the manliness, honor, and obedience that were essential to worthy householders and noblemen. Castlehaven protested that the real danger lay in the prosecution's carelessness, not in his character. Both sides drew upon the same assumptions about the responsibility of a head of household, although each emphasized different aspects of those obligations. Demonizing Castlehaven offered the jurors an opportunity not only to disassociate themselves from the Earl, but also to allow themselves as good patriarchs to counteract a bad one. If the jurors believed the realm's officials, a decisive guilty verdict would renaturalize patriarchal governance, reaffirming its power to protect subordinates from internal as well as external threats. Castlehaven argued for a different path to the same end. He contended that by pursuing a case built from the testimony of inferiors, the prosecution had undercut the authority of all heads of households, whether they were peers or more ordinary men. By acquitting him, the peers could uphold patriarchy, piety, and honor, and at the same time, demonstrate their dedication to an order based in the privileges of status and the traditions of the common law. They could overturn the treachery of his (and, by extension, their) enemies.

These arguments were no more conclusive than the analogies upon which they rested, but that made their reaffirmation all the more important. Both sides argued not guilt-by-association, but rather guilt-by-explanation, each hoping to elucidate how one transgression (impiety or greed) conflated with and bled into all the others. In framing this story in terms of manhood, honor, and good governance, both the prosecution and defense folded it into predicaments faced by many privileged men in early modern life. By their rhetoric (deliberately or not), they made this a case about much more than a single man or a single family, exposing unresolved (and probably unresolvable) tensions within the prevailing social organization. The Castlehaven trial, despite the unimportance of its defendant (or perhaps because of it), became a canvas upon which an entire palette of social anxieties could be exhibited.

The jury deliberated for about two hours. When they returned, twenty-six of the twenty-seven peers condemned Castlehaven for abetting Giles Broadway in the rape of the Countess. Only Lord North, a peer of "spirit and flame" who had retired to the country years earlier when his quest for favor at court ended in frustration and poverty, voted for an acquittal. There is little doubt that the accusation of rape against the Earl was more shocking than the accusations of buggery. And despite the unresolved conflict over whether Broadway had actually penetrated the Countess, despite murmurs about the fact that neither Broadway nor the Earl had been able publicly to confront the Countess, better evidence supported the charge of rape than the charge of sodomy. While willing to assure the capital sentence that the King no doubt desired, many of the jurors balked at returning guilty verdicts on the counts of buggery. According to an anonymous contemporary, the jury argued bitterly about whether the requirements of the law on buggery had been met and about whether on this matter their own opinions or those of the judges should prevail. About half of the jury apparently believed that the evidence fell short, that the judges' interpretation was "contrary to the grammatical sense of the indictment," and that, outside of their own courts, the judges had no sovereignty. Three times during their deliberations, the peers consulted with the Lord High Steward as well as with the Lord Chief Justice. After the Chief Justice appeared "in the name of all his brethren to declare the law," two of the dissenting jurors agreed to change their votes. The final tally on the counts of buggery was fifteen for conviction and twelve for acquittal. That met the necessary threshold of a majority of at least twelve, but only barely.[37]

The twelve dissenting peers included four of the privy councilors: the Earls of Pembroke, Salisbury, Dorset, and Holland. They were joined by the Earls of Kent, Worcester, Bedford, Essex, Leicester, and Berkshire as well as by Lords North and Howard. In the main, the dissidents were the jurors who superficially resembled Castle-haven most directly: men within five or so years of the Earl's age of thirty-eight, with living sons, and of "ancient" families. Dorset, Essex, and Pembroke had themselves been the subject of earlier moral scandals. Of the ten jurors between the ages of thirty-five and forty-five, seven joined in the dissent; conversely, only one of the eight jurors over fifty did.[38] Only two of the seven jurymen who had no living male heirs were sympathetic. Only three of the twelve men who owed their peerages to the Stuarts were willing to acquit the Earl of buggery, and these three were all the younger sons of families with more established titles.[39] Even more strikingly, with the exception of Lords Percy, Strange, and Clifford, it was the dissenting rather than the convicting votes that contained all of the most familiar surnames: Russell, Somerset, Sackville, Devereux, Grey, Sidney, North, Herbert. Most of the jurors related to the Countess wanted to condemn the Earl for buggery, but not all; Pembroke and Bedford, for example, voted for acquittal despite such ties. Affinities of religion and geography had similarly mixed effects.[40] And as one might expect with a group based on heredity, some members of extended families found themselves united and some divided: the brothers Berkshire and Howard agreed; the brothers Holland and Warwick did not. The vote linked one set of brothers-in-law (Berkshire, Holland, and Essex), and separated three others (Leicester and Percy, Salisbury and Clifford, Worcester and Petre). There were Howards and Cecils in both groups.

But the dissent appears to have been more than solidarity built around a demographic profile. This was in no way a division between courtiers and others; with a selected jury, most men on both sides had close connections to the royal court. However, there were clear distinctions. The group voting to convict contained most of those known more for charm than talent, men such as Carlisle, Clifford, and Goring. The most obviously able men who joined them (Manchester, Weston, Dorchester, Conway, and Wentworth) were also those most immediately dependent upon the King.[41] In contrast, the dissenting group was more independent and while unquestionably supportive of the monarchy, included three of the four jurors who vigorously had opposed the Forced Loan and/or supported the Petition of Right. The most important influence on the jury was undoubtedly, as our unknown contemporary observer suggests, a reluctance to condemn the Earl for buggery when the evidence suggested "a degree thereof which the law makes not mortal." But having condemned the Earl, the jurors were also freer to register a protest against what they may well have seen as an instance of all-too-familiar legal legerdemain. Charles I's approach to Castlehaven's guilt was not that dissimilar from his approach to constitutional issues generally; as L. J. Reeve has argued, the King "assessed his actions in a moral and not a legal way."[42] Opinions about the state of England would shift and change many times throughout the 1630s, but there is a clear duplication between the dissenting jurors and those who eventually took arms against the King. Of the eighteen jurymen alive at the outbreak of the Civil War, six of the eight who had voted to convict the Earl of buggery (the other two perhaps being the jurors who changed their votes at the last minute) allied with Charles; only three of the ten remaining dissenters (two of them Catholics) did so.[43] Anxieties about the autonomy of both the peerage and the law seem a reasonable explanation for this pattern.

DEATHS AND QUESTIONS

When on 25 April 1631, the Lord High Steward formally condemned the Earl of Castlehaven to death, few people present probably expected that the sentence would be carried out. No English peer had been executed for a crime apart from treason in close to a century; James I had freed and eventually pardoned the Earl and Countess of Somerset after equally sensational convictions.[44] Pardons such as these were not always popular, but given the power of most nobles, they were hardly surprising. Moreover, the process of asking for a pardon and having it granted confirmed the King's munificence as well as the submission of the condemned. The Earl, it was said, "seemed much amazed" when the justices ruled that his actions constituted buggery. He was not alone in his astonishment. In 1632, the London attorney William Drake referred to the case as one in which "that was made buggery which was never accounted so before." Drake believed that because the law was at issue, the Earl ought at least to have been given the counsel that he requested.[45]

Here was a crime defined after the defendant had been indicted, a trial in which a wife had testified against her husband, a verdict reached by trusting the word of women, servants, and a Roman Catholic Irishman over the word of a man of rank and family. And no warrant for the Earl's execution was immediately forthcoming. By the first week in May, rumors were circulating widely about Castlehaven's fate. Correspondents reported that the judges of the common law thought that the Earl should be spared until Broadway and Fitzpatrick were tried and convicted; that the judges were uncertain if in the instance of a common felony, the King could change the Earl's punishment (as was customary in the case of a condemned aristocrat) from hanging to beheading; that Castlehaven had been or was about to be reprieved, if not pardoned. The longer he lived, some said, the more rumors that he would continue to live would gain legitimacy.[46]

Charles I ordered the Attorney-General on 7 May to prepare a warrant for Castlehaven's execution, and pleas to pardon the Earl arrived soon thereafter from at least four different sources. Three of the Earl's four living sisters immediately sent a petition to the King, begging him to investigate Castlehaven's claim of a conspiracy. They accused no one specifically, but assured the Monarch that such an inquiry would be a means "to conserve the honor of your justice and the peace of your tender conscience, by preventing the effusion of noble, Christian and innocent blood."[47] John Beaulieu reported that Lord Audley now offered "large moneys, and to take in his wife again" if the King would spare the Earl. Audley wrote to Castlehaven, rescinding none of his accusations, but enclosing copies of two petitions (now lost), and promising to pursue "any way better for your safety" that his father might suggest. The Queen herself, it was believed, sued for Castlehaven's pardon.[48]

Sir Archibald Douglas, the husband of Lady Eleanor Davies Douglas, Castlehaven's fourth sister, was the most assertive. Douglas went himself to the King's Bench and Fleet prisons and interrogated Fitzpatrick and Skipwith respectively. According to Douglas's report to the Privy Council, Fitzpatrick admitted that he had "had many fair promises made him" by Lord Audley and his counsel William Wroughton, including one that Fitzpatrick could become a footman to the Queen. Skipwith claimed to know that Wroughton had unsuccessfully offered one servant £80 to testify against the Earl. Skipwith reported as well that Giles Broadway had assured his father that he and the Countess had not successfully had intercourse, but even more critically, that the Countess had said that "she did nothing that might take away the life of her husband." Douglas had witnesses to these revelations. Fitzpatrick had declared that, having been once betrayed, "he would never speak a word till he was assured of his life," but Skipwith, Douglas said, was willing at any time to repeat his statements under oath.[49]

The entreaties left the King unmoved; they may even have hastened the date of Castlehaven's death. Given the power of the Countess's relatives, there were most likely active voices at court against mercy as well as for it. Charles I was particularly unsympathetic about breaches of sexual decorum; these years saw him support not only Castlehaven's execution, but also the severe punishment of a Scottish laird and an English knight in two instances of what the seventeenth-century English considered to be incest. As his pretrial proclamation about the consequences of attending Castlehaven's trial suggested, the King believed that even condemnatory public discussion of such matters could be contaminating. So he was unlikely to be sympathetic to or impressed by witnesses whose confessions of subornation might also get them out of prison. Nor was he likely to find Sir Archibald Douglas, whose prophesying wife had been banned from the court for her disruptiveness, to be a credible unveiler of conspiracy. Instead of freeing Castlehaven, on 11 May, the Council ordered the indefinite confinement of Douglas in the Fleet prison.[50]

Most important, the King was unlikely to be moved to mercy where he saw no sign of repentance. The link between grace and penitence was integral to not only English Christianity, but also English law enforcement. Free pardons were rarely free in either fiscal or spiritual terms. Nothing could guarantee a pardon, but a convict's refusal to validate the verdict of the Crown by confession almost guaranteed that no pardon would be granted. Mercy, in such circumstances, would have been an implicit admission of injustice. Contrition served an integrative function, transforming a trial from an adversarial contest into a ritual of recuperation. It legitimated the authority of the King and suggested that the seductiveness of the law lay in its justness as well as in its might. The critical act freeing the King to grant a pardon would have been the Earl's submission. Yet just as the Earl was problematical as a patriarch, so, too, he was problematical as a subject.

Castlehaven continued to insist upon his innocence. Despite heated urging from the Lord High Steward, the Earl refused to confess even after the jurors had rendered their verdicts. The earliest texts say that despite this recalcitrance, he asked the peers to convince the King to banish rather than to execute him; however, once back in prison, his resolve seems to have toughened.[51] He refused at first even to ask that Charles I remit his hanging to the more dignified beheading, proclaiming, one correspondent wrote, that he was "no more ashamed—he says—of hanging in a rope, then Christ was for his sins upon the cross." When the threat of losing access to communion did not draw a confession from him, even the chaplains sent him by the King grew shaken. On the scaffold Castlehaven remained determined, telling the assembled spectators that "for those two deeds and offenses whereof I stand accused I deny them for that I am not guilty of them, but do here clear myself of them at the hour of my death." Such self-assurance against the will of law and Crown made the sparing of his life not just improbable, but impossible. In respect for Castlehaven's "ancestors who had done good services to the Crown," Charles I did mitigate the sentence of hanging to beheading; at whose request we do not know. Three weeks after his condemnation, the 2nd Earl of Castlehaven was executed on Tower Hill.[52]

Most persons executed in early modern England died painfully and silently, with few spectators and even less attention to their dying words or wishes. But a felon's death was a moment of public spectacle and public education, a moment given special purchase by the importance that early modern men and women put on dying moments. Executions were supposed to remind the condemned and the spectators of their own fallibility, of their need for discipline, of the price of human vanity. And they were also visible reminders of the expectations of God and King. The public ceremony, the scaffold speech, even the grisly business of the death itself, were literally expected to embody the wisdom of obedience and the futility of defiance.[53] The essence of dying well, on the scaffold as elsewhere, was the recognition of one's humanity and a concomitant resignation before God's will. A good death on the scaffold legitimated the governmental claim that judicial murder had a didactic as well as a terroristic purpose. The ideal felon's death, then, was one that publicly endorsed both the power and the moral authority behind his or her fate. In death as in life, Castlehaven defied such expectations. He appeared as confident in his own innocence as he was resigned to his public fate. His refusal either to resist or to confess drove a wedge of doubt into the complementarity of law, King, and God.

The Earl seems to have devoted the time between his conviction and his execution primarily to spiritual matters. A correspondent of the Earl of Newcastle reported that Castlehaven "now speaks, prays, weeps, tells the confession of his sins, writes the confession of his faith. . . . Never man more humbled and wonderfully cheered by the receipt of the communion." He prayed regularly with the chaplains whom the King had sent to him, took the sacrament weekly, and published a signed testament to his faith in the Church of England. It was said that when the warrant for his execution arrived, Castlehaven had his coffin built and brought to him to contemplate. "I never took so much comfort as I do in this, which the world calls misery and affliction," he allegedly wrote to his sisters. Edward Hyde, visiting him the night before his death, found the Earl "as full of pity as ever any martyr was, and as void of passion."[54]

Castlehaven's execution, like his trial, attracted a considerable audience.[55] The behavior of a felon facing death and of the crowds observing him or her were always unpredictable, and the spectacle of execution could quite easily turn against the state. A convict too bold or too fearful in the face of death undermined the desired mix of deterrence and spiritual outreach. A delinquent who resisted or an official who seemed sadistic could incite a crowd to violence. A convict who combined the stoical qualities of a good death with an unremitting rejection of guilt destroyed the intended administrative and symbolic closure of the occasion. The Earl spent most of his time on the scaffold in private prayer, addressing the crowd only after repeated urging from the chaplains, and claiming that his long "affliction of imprisonment" had left him forgetful and virtually blind. When he did speak, he acknowledged himself to be a sinner who had squandered great worldly and heavenly privilege. Despite his continued avowal of innocence, he accepted the King's right to confine him and God's right to take his life.

And yet, while forgiving those who had accused him, he refused to legitimate their claims. He admitted having "wavered" in religion, yet insisted that the issue had "a long time been settled."[56] To prove it, he ordered one of his attendants to read aloud a detailed confession of his faith. Castlehaven thanked Charles I for earlier favors, for the trial, for the time to prepare for death, and for access to the chaplains. He prayed that the Stuarts might reign happily "as long as the sun and moon shall endure." But he added sotto voce to his thanks the statement that he had been condemned "upon as weak evidence as ever nobleman was condemned." One alleged eyewitness said that Castlehaven also prayed for the preservation of the King and Queen of Bohemia, a request that could have been understood to ally the Earl with a muscular Protestant foreign policy at odds with the accomplishments of Charles I.[57] Although some later commentators suggest that at the last moment, the Earl's courage wavered, the early texts say that he faced death "very confidently." His last request, out of "a kind of modesty," was to be interred fully clothed rather than in a winding sheet. His servants apparently did that and laid him to rest in the Tower's chapel.[58]

The Earl's performance on the scaffold transformed a ritual focused on his own spiritual condition into one that questioned the spiritual health of others. Implicitly undermining the Monarch's authority while accepting his coercive powers, such a death confused simple equations of conviction with guilt. John Bladen told Sir Thomas Fairfax with disgust that Castlehaven's mixture of penitence and defiance "has given cause to some to apologize for him." Joseph Mead concluded that the Earl "had been guilty of crimes of as high a nature as these and it may be of the same kind; yet was falsely accused of those two facts." Dorothy Randolph wrote to Lady Jane Bacon that Castlehaven "was much lamented; his son and wife as much hated." And Hyde, who had earlier derided "the rabble" who confused demeanor with innocence, declared himself converted after the execution. "On my conscience [I] think he is in heaven . . . ," Hyde wrote to his father.[59]

The trials and executions of the two men charged as the Earl's associates did little to allay disquiet.[60] Five weeks after Castlehaven's execution, Giles Broadway and Florence Fitzpatrick were tried before the Court of King's Bench for rape and sodomy, respectively. Realistically, neither man could have been acquitted. To have freed them would have been to vindicate at least partially Castlehaven's claims of innocence and, therefore, to indict the government for wrongful execution. As the judges advised the Lord Keeper:

> We for our parts thought it to stand with the honor of common justice, that seeing their testimony had been taken to bring a peer of the realm to his death, for an offense as much theirs as his, that they should as well suffer for it as he did, lest any jealousy should arise about the truth of the fact, and the justness of the proceedings.

On the 6th of July, Broadway and Fitzpatrick were both hanged at Tyburn.[61]

Despite their earlier confessions, at their own trials both men pleaded innocent. Broadway repudiated his prior statements, saying that he had not understood their implications. He insisted again that there had been force, but no carnal knowledge (and so no legal rape), between him and the Countess. As the Countess was now the only other witness to the alleged rape, his denial forced her to testify. She came to the court and confronted him, but their stories remained unreconciled. Fitzpatrick, acting, the judges said, as "one very ignorant or rather senseless," insisted that his examination had condemned the Earl, but not himself, and that in any case, he could not be convicted solely upon his own testimony. The Chief Justice acknowledged that self-incrimination was irregular, but said that in a capital case where culpability was mutual, the confessor as well as the accused must suffer. When the jurors asked the judges whether Fitzpatrick was a principal or merely an accomplice, the Chief Justice reminded them that all parties were principals in buggery, and maintained that the footman's age, understanding, and physical strength precluded any claim that he had been intimidated.[62]

At their executions, the condemned men were more conciliatory, but their behavior did not settle any questions about the uprightness of the proceedings of the last three months. Broadway and Fitzpatrick cleared Lord Audley of all wrongdoing and blamed their misfortunes on the Earl's "persuasion," yet, in different ways, each also supported the notion of a conspiracy. Broadway impressed observers by accept-

ing his death as "a true penitent," but he used the occasion not only
to insist again that he had never had intercourse with the Countess,
but also to portray her as promiscuous and murderous. Having been
asked by a "fat gentleman" in the crowd if the Countess had desired
him, he admitted not, but said that had he wanted to sleep with her,
doing so would have been effortless. "Skipwith and Anktill" he said,
"lay with her commonly." She had "made away" with her own bastard. She was "the most wicked woman that lived and had more to
answer than any one under the sun."

Fitzpatrick, whose enthusiastic declaration of Catholicism inspired jeering from some in the assemblage, was a less sympathetic
figure. And his story was still more damning. He held to what he had
said at Castlehaven's trial: they had engaged in mutual masturbation,
but not in penetrative sex. Yet he also alleged that his testimony had
been suborned. He said that after he had been in prison for three
days, the Earl of Dorset, speaking as if for the full Council, visited
him and encouraged him to implicate Castlehaven, promising that
"whatsoever he delivered should no ways prejudice himself."[63]
Broadway's aspersion of the Countess upheld the Earl's denunciation
of her and Fitzpatrick's tale of inducement (even with the parties
changed) bolstered Castlehaven's (and Douglas's) contentions of
intrigue. The words of two "mean" felons could easily be discounted,
but accompanying the protests at the trials and the Earl's conduct
when he faced execution, they complicated rather than settled
doubts about what had happened.

Could the Earl of Castlehaven have been so wantonly self-
destructive? Absolutely; he might have so hated his wife and son,
or so loved Broadway and Fitzpatrick, or so believed in his own prerogatives that he brought himself to ruin. In a society where neither
divorce nor disinheritance was an option, where the law traditionally defined crimes such as rape and sodomy conservatively, where
the stability of women and children was always suspect and a preference for male company not only accepted but expected, Castlehaven could genuinely have believed himself to be innocent of
crimes for which we might condemn him. In a largely self-sufficient
household, a "little commonwealth" ruled by its patriarch, the occasions for such abuse were manifold. Could the Countess, Lord Audley, and the servants have conspired successfully against the Earl?

Certainly; they could have found him so distasteful, or so untrust-worthy, or so long-lived that they decided to be rid of him. In a soci-ety where estate was status, where the heart of the law was judicial discretion, and where women and servants were seen as vulnerable as well as unreliable, the case against the Earl could easily have cohered around what we might label avariciousness, intimidation, and betrayal. In an economy with chronic underemployment and cir-cumscribed access to real property, the opportunities for and attrac-tions of conspiracy were numerous.

Could members of the Privy Council or even the King himself have wanted Castlehaven condemned so much that they were will-ing to be less than punctilious about procedure? Undoubtedly; they might have believed him to be so irresponsible or so dangerous or the law to be so vague that it justified exceptionally creative jurispru-dence and perhaps bribery. In a court where there were always nobles eager for forfeited property, where the King was better attuned to ends than to means, where the law could be frustratingly ambigu-ous, where indecorousness seemed an ever-present danger and obscurity almost the equivalent of death, the opportunity presented by Lord Audley's complaint against his father might have proven overwhelming.

Neither side in this case produced irrefutable evidence, but the nature of the allegations made such evidence unlikely. Castlehaven had credible motive, capability, and opportunity to do the deeds of which he was accused; but so, too, did his wife, son, and servants. It would be comfortable to use Castlehaven's guilt or innocence to fix our reactions to him and to those around him. But it would also be deceptive; our knowledge is different, but not necessarily less par-tial, tainted, or bewildering than the information available to con-temporaries. The enigma of Castlehaven's guilt or innocence is irre-solvable, but we can say a considerable amount about how and why the Earl was convicted and executed, and about why doubts con-cerning the case persisted. This trial touched upon some of the most dearly held categorical ideas in early modern English life and revealed them to be uncomfortably pliable. The belief of both the King's attorneys and the Earl that the sanctity of household and king-dom was at issue made the case about manhood and kingship as well as rape and sodomy. Moreover, it exposed unanswerable dilemmas

about identity and the proper limits of obedience. The belief of both
the jurors and the Earl that the sanctity of the law and peerage was
at issue made the case about the Constitution, while suggesting that
constitutional ambiguities were neither an always negotiable nor a
secure refuge.

One can imagine circumstances (say similar accusations against
a peer such as Arundel or Manchester) in which the strategies that
the prosecution employed here would simply not have worked. But
Castlehaven was a peer with few friends and well-connected enemies,
a nonentity with undeniable ties to Catholicism, Ireland, and disreputable relatives. Whatever actually happened at Fonthill, the
prosecutor's triumph was making Castlehaven's exculpation seem
more dangerous than the legal curiosities of the case or the use of
witnesses whose reliability normally was suspect. The Earl's attempt
to portray himself as a victim of a conspiracy against his position and
the protections of the law made him still more threatening. Castlehaven was found guilty because he had neither the reputation nor
the patronage to appear credible and because the tale he told was as
frightening as the one that he refuted. His obscurity made any accusation against him plausible, his legal acuity (however fortuitous)
made his acquittal dangerous, and his obstinacy made his death
inevitable.

CHAPTER 4

A HOUSEHOLD BROKE
BEYOND REPAIR

hen the 2nd Earl of Castlehaven entered court on the morning of 25 April 1631, he faced a cohesive, but temporary, assemblage of arbiters, most of whom knew him or knew of him. His fate rested, as we have seen in chapters 2 and 3, partly on ground laid open during the proceedings, and, as we have seen in chapter 1, partly on ground bared long before. When, after sentencing the Earl, the Lord High Steward broke his staff at the end of that Monday, he dissolved the court, symbolically declaring that the issues before it had been resolved. For most contemporaries, the story of Castlehaven's household was a six-month wonder, worn out by the time of his execution in mid-May or, if not then, at the latest, by the trials and hangings of his servants in the first week of July.

But for some people, this was emphatically not so. In important ways, trials do not end with verdicts or even with the punishment or release of defendants. Going to law had and still has social consequences that can extend far beyond a judgment. Castlehaven's trial changed the lives of all the principals, accusers as well as accused, dramatically and irrevocably. Closure was elusive and unpredictable in a scandal that breached as many conventions as did this one. Ironically, the Earl was the participant who might have been the most pleased by what followed his beheading; his surviving favorites were left richer and his surviving relatives poorer than they had been. For every major figure in the trial—not just the executed felons

Castlehaven, Broadway, and Fitzpatrick—death, not the breaking of the Steward's staff, marked the real conclusion of the case.

Lord Audley had said that he turned to Charles I in "the hope to find him a father," a convention that gained real substance after Castlehaven's death. Because the Earl's lands were forfeited to the Crown, as were the lands and chattels of every felon, the royal obligation to oversee the subjects' welfare became hands-on administrative responsibility. The law of forfeiture did not apply to titles or land in Ireland, so Lord Audley was made neither destitute nor a commoner by his father's death, but the future of the family's English property was left unsettled. The executed Earl's wife, daughter-in-law, and younger children were all in need of support. Debts were owed and wages unpaid. And there were innumerable other matters to be settled; should Charles I restore the family's ancient English barony, their properties, or both? Would he pardon the now Dowager Countess of Castlehaven and her daughter, the new Countess of Castlehaven, for their roles, however involuntary, in the scandal? Would he reunite the 3rd Earl and his now dishonored wife? Forfeiture made a felon's household literally the King's. Whatever Castlehaven might have given away to his favorites, had he died naturally, his son would have inherited the estates protected from alienation by entail. The price of Lord Audley's successful complaint was the loss of his right to those entailed properties; by his father's condemnation, Audley had traded one master for another.[1]

PROPERTY AND FORGIVENESS

Since the family's English estates fell to the Crown after Castlehaven's execution, the household at Fonthill Gifford had to be dismantled. The 3rd Earl of Castlehaven (the former Lord Audley) could be expected to reconcile with and provide for his wife (the former Lady Audley) and his younger siblings. The logical home for the 2nd Earl's wife was with her mother, the Dowager Countess of Derby. But there were problems. The 3rd Earl showed little interest in reunion; his wife showed even less. The Dowager Countess of Derby resisted accommodating either her daughter or granddaughter until and unless they repented, received pardons, and secured some form of annuities. She considered them both to have been tainted by their "wicked crimes" and was particularly angry that, against her advice, the former Lady Audley continued to spurn her lawful spouse. "And I am fearful," she wrote to Secretary of State Dorchester, "lest there should be some sparks of my grandchild Audley's misbehavior remaining, which might give ill example to the young ones which are with me."[2]

After several false starts, the King managed to broker an agreement among the principals during the summer of 1631. The new Earl and Countess of Castlehaven would not be reunited, but he would contribute to her maintenance. A £500 annuity drawn jointly from the incomes of the new Earl, the Dowager Countess of Castlehaven, and the Dowager Countess of Derby would provide the young Countess with an allowance. At the age of sixteen, she was effectively cast out of both her marital and her natal families.[3] Castlehaven's widow would return to her own mother's care. Only after they had accepted this settlement did Charles I pardon either the Dowager or the current Countess of Castlehaven, forgiving the one on the grounds of a wife's frailty before her husband and the other for a frailty "made more considerable by her tender years" which rendered her more "apt to be deceived by the allurements which were used to mislead her."[4] The younger children from the Dowager Countess's Chandos marriage remained with their Derby grandmother. Two of the younger Touchet siblings stayed with members of their natal family: George with his sister and brother-in-law, Dorothy and Edmund Butler; Frances in the custody of her uncle Ferdinando. Frances received the respectable sum of £2,000 to be used as her marriage portion. The arrangements for the two youngest Touchet children are unknown, but they may have continued with their schoolmasters in Salisbury. The Council paid off Castlehaven's debts and his servants with revenue from the forfeited estates.[5]

Over these same months, the Council set out to discover exactly what the Crown had gained fiscally by the 2nd Earl's condemnation. Rumors circulated that his English estate was insignificant, depleted in both real and movable property by Castlehaven's openhandedness. The common belief was that the dead Earl had actively attempted to defraud his heirs.[6] The 3rd Earl had estimated the value of his father's movable gifts to Henry Skipwith at approximately £12,000. The Crown's auditors noted only £1,000 worth of goods received into the Exchequer from the estate. Walter Tyte, the family steward whom the Council now authorized as its agent, calculated the family's rent roll for England and Ireland together at just slightly more than £2,000. Tyte, however, had earlier acknowledged that Castlehaven kept "all himself in his own custody" the deeds for the properties which he had conveyed to Skipwith.

In the middle of June 1631, Castlehaven's cabinet of "writings" was brought to London to be opened by the Attorney-General in the presence of the 3rd Earl or his counsel. After an inquisition held in Wiltshire later that summer, Heath had most of the conveyances arranged by the 2nd Earl declared as fraudulent, and the lands resettled upon the Crown. This more than doubled the King's profits, raising the estimate of the family's realty in England alone to £4,000 per year. And Heath was equally assiduous about movable goods. The final inventory of Castlehaven's estate no longer survives, but we do know that it filled nine hundred sheets of paper. One commentator thought the goods so valuable that he expected the High Commission to fine Skipwith £40,000 for their illicit possession.[7]

By the start of 1632, King and Council were ready to begin the less sensitive, although not necessarily less complicated, issue of disposing of Castlehaven's belongings. In January, the King returned the 2nd Earl's household goods to his son, but the plums in the pie were the realty. The deceased Earl had held property throughout Wiltshire, in London, and in several other shires, but, of course, the biggest plum was Fonthill Gifford. The 3rd Earl was the most prominent suitor for these lands. He had reason to be hopeful, for monarchs often granted at least part of a prominent felon's estates back to the former heir.[8] However much he disapproved of the estrangement of the young man from his Countess, Charles I could not ignore the fact that it was the 3rd Earl who had made public the disarray at Fonthill Gifford, or that he had done so specifically in defense of claims to property. The new Earl could expect that the King would recognize his loyalty by restoring his rights in the family's English lands.

The new Earl of Castlehaven had powerful competitors in that quest. Before his father had even been indicted, the Bishop of Salisbury had reminded the Council that by "ancient charter," goods taken from convicted felons in Salisbury (where Castlehaven had a townhouse) belonged to him. He reiterated the claim within a week of the 2nd Earl's condemnation. Later that spring, William Belou, a man who, by royal grant, had been given rights in the properties forfeited by felons, complained to Lord Treasurer Weston that his privileges were useless if the King insisted upon giving forfeited estates away. He asked for whatever monies the Crown would receive if it regranted Castlehaven's properties.[9] But the 3rd Earl's most significant rival had no need to write petitions for largesse. He was Francis Cottington, privy councilor, Chancellor of the Exchequer, and protégé of the Lord Treasurer. One of Charles I's confidantes on foreign policy, in July 1631, Cottington had become Baron Cottington, but he held no estate appropriate to his title. The Crown owed him tens of thousands of pounds for monies he had spent on the King's ill-fated 1623 trip to Spain. Cottington's requests were hard to ignore, and in September 1632, Charles I granted Fonthill Gifford and its ancillary properties to him and his heirs in consideration of £10,500 paid into the Exchequer and £6,000 paid to the 3rd Earl of Castlehaven. Official business often kept Cottington away from Wiltshire, but he kept house at Fonthill Gifford whenever he could, living there, a visitor wrote to Thomas Wentworth, "like a great Don of Spain."[10]

In May 1633, two years after Castlehaven's execution and sixteen months after the return of the miscellaneous household movables to his son, the King restored the Touchet family's English barony. Making the 3rd Earl of Castlehaven once again Lord Audley in England, Charles I also granted him his grandfather's precedence and (except for Fonthill Gifford and the lands that descended with it) his dead father's "manors, castles, lands, tenements, and hereditaments" in England. But the King expected the 3rd Earl to accept more than the surrender of Fonthill. Part of his reinstated revenues were to go toward "the maintenance of the Lady Elizabeth his wife, whom he receives, and of the children to be begotten between them."[11] Here was the reconciliation that both the King and the

Dowager Countess of Derby had sought unsuccessfully in 1631. More likely than not, the two reunions of 1633—of the new Earl and his Countess, and of the new Earl with his ancient English title— were dependent upon one another.

Charles I did not slight the 3rd Earl, but neither did he satisfy him. The younger man was compliant, but not resigned to either the loss of Fonthill Gifford or to the resurrection of his marriage. In December 1640, in the second month of the Long Parliament, he took advantage of the growing pressure upon royal councilors such as Cottington to introduce a petition in the House of Lords "about hard measures" in the loss of his estate. By February 1641, he had two separate, but linked petitions before the House: one to reverse his father's attainder, and, consequent upon it, another to restore Fonthill Gifford to the Touchets. He claimed that procedural irregularities invalidated both his father's trial and the transfer of property to Lord Cottington. The 2nd Earl, his son now argued, died the victim of an "unlawful conspiracy," but one directed from the Privy Council rather than from within the family. The son of Castlehaven's steward testified that his father, returning from an interview in December 1630 with Cottington's ally the Lord Treasurer, had said "Fonthill was the thing that was aimed [at]." At the center of the plot, as the 3rd Earl now described it, was "some powerful person," who had targeted Castlehaven "for his estate and especially for his principal house and manor of Fonthill, which has been since wrested from your petitioner." The 3rd Earl pleaded that members of the Council had taken advantage of his youth, bribed their way into the confidence of his attorney, and tricked the confused heir into signing away his birthright. His petition named no names, but it clearly implicated Cottington. After six months of investigation, interrupted repeatedly by more pressing business, the House rejected the 3rd Earl's petition. "My Lord Cottington, I see," William Calley wrote to Richard Harvey that July, "has blown away the little Earl of Castlehaven's pretenses." The spectacle of accuser turned exonerator was surpassed only by its unseemly context. The 3rd Earl, a staunch supporter of the King, pursued one of the King's most important ministers against the backdrop of debates over fundamental relationships among Crown, Church, and Parliaments. Castlehaven may have been "blown away," but in the interim, Cottington had resigned his major offices, retiring to Fonthill Gifford on the putative grounds of ill health.[12]

THE SOLDIER AND THE "JADE"

The later history of the alliance between the 3rd Earl and Elizabeth, Countess of Castlehaven, is obscure. He did send for her within a few months of his return to Ireland in 1633 and we know that in June 1637, she was at the family's house at Maddenstown near Dublin. That summer, the couple either quarreled over, or colluded to delay, the virtually completed sale of Stalbridge, Dorset, to the Earl of Cork. To prevent foreclosure on Maddenstown, Audley had sold Stalbridge for £5,000, one-fifth of which was to be rendered immediately in cash. Cork had paid the £1,000 plus the first of two £2,000 installments when the Countess refused to concede what she maintained were her rights in the estate. With considerable annoyance, Cork asked the 3rd Earl to command his wife's cooperation; when he did not, Cork claimed that the two, having gotten the necessary mortgage money in hand, were conspiring to obstruct the sale. It is unclear whether Audley and his wife were allies or at odds, but in November 1637, with the sale still unfinished, the 3rd Earl departed for a three-year sojourn on the Continent, apparently without the Countess. In 1639, Cork referred to her as "formerly married" to Lord Audley. By the mid-1640s, although the finances of the Earl and Countess were still entangled, correspondents described a gun-running confidence woman named Katherine Stamfort Downes (probably the 3rd Earl's mistress) as "now wife to the Earl of Castlehaven." The 3rd Earl spent most of the years between the mid-1640s and the mid-1680s on the Continent or in Ireland; as far as we can tell, the Countess spent them in England. The only later evidence that places the spouses together is a pass issued on 8 March 1679, for the Earl and "Elizabeth, his wife" to travel "beyond seas." The Countess was probably alive on 8 March, but she was buried in London eight days later. When the Earl set out from England on 30 June, he had already married one Elizabeth Graves. The earlier pass, in fact, more likely refers to this second Elizabeth, even though in March she had not yet legally married Castlehaven.[13]

The itinerancy of the 3rd Earl suggests the disappointment of his fortunes and perhaps his own desire to escape the past. As he had feared, although not quite in the way he had imagined, estrangement from his father had lost him the bulk of his inheritance. He spent the middle 1630s in Ireland with his sisters, often in the company of his youngest brother, Mervin. Despite his title and a loose alliance with Lord Deputy Wentworth, his public role was minimal. Although in 1643, he insisted that "the main of my estate lay [in England]," over the 1630s, he had sold off many of his English properties. He spent his years on the Continent traveling and soldiering until Charles I summoned him back from Rome in 1639 for help in the worsening Scottish conflict.[14]

Back in England, the 3rd Earl's activities fell into a pattern that would repeat with only slight variation for the next two decades. He hoped to find a way to serve his purse, his religion, and his King with honor, but the turmoil that engulfed Britain in the 1640s and 1650s was hardly a secure place for a Catholic loyalist domiciled in Ireland. He attended the King's Council at York, the Short Parliament, and the first session of the Long Parliament, speaking at the latter in defense of the loyalty of most recusants.[15] By the fall of 1641, he was back in Ireland, disgusted, he later wrote, by "the affronts daily multiplied on the King and Queen and other intolerable insolences tending to the destruction of monarchy and establishing of popular government." When later that year, some Irish Catholics mounted a rebellion against English rule, he offered to help subdue the rising, but was told by the Privy Council in Dublin that, as a Catholic, "uncapable of trust," he could neither join the government in the field nor leave the island to join the King. Despite his successful rescue of several English Protestants from the hands of Catholic rebels, within a year he found himself indicted (wrongly he insisted) for high treason. The Irish Privy Council ignored not only his pleas of innocence, but also complaints that his father would have seconded to discount accusers of "base condition," and a jury foreman who "associated himself with the Irish, changed his religion and went to mass." Disabused of any confidence in the government in Dublin, the 3rd Earl escaped and fled into the Wicklow mountains.

He intended, he later insisted, to join the King in England. Instead, the rebels convinced him to join them as a General of the Horse. For the next three years, he fought with the Catholic Confederates, but in 1646, he again changed sides, championing an agreement with the King's Protestant commander, the Marquis of Ormonde. Both the Papal Nuncio and the leaders of the Confederacy refused the proffered settlement. Disappointed, Audley left Ireland for the Stuart court-in-exile at St. Germain. He divided his time in the late 1640s and the 1650s between failed attempts to restore a Royalist government to Ireland and successful attempts to earn himself military rewards on the Continent. He joined Ormonde and the now combined effort of Royalists and Confederates against Oliver Cromwell, but by 1651, he was back on the Continent, fighting beside the Prince of Condé in the Fronde and, later, for the Spanish as a Major-General in charge of Irish regiments.[16]

Despite his loyalty, the Stuart restoration made surprisingly little difference to the 3rd Earl's status. He was welcome at the court of Charles II, and a participant in its pleasures, but his income (he felt) remained precarious. Charles II repaid Audley money that he had loaned to the Crown in the late 1650s and early 1660s. The 3rd Earl also received a pardon for his alliance with the Irish rebels, the restoration of some of his Irish properties, a partial grant of assessments owed the Crown (to be collected at his own expense), and eventually an annuity of £400 (later raised to £500).[17] The annuity was more easily promised than realized. The 3rd Earl's pleas for payment are a repeated theme in the State Papers of both Ireland and England from the Restoration until his death in 1684. He claimed hyperbolically in 1674 that only the annuity would ensure "that those I leave behind me which are most dear, may not fall to be maintained by the parish"; and in 1676 that only the money due would allow him to stay in a command that brought "a great deal of honor, but little or nothing to support it." His financial situation ensured that he was also a ready voice whenever the misfortune of others seemed likely to make new funds available.[18]

Once again, military engagement seemed his best hope for both needed funds and glory. Between 1660 and 1684, the 3rd Earl volunteered twice to help Venice against the Turks, fought on both sea and land in the two Anglo-Dutch wars, and commanded a regiment for the Spanish in their battles against Louis XIV. He acquitted himself honorably, but not lucratively, and learned that the Spanish government was no better than the English at meeting its financial obligations. Despite his clear willingness to go anywhere to fight either the French or the Turks, the labyrinth of international diplomacy in the late seventeenth century was considerably beyond his political skills; he was distrusted by and distrustful of seemingly all of his European colleagues and commanders.[19]

He was no happier with or more adept at politics at home. A minor companion of the King, Audley's name was associated with royal amusements rather than with policy. His attempts to influence either foreign or domestic affairs came to little. When he spoke in the House of Lords about Louis XIV's expansionism, his remarks were "thought by some very rash and hasty and accordingly undervalued." In the spring of 1678, he introduced a private bill to confirm his titles, register the voluntary surrender from the family succession of his brother George (who had become a Benedictine monk), and reverse their father's attainder. The bill became law, but only after amendments struck out the phrases that would have negated the family's earlier disgrace.[20] That fall, as rumors of popish plots raged through the capital, the 3rd Earl spoke out movingly, but unsuccessfully, when a bill threatened the right of Catholics to sit in Parliaments. "And all men agree," one correspondent wrote to Ormonde, "that never man spoke in any case with more eloquence or more art against this bill than he did." When the legislation passed in late November, the 3rd Earl was one of seven peers who withdrew from the House rather than take the required oath of allegiance. In recognition of "the great actions done by his ancestors in France in former times," the Lords recommended the 3rd Earl to the Crown's special favor. But as if to emphasize the durability of the family's other legacy, within months of the recommendation, a pamphlet appeared rehearsing the events of 1631. The nuances of its retelling will be discussed below, but it gave more credence than any other text to the inference that the Catholic Audley had entrapped his Protestant father.[21]

A less salacious, but more personal, literary humiliation was to follow. In 1680, in anticipation of a published history of the Irish rebellion that would have little good to say about the role of

Catholics, the 3rd Earl produced his own memoir of the Irish wars. Hoping again to prove that loyalty and Catholicism were not incompatible, his treatise was a Catholic-Royalist account. Not surprisingly, he had little good to say about the English officials who in 1641 had refused his assistance and then imprisoned him for treason, and little bad to say about himself, but the narrative was no more biased or self-aggrandizing than most personal recollections. As in 1640, however, the Earl's timing left something to be desired; his plea for religious understanding, published in the face of both the Exclusion Crisis and the Popish Plot, came at a low moment in English interfaith relationships. Ormonde, Castlehaven's relative, compatriot, and now Lord Deputy of Ireland, dismissed his work as "foolish and unseasonable." Edmund Borlase, son of one of the men who had angered the Earl in the 1640s, pronounced the text "a calumny on the government." Denunciations and defenses flew back and forth from the London presses, buoyed not only by the general political situation but also by factionalism within the government. In 1682, the Privy Council denounced both the Earl's *Memoirs* and the responses, but the literary sparring continued. A new edition of the Earl's text, retitled *The Earl of Castlehaven's Review,* and carrying his story into the 1670s, appeared in 1684. That same year he died unexpectedly at his sister's home in Tipperary.[22]

Unlike his father, the 3rd Earl of Castlehaven had lived largely in the public eye, as a soldier, as a courtier, and as an author. He was a known devotee of hunting and concerned enough about his table to hire a cook who had been trained in Paris. Ambition, royalism, and the conviction that Catholic loyalism was not an oxymoron animated his career. He was the longest-lived principal of the Castlehaven trial and the one who might most easily have outgrown its associations, yet he never escaped its shadow. More than half a century after the event, the diarist John Evelyn would still identify him as "the son of him who was executed fifty years before for enormous lusts etc."[23]

Repeated laments about finances and public reputation also punctuate our glimpses of the later life of Elizabeth, Countess of Castlehaven, but, unlike her husband, she could neither represent herself as the aggrieved victim of 1631 nor as an heroic devotee of the Stuarts. Despite (as her pardon said) her "tender years," the then Lady

Audley had fled from the investigation, and she had admitted to adultery with Henry Skipwith. But she was not much more than a child, trapped in an unhappy marriage not of her choosing, and deserted by virtually everyone around her. If she had willingly slept with Henry Skipwith (as he suggested), then not only her husband, but also her lover had betrayed her. If she had accommodated herself to Skipwith only under Castlehaven's increasing threats (as she suggested), then, like a prisoner in some erotic war, she had exchanged the terror of being blackmailed for the derision of those who could not acknowledge the power of nonphysical coercion. Whether she was willingly unchaste or woefully exploited, by the time of her step-father/father-in-law's execution, Lady Audley was without a willing husband, a lover, a supportive family, or any protector. Although she had not been a defendant, she might reasonably have felt that she had been convicted.

The new Countess's options for reclaiming her honor were distinctly limited. Since divorce was virtually impossible, the accepted female occupations of housewifery and childbearing were open to her only if she and her husband reconciled or he predeceased her (which he did not). Since her grandmother considered her immoral, and her brothers were young children, she could not expect the help of her natal family. Since her income, while respectable for a gentlewoman, was unexceptional for a Countess, she could not retire easily abroad.[24] Her best alternative was to return to her husband, a man with whom she apparently shared little more than the certitude that permanent amity between them was impossible.

By her early twenties, the Countess had apparently been left to live by her wits, and live by them she did. Whether by temperament, self-fulfilling prophecy, or sheer necessity, she matured into a wily survivor and a disorderly woman. When the Earl of Cork wanted her to confirm that she had no claims on Stalbridge manor, she refused unless given "one hundred pieces [i.e., money] before hand." Back in England in the 1640s, she deceived the Committee for Compounding (which allowed her her income even though her husband had fled to the Stuart court in exile) into thinking that her annuity was larger than it really was. In 1653, she used her immunity as a *femme covert* to avoid prosecution by her creditors. At the Restoration, claiming a poverty engendered by her loyalty, she asked for and received a portion of what was due the Crown from delinquents in Wiltshire. Her frequent companion was the notorious Lady Petre, also estranged from her spouse, also continually dogged by debt. In August 1655, a constable incarcerated both women for a night in "the cage" by the church in "the Common Garden." The diarist Samuel Pepys described Lady Petre as "an impudent jade," and that label struck at least one modern commentator as equally appropriate for Lady Castlehaven. No further evidence survives about her until a notice of her death in 1679; she was buried in London in the church of St. Martin's in the Fields. Whether the "sparks" that her grandmother had feared were cause or effect of her position (or both), the Countess's involvement in the trial, however incidental, seems to have defined both her later life and reputation.[25]

THE WIDOW

In contrast to her daughter and son-in-law, the Dowager Countess of Castlehaven, Anne, almost never appears in her own behalf in the records of events after 1631. Most of what we can discern comes from comments about what others did for her or to her or said about her. We know that as the only living witness against Giles Broadway, she confronted him in person at his trial; that a few years later, she signed a marriage agreement for her younger daughter Frances; that in the 1640s, she petitioned the Committee for Advancement of Money not to sequester her jointure property. But beyond that, we know very little. The Dowager Countess appears to have lived quietly with her mother at Harefield, Middlesex, until the latter's death in 1637. Although her mother had said that Castlehaven left her daughter penniless, the Dowager Countess had a £600 annuity from the Chandos estates as well as income from Compton manor, Wiltshire, and lands near Brinksley Town and Bockingfold Park in Kent. She received occasional, but not significant, help from her brothers-in-law, the Earls of Bridgewater and of Huntingdon. And the Dowager Countess of Derby's death brought to her "dear daughter" bequests both ornamental and practical: jewelry, a furnished coach, six milk cows, and a "competent" number of swine and poultry. Having given up her life interest in Harefield in order to pay her debts, the Dowager Countess of Castlehaven spent the remainder of her life in residence at Heydons, a mansion originally intended for her younger son.[26]

The Dowager Countess always insisted upon her innocence, and in theory, her husband's condemnation should have vindicated her. Testimony at the trials of Castlehaven and Broadway had alleged that she was a whore, a reprobate, and a deadly schemer, but contemporaries apparently found these charges if not incredible, at least unproved. If she was (as Broadway later called her) "the most wicked woman in the world," then she escaped relatively easily; if (as she claimed), she was a hapless victim, then her life after 1631 was a very partial exoneration. Her husband's execution speech carried accusations against her to a new audience, as did Giles Broadway's speech at Tyburn. Every manuscript or pamphlet rendition of the case did the same. The most popular verse circulating after the trial portrayed Castlehaven as a cuckold rather than the Countess as a victim. Castlehaven's sister, Lady Eleanor, denounced her as a Jezebel, first in a private petition to the King and then in two published pamphlets, one of which displayed the Stanley arms upon its title page, flanking them with anagrams that "revealed" the Stanley character. The Dowager Countess (rechristened Ana) became "A Lye Satan." And in his fruitless quest to regain Fonthill Gifford in 1640, the 3rd Earl specifically brought his stepmother's chastity once again into doubt before a public forum.[27]

The most enduring monument of the Dowager Countess of Castlehaven, however, was more positive, another bequest from her mother. In the upper chancel of the parish church of St. Mary's, Harefield, stands an enormous hearse tomb, built shortly before her death by the Dowager Countess of Derby. Beneath her full-length effigy, representations of her daughters, complete with inscriptions and coats of arms, kneel in niches carved into the west wall of the tomb. Despite the great pride that her mother had taken in having three daughters become Countesses, the Dowager Countess of Castlehaven appears here as Anne Stanley Brydges, Lady Chandos. Her second marriage earns no mention. The inscription was both a rewriting of the past and a hope for revision in the future. It is no small irony that the tomb, which still dominates its setting, is now the most public, accessible, and permanent reminder of the Dowager Countess of Castlehaven and, for those who know her history, of the Castlehaven trial.[28]

THE MASTER'S OTHER CHARGES

Castlehaven's trial had the least impact on the youngest children in the family; not having been directly involved, they seem to have been more able to leave 1631 behind. Like their eldest brother, as adults, the younger Touchets were more central—socially and politically—than their father had ever been. Castlehaven's younger sons were companions, albeit peripheral ones, to both Charles II and his Queen. George became a monk in 1643. Known in religion as Father Anselm, he published a history of the English Reformation and became a chaplain in Queen Catherine of Braganza's household. Exiled from England with the rest of the Queen's English chaplains in 1675, Anselm removed himself from the family succession. He died in France in the late 1680s.[29] Colonel Mervin Touchet was a Catholic loyalist who acted as an intermediary for the 3rd Earl during the Irish troubles, and (according to later claims) was "instrumental" in protecting the future King from harm during the civil wars. Charles II rewarded him with land and protection from persecution as a recusant. He married Mary Talbot Arundel, the daughter of the 10th Earl of Shrewsbury. He became the 4th Earl of Castlehaven at his brother's death in 1684, but died himself two years later.[30] After 1631 as before, the Touchet children married into some of the "best" Irish and English Catholic families. Mervin Touchet wed a Talbot; his sister Frances married Richard Butler, brother of the then Marquis (later Duke) of Ormonde; and following John Anktill's death in 1638, Lucy Touchet Anktill married the younger son of Lord Kerry. These marriages were grander, in fact, than those of the family's Stanley half-siblings.[31]

Castlehaven's surviving favorites did well for themselves in the years after the trial. John Anktill remained the Touchet collector of rents in Ireland. Other Anktills acted as attorneys and land agents for the family. The son of Anktill's marriage with Lucy Touchet inherited an estate in County Cork; their daughter married into a genteel family in County Clare. Henry Skipwith retreated within a few years to the obscurity that had cloaked his life before the 1630s. But not immediately. In January 1632, the Council reprimanded the Warden of the Fleet for allowing Skipwith, still a prisoner, to "walk abroad at his pleasure." To the embarrassment of the 3rd Earl of Castlehaven, the former servant boldly conducted business from a coach and four on such excursions. By the end of the year, the 3rd Earl and his old rival had brokered an agreement, one likely encouraged by Skipwith's continued incarceration. In exchange for an undisclosed sum of cash, Skipwith restored to the Touchet family Bishopstrow manor, Castlehaven's townhouse in Salisbury, and any and all other lands that had once been the property of the 2nd Earl. No evidence exists of any continuing relationship between Skipwith and the young Countess of Castlehaven; no record at all survives of either Skipwith or his own wife after 1632. The indenture surrendering the lands referred to both Skipwith and his father as gentlemen. Whatever the depth of fiction in that designation, the claim was more credible than it would have been a decade earlier. Their association with the Touchets had almost cost Anktill and Skipwith their lives, but having escaped that danger, both men had clearly risen in the world.[32]

The effect of the Castlehaven trial upon the 2nd Earl and his co-defendants is obvious, but the case altered the lives of all of those closest to it. The 3rd Earl, his Countess, and the Dowager Countess of Castlehaven grew poorer in terms of both material possessions and reputation. Henry Skipwith and John Anktill grew richer and more genteel. There were to be no more scandals, but reminders of the trial were always present—for the disinterested as well as for the participants.

CHAPTER 5

RETELLINGS

bout twenty-five years after Castlehaven's execution, his grave was apparently unsealed to make room for a "kinswoman" of the Lieutenant of the Tower. The Earl's silk stockings were still there, "so fine and good" that they were marketable. They were promptly sold, and then resold for an exceptionally good price.[1] This macabre recycling of Castlehaven's clothing was not so different from what happened to the Castlehaven story—it did not end with the death of the principals; instead of putrefying, it was repeatedly repackaged and reused; its serviceability reflected both quality and commercial appetite. Any catalog of Castlehaven "sightings" must be incomplete, just as will be any discussion of the story's possible interpretations; over three centuries writers have used the example of Castlehaven in arguments about (among other things) cuckoldry, tyranny, degeneracy, redemption, marital abuse, marital reform, toleration, and homophobia. A cautionary tale addressed to every genteel householder has served many morals: among them the promise of redemption, the horrors of aristocratic decadence, the power of English justice, the value of spousal authority, and the irrepressibility of sexual difference. The persistence of many of the issues with which the trial engaged—familial responsibility, aristocratic privilege, sexual politics—has strengthened its resilience. Realigning the events with their original meanings is important for an historical assessment of the trial, but the later reconfigurations tell us something about how

the scandal was understood by different audiences and how, therefore, its history has been made and remade. What we find is that Castlehaven remains as indeterminate dead as he was when alive.

We think of judicial trials primarily as mechanisms geared to the resolution of legal conflict; through the trial process, we collectively allot blame, vindicate innocence, and assign punishment. And almost as if the adversarial format of modern common law demanded it, we tend to identify with either the defendant or the representatives of the state, but not with both. In early modern English society, trials had a different resonance. They were less about proving and more about testing—testing the character of the defendant, testing the impartiality of the jurors, testing the power of repentance. Since Christians believed that the law was one aspect of a continual and often unsuccessful struggle to distinguish Divine truth from satanic deception, verdicts were temporal, not absolute, solutions. God chose to punish the most visible of sinners through the legal process, but since one and all were sinners, categorizing a defendant as "other" was a difficult and potentially hubristic exercise. Trials and executions were (albeit in exceptionally graphic form) a reminder of the choices that every Christian faced and for which each would be expected to account. Unlike their modern counterparts, then, early modern trials were supposed to be tools of both discipline and inspiration.

Stories of criminals condemned and criminals redeemed, therefore, were an exceptionally effective (perhaps the most effective) secular medium for showing people what they could be, what they might become, and the paths between those possibilities. Condemned criminals who died "well" made ideal subjects for such retellings because from a believer's perspective, the drama of each conversion added to the power of the Christian message. By the seventeenth century, the spread of literacy and cheap printing had stimulated a healthy market in England for broadsheets and pamphlets that narrated criminal odysseys from degradation to redemption.[2] A combination of spectacle, civic lesson, and hellfire sermon, stories about convicted criminals extended the lessons of law and punishment beyond their immediate observers. The stories were intended to amuse, to scare, and to show the tenacity of God's love. Such tales illustrated what united all Englishmen and women as well as what distinguished criminals from their law-abiding counterparts.

No printed rendition of Castlehaven's trial appeared in England until the 1640s. Although telling tales of criminals was useful, it could also be dangerous; where the upright saw warning, the weak might see inspiration. With this trial in particular, introducing the proper lessons—the honorable paternalism of the King, the power of the law, the inevitable punishment of evil—without also introducing the means with which to challenge, if not undo them, seemed impossible.[3] However it was told, the story of Castlehaven's trial was an embarrassment. Yet the Earl was a repeated, if oblique, presence in a variety of media throughout the 1630s. The printed references were asides rather than full-length reiterations, but he was there as an unnamed example, an unexplicated reference, an expected but absent presence. With the exception of his sister's cryptically prophetic pamphlets, all of these gestures reinforced the lessons that Castlehaven's prosecutors had hoped to teach.[4]

In 1632, for example, new editions of several fictions concerned with rape and family came into print: Shakespeare's *Rape of Lucrece,* Claudius Claudianus's *Rape of Proserpine,* Thomas Heywood's *The Iron Age,* and the anonymous *The Nightingale Warbling Forth* (or *Philomele*). Most of this material had long been popular, but so many reprintings within a single year was highly unusual.[5] In 1633, William Prynne's caustic antitheatrical (and antiroyal court) tract, *Histrio-matrix,* reassured readers that sodomy was a capital offense in England by referring to "a late example of a memorable act of justice on an English peer." In pursuit of patronage rather than reform, Sir Henry Wotton in the same year pointed to Castlehaven's execution as evidence of King Charles I's commitment to impartial justness. A meeting of the Irish Parliament in 1634 so fractious that it was expected to refuse all criminal legislation, nonetheless approved the passage of Ireland's first "Act for Punishing the Vice of Buggery."[6] And in 1637 came the first published edition of *Comus,* a masque by John Milton and Henry Lawes that had been written and performed in 1634 to honor two of the dead Earl's in-laws, the Earl and Countess of Bridgewater. The masque's theme was the triumph of virtue over dissipation. Like Castlehaven, *Comus* was a procurer and a pander enslaved to lust; he used a protective guise (as a shepherd) to hide predatory intentions; and his aim was the corruption of a happy family. Comus and Castlehaven each denied in act and speech the piety of temperance. The message of the masque, like the message of the trial, was that "evil on it self shall back recoil."[7] Yet despite such reaffirmations, the prosecution's view of the case was never the only one; the printed references of the 1630s were a veneer covering more complicated and ambiguous interpretations.

LETTERS AND LIBELS

Although there was no formal means of mass communication in early-seventeenth-century England, networks for passing important or interesting information were well established and well used. Gossip was a mainstay of alehouses, country houses, and everything in between. One of the informal obligations of visitors to London (as well as to smaller towns) was to keep friends and relatives at home apprised of news. Genteel and merchant families who sent representatives to the capital on legal, economic, or social business expected a regular flow of miscellaneous information, and some households employed agents specifically to provide them with weekly missives. Trials and executions, marriages and estrangements, rises and falls in favor; these were part of the spectacle of London and, given the speed with which favor waxed and waned, as important in their own way as news of wars or Parliaments. The demand for news was reliable enough that by the early seventeenth century, a few men earned their livings and many more supplemented them by selling reports culled from visits to Westminster, Whitehall, and the Exchange.[8]

Timeliness, even more than accuracy, was vital to the credibility of such accounts; old news, after all, was no news. Castlehaven's trial figured in correspondence sent as far north as Yorkshire and as far west as Massachusetts Bay. Most details of the scandal left London within a week of the events being discussed, sometimes on the same day. When John Bladen took two weeks to report on the Earl's death, he expected that Sir Thomas Fairfax, in Yorkshire, would already have heard his news.[9] Most of the correspondents who wrote about the case relied upon informants, but some witnessed the events that they reported. A neighbor of Castlehaven was said to have provided the assessment of the Earl's character that Joseph Mead passed on to Sir Martin Stuteville in December 1630; one of Castlehaven's final confessors allegedly revealed the details of the Earl's last moments for another report in May. Edward Hyde and at least one of the anonymous reporters attended the trial. Hyde also visited the Earl in prison after his condemnation. Another observer claimed to have been present at the execution.[10]

The overall stance of the correspondents was remarkably consistent. To them, the trial was about more than the indicted crimes; it was about disrespect between father and son, abuse of power between husband and wife, and dangerous shifts of authority between master and servant. These things were what both accounted for the indictments and made sense of them. Although some believed the evidence "very full and clear," others, as we have already seen, thought that the conduct of the trial and the conduct of the Earl left troubling questions. Castlehaven, who in December could be depicted as a man whose "whole delight was to damn souls," had by the time of his death become, for some commentators, something much more enigmatic.[11] Unlike the image derived from the speeches in court (whose purpose, after all, was to demonize the defendant), the epistolary Earl is a more sympathetic creature than we have understood: delinquent, but not entirely evil; ineffectual, but not completely irredeemable.

One of the best examples of the Earl's ability to impress those with whom he came into contact comes from Edward Hyde, the future Earl of Clarendon—not from the already cited letter about Castlehaven's last days, but from another written fifteen years later. Hyde was in most ways Castlehaven's opposite: cautious where he was brash, steady where he was volatile. Yet the conversion in his views about the Earl which he acknowledged in 1631 stayed with him. In the depths of the winter of 1646, as the royalist cause to which he had devoted himself was foundering, Hyde invoked Castlehaven to urge calm upon fellow Royalist Sir John Berkeley. The reference is so surprising that it deserves to be quoted at length. Discussing whether he and Berkeley ought to flee the country or to seek a pardon from Parliament, Hyde advised:

> Let us not share with them in the guilt by wishing anything to be done, but what should be done. I remember the next day after the Earl of Castlehaven was condemned, I was carried by curiosity, and a friend, to visit him in the Tower; and amongst other things, I asked him, whether he had petitioned the King to change the manner of his death from hanging to [be]heading; he told me no . . . he would suffer that judgment which the law had laid upon him, out of his duty and obedience to the law, but his own conscience would not give him leave to bring any other death upon himself, knowing that he was innocent and deserved not to die. Though I then thought that scrupulosity unseasonable . . . yet in earnest, Jack, the logic of it is not at all ridiculous in our case, and we may very well bear and submit to such a peace, to the making whereof we do heartily disagree.[12]

To find the man generally considered as one of the age's finest statesmen citing in time of misfortune the man generally considered as one of the age's greatest embarrassments is something of a shock, but it reveals how equivocal Castlehaven's contemporary reputation was. Hyde thought the Earl's position philosophically sound even if it was also pedantic. Hyde's recollection epitomized the ambivalence of the contemporary correspondents. His Castlehaven was not clearly guilty, and he was clearly, but improbably, capable of behavior worth emulating.

Private correspondence and word of mouth were not the only outlets for opinions about the scandal; commentaries in verse were also available almost as soon as the Earl was dead. These lyrics were almost all short, cheap, and public, drawing their authority from humor and an alleged immediacy to their subject matter. They appeared (or at least this is where later copies claim that they appeared) affixed to hearses, statues, or anything available where a literate person might find, read, and recite them. The verses refracted rather than reported events, using wit to distill detail into moral. But as with correspondence, the moral that one might draw from such materials was not necessarily what the prosecutors had intended.

The most popular and probably earliest extant verse about the Earl was known as his epitaph.[13] It purported to have been written by

Castlehaven, and its target was the Countess. The Cheshire diarist, William Davenport, noted that the epitaph had been "set on his [Castlehaven's] tomb after his beheading"; other memoirists said that the Earl had sent the poem to the Countess or that it had been found "in the Earl's chamber."[14] Whether or not the Earl actually composed the lines, his voice was certainly the most plausible one for the interpretation of the trial that they presented. Framed as a warning to other men, the epitaph replayed the Earl's contention that lust had driven the Countess to use the law against him. In this lyric, Castlehaven appears not as a bugger nor a reprobate, but as a cuckold:

> I need no trophies to adorn my hearse
> > My wife exalts my horns in every verse
> > And places them so full upon my tomb
> > That for my arms there is no vacant room
> > Who will take such a Countess to his bed
> That first gives horns and then cuts off
> The head?[15]

The epitaph reduced the relationship of Castlehaven and the Countess to that of cuckold and adulteress. Gone were rape and sodomy, disinheritance and patriarchal irresponsibility. In their places was a simple argument between husband and wife over fidelity and danger. The verse portrayed the Earl as hapless, not monstrous; the willful evil belonged to the Countess. The lyric suggested that the adultery of a wife defined a man more thoroughly than did any of his own actions. Appended to the story of the trial, as it sometimes was, the epitaph reopened the possibility of Castlehaven's innocence; detached from its legal context, as it sometimes also was, the verse encouraged readers to rewrite the case completely. Not surprisingly, the epitaph was the only remnant of the trial to appear in the often bawdy and usually male-compiled pages of commonplace books. Its lesson seemed timeless: women, the verse said, are dangerous; reputation is critical; infidelity revealed is social, if not always actual, death. The message was so universal that by mid-century, one commonplace book writer credited the lines to the Earl of Newcastle about his very different sort of wife.[16]

But not all verses adopted a male perspective. Appended to about

one-third of the known copies of the epitaph is one of two verses
attributed to the Countess.[17] Both of these rejoinders reversed the
epitaph's moral trajectory. The Countess was chaste, they argued; the
Earl a procurer who made himself into a cuckold. His death came
at his own hands, not by hers. The Earl alone was guilty and responsible for his family's disgrace:

> Tis true you need no trophies to adorn your hearse
> Your life being odious and below all verse
> Nor was it your wife who came chaste to your bed
> That did you horn; your own hands horned your head
> Twas fit your head should of then most men censure
> That you that lived so, should die a monster.

These verses rejected the attempts of the epitaph to generalize
from the Earl's predicament; they reinstituted images created during the trial by the King's officials: Castlehaven as a "beast" or a
"monster" whose abuses were only superficially related to the conduct of any decent man. The epitaph's answers, most probably (but
not certainly) composed by men, represented a restatement of patriarchal responsibility and control; not an ideal of woman necessarily, but an ideal of a wife.

Two more complex poems about the trial of the 2nd Earl also have
survived, each longer than the epitaph or its answers, and neither
in the voice of a participant. They, too, however, can be read as competing attempts to settle the unsettled meaning of the trial. The
briefer of the two, entitled "Upon the Lord Audley's Conviction
April 1631," saw in the Earl's condemnation a vindication of English justice. The Earl, the verse opined, had outdone the gravest sins
of ancient times. He had committed acts too horrid to be believed;
"to rape himself and make one rape prove two," "to get an heir his
blood to disinherit." Royal justice had exposed the "riddle" of the
Earl's monstrosity and, properly, left it to God to pardon. The longer
set of verses lampooned not Castlehaven, but the trial itself. The text
was a parodic narration of the event, summarizing the major
speeches of all the principals as well as the judicial commentary.[18]
The author ridiculed the Lord High Steward as vain, the Attorney-
General as hypocritical and long-winded, the Clerk of the Crown as

comically obese. He or she questioned not only the impartiality, but also the scrupulosity of the verdict, declaring:

> Competent judges they were none
> For by the closeness of their beard
> Twas more than to be feared
> They were Eunuchs every one.

Contempt for the judges was, of course, not synonymous with support for the defendant. With a satirical form such as the libel, it is particularly difficult to uncover the sentiment behind the mocking. But clearly words such as "eunuchs" and "the closeness of their beard" were intended to suggest a lack of wisdom and a lack of independence; these were terms traditionally associated with immaturity and subservience. Taken alone, the verse would not have reassured any reader's faith in the integrity of either the judges or the attorneys; read with the epitaph's depiction of female cunning triumphing over justice, its message might have seemed still more damning.

CASTLEHAVEN AND THE STUARTS

Manuscript narratives of Castlehaven's trial began to circulate even before the Earl's execution. Handwritten texts were the preferred form of "publication" among the English elites; such texts were reproducible, but controllable, commodities of privilege. The affluent regularly copied or had copied texts that appealed to them and relied on manuscript collectors the way that we rely upon libraries. These renditions of the trial were unlikely to have had popular counterparts before the story reached cheap print in the 1640s. Even within genteel circles, long manuscripts had a smaller and more selective audience than did lyrics: they were less portable, more expensive, and more esoteric. Still, early copies of Castlehaven's tale found their way into the collections of families such as the Cavendishes, Grosvenors, Myddletons, Hattons, and Ishams.[19] In contrast to the correspondence or versifying, these narratives claimed to be educational rather than merely informative or entertaining.

Some of these renditions narrated the trial, the execution, or the servants' stories at full length; others abridged the materials. Some were discrete texts; others became part of miscellanies devoted to law, history, or politics. All strove for credibility: some claimed firsthand knowledge of the events, some reported testimony as verbatim dialogue, some incorporated evocative (but probably imaginary) details such the Earl's putative desire to be banished to Virginia so that "I might labor for my bread and have time to reconcile myself to almighty God."[20] In this bewildering array, some variations are obviously errors in copying, but other disparities are probably intentional. Here, as in other forms, one finds at least two very different Castlehavens: one pure villain, one more equivocally evil and a victim as well. The earliest narratives were unsympathetic to the Earl, but within months and maybe even weeks, these texts were joined by ones that replotted what had happened as a redemptive tragedy.

The apparently earliest texts and those derived from them paid less attention to Castlehaven than to his accusers; in contrast to the epistolary commentators, these authors produced a story that, by implication, supported the verdict of the court. The dynamic here was the Crown's: accusation, prosecution, conviction. The accounts read as rough elaborations of notes taken on the spot, with little explicit commentary. Castlehaven's response became a blanket denial. The inclusion of Heath's derisive rejection of what the Earl had said, the lack of a description of the jury's deliberations, and the occlusion of Lord North's dissent suggested to readers that Castlehaven, in fact, had presented no defense. Some of these texts ended with the Earl's condemnation, but even those that included a description of the execution used it simply to reinforce the Earl's obdurateness. These texts focused on action, not explanation; they displayed no sympathies toward Castlehaven and no interest in the paradoxes of the scandal.

A later rendering, composed at only a slightly greater distance, was more overtly narrative and more overtly edited. The story grew to incorporate both a dramatically evocative beginning (the "theater" built to house the court) and a morally uplifting conclusion ("the Earl's mental description in these later days"). A structure of denial, remorse, and redemption complemented the earlier trajectory of accusation, prosecution, and conviction; the perspective shifted from what the Crown did to what the Earl felt. A detailed report of Castlehaven's rejoinders, including the contention that his was the plight of every patriarch, made him seem less petulant than genuinely aggrieved; an acknowledgment of the jury's difficult deliberations off-set Heath's dismissal of Castlehaven's plaint. The editor hoped to inspire "a fixed aversion and a settled detestation" of Castlehaven's baseness, but it was hard to avoid the sense that the story now began rather than concluded with the Earl's conviction. Castle-haven's humiliation was also his spiritual opportunity; his execution was so moving that, like Hyde, the writer of this text found elements of the Earl's behavior worthy of emulation.

> Thus have you (good reader) the epitome and abridgment of the late Earl's behavior, and wherein what to fly, what to follow; with Mary choose the better part, his life and death seeming to me a real comment of the apostle's speech, where sin abounded there grace did much more.[21]

In both of these redactions, the recital of events was more involved, but also simpler, than in the correspondence or the lyrics. The looser story of divided verdicts, divided sympathies, and divided character was fine as news, but retelling the tale at length, and in a form suitable for circulation, demanded a clearer message. The manuscript narratives accomplished this goal by sacrificing ambiguity for closure. The story became edificatory rather than merely scandalous; both versions obscured the details that letter writers and diarists had pondered over, both downplayed rather than emphasized the irre-solvable contradictions. The narratives suggest a contemporary desire not only to know the facts of the Castlehaven trial, but also to distill from those facts some broader meaning. The significances of that meaning, however, remained manifold.

If the politics of England in the seventeenth century had been less volatile, Castlehaven's story might have faded as the decades passed into an oddity noted only by antiquarians or legal scholars. Instead, it retained and even broadened its appeal. Where the manuscript nar-ratives worked toward a fragile closure, their printed counterparts dexterously revisited and exploited the uncertainties of the trial. Pamphlets about the case appeared in 1643, 1679, 1699, and on into the eighteenth century, each fulfilling the Earl's prediction that his predicament was not and would not be only about himself. The sort of analogies that the prosecution had tried so firmly to preclude— particularly between the Earl and other aristocratic or royal patri- archs—breathed new life into the story. Castlehaven's failings became marks of statural, rather than of human, weaknesses. Published tracts about the trial focused less on the prosecution or the Earl's repentance than on the parallels between Castlehaven and other priv- ileged hereditary rulers.

Despite its potential as a salable commodity, the life of the case in print really began only in 1643, not coincidentally after the tem- porary collapse of the system of governmental licensing. The first pamphlet appeared about six months after the formal outbreak of the Civil War, just as people were beginning to realize (after failed diplomatic as well as military initiatives) that hostilities were likely to continue. London in particular buzzed with political argument, moral exhortation, and uneasy bargaining. In 1643, the propaganda value of the Earl's trial, judiciously retold, as a weapon against Charles I would have been considerable; this was, after all, the story of an allegedly decadent and allegedly Catholic peer produced dur- ing a war in which most peers and virtually all English Catholics were on one side. The charges against Castlehaven fitted contemporary ideas of Catholic and Irish failings at a moment when both groups were the particular focus of near hysteria. And the story comple- mented the sexual slanders about aristocrats that were quickly becoming a staple of both the royalist and the parliamentary presses.[22]

The editor of *The Arraignment and Conviction of Mervin, Lord Audley* . . . (1643) exploited these possibilities. Castlehaven's guilt here was presented as unambiguous. His alleged sexual machinations grew to include (in addition to his wife's rape, his own sodomy, voyeurism, intercourse with servants male and female, and the pair- ing of his stepdaughter/daughter-in-law with Henry Skipwith) sodomy with Skipwith as well as attempted liaisons between the Countess and Skipwith, the Countess and Anktill, and Lady Aud- ley with two former servants. The Earl's challenges to his accusers vanished, leaving a plea against self-incrimination as his only sub- stantial response. His later affirmations of Protestantism, innocence, and loyalty to the state disappeared as did his insistence that his dilemma should resonate with every head of household. The jury's deliberations, in reality long and rancorous by contemporary standards, appeared as smooth and entirely unexceptional.[23]

The pamphlet complemented and may have even been inspired by two publications of the previous year accusing John Atherton, the Bishop of Waterford and Lismore, of sodomy. Taken together, the association of an Irish Earl and an Irish Bishop with buggery, an act associated with the deepest forms of disorder, reinforced not only slurs against the morality of the Irish (although both men were in fact not Irish, but English), but also the belief that under Charles I, the aristocracy and the episcopacy were decadent at their core. *The Arraignment and Conviction* muted Charles I's unequivocal censure of the Earl, while retaining the boast that the King granted Castlehaven "more favor than ever any man that came to this bar." It portrayed a Monarch so interested in mercy over justice that he failed to protect his people. And since the piece concluded with Castlehaven's condemnation rather than with his execution, it left the reader only indirect clues about the King's determination to see Castlehaven punished. Reminding readers of the affinities between an aristocrat and a King, the tract neatly then closed off sympathy for either. In 1643, Castlehaven's story was used to challenge not only the Earl's but also the King's manliness, honor, and loyalty, to challenge the benefits of not only household patriarchialism but also the patriarchialism of the Monarch.[24]

Castlehaven's sister Eleanor challenged the simple equations of King and Earl, and Earl and guilt, with two of her own versions of the trial published as the wars continued. She argued that the image of Charles I in tracts such as *The Arraignment and Conviction* was correct, but not the image of her brother. To her, the King was a feeble patriarch who trusted unreliable women, Catholics, and the *nouveaux riches* instead of members of the kingdom's ancient families. Bad advice and flawed decisions were the inevitable results. In *The Word of God to the City of London* (1645), Lady Eleanor revived the image of her brother as a victim, although this time the victim of a conspiracy of Catholics furious at his rejection of their religion. *The Crying Charge*, printed four years later, was even more specific. Intended as a gift of evidence for the court created to try the King, this was a detailed recitation of the errors in the conduct of Castlehaven's trial:

ineligible and absent witnesses, unsworn and suborned testimony, unsound and unprecedented process. Castlehaven, wrote Lady Eleanor, had died, "like Isaac rather sacrificed . . . for the misdemeanors of an unruly household suffered by him, laying on him their faults."[25]

After thirty years of silence, in 1679 a new pamphlet devoted to the trial appeared, again in a moment when governmental censorship had faltered, again apparently inspired by and integrated into a time of heightened political tension. In the autumn of 1678, the accusations by Titus Oates had triggered the hysteria of the Popish Plot, but Oates's match flared so dramatically because it struck a woodpile already flickering with fears of Catholic deceit and degeneracy. The aristocracy and the royal court were a central focus of these fears; the situation made these years exceptionally productive ones for all sorts of politically daring books and pamphlets. Close to four decades after the fact, Castlehaven's humiliation still proved a useful weapon, now one that could be used to denigrate a new cast of characters: the 3rd Earl, King Charles II, and the King's Catholic brother, the Duke of York.

The Trial of the Lord Audley, Earl of Castlehaven . . . (1679) differed dramatically in content and in tone from the text of 1643 and from the pamphlets of Lady Eleanor. Using a reportorial third person, the 1679 tract summarized rather than retold the trial and devoted nearly one-third of its space to a description of the Earl's execution. Given the date of its appearance, one would expect *The Trial of the Lord Audley* to be a bludgeon with which to batter English Catholics; in part it was, but more creatively than one might have predicted. While fulsomely praising the prosecution, and condemning the alleged crimes, the pamphlet allowed the dead 2nd Earl to denounce the living 3rd Earl, his own accuser, an uncompromising Roman Catholic, and as we have already seen, a tempting target for attention because of his more than customarily vocal recent defense of loyalist Catholicism. The title itself evoked the conflation of identity in aristocratic families; without Christian names or ordinal numbers on the title page, the reader was left to wonder initially which Lord Audley had been on trial. Having allowed the possibility that the current Earl might be guilty of rape and sodomy, the pamphlet then denigrated him in the act of exonerating him. For the first time in print, a narrative of the trial included the specifics of Castlehaven's contention that his son and wife had framed him. *The Trial of the Lord Audley* reported the jury's difficult deliberations and its inability to return even a single unanimous verdict. The tract emphasized Castlehaven's affirmations of his loyalty to the English Church, dismissing his flirtation with Rome as a temporary aberration encouraged by the "persuasion of his neighbor Roman Catholics" (the most prominent of whom was the grandfather of the Arundel of Wardour languishing in the Tower in 1679 upon a charge of treason). Castlehaven, the tract said, faced his death with equanimity. "A world of people," the pamphlet said, attended his execution, "such was the concourse and press of people, both men and women, to see him, that his person was scarce free, but even borne along in the throng." "And thus," the tract concluded, "dies the Great Lord of Castle-haven."[26] The pamphlet never endorsed Castlehaven's innocence, but it allowed a lot of questions, all of which impugned the integrity of the surviving Earl.

Yet *The Trial of the Lord Audley* cast aspersions upon more than just a minor courtier. The pamphlet spared Charles I, who was merely a background presence, but it did not spare the Stuarts. The pamphlet introduced a new generation to the association of Castlehaven with deceit and lasciviousness, qualities that in the 1670s were routinely associated with Charles II and his court. To many contemporaries, the crises of the late 1670s were crises of immoderation, and Charles II was the embodiment of that vice. Like the 2nd Earl, the 2nd Charles appeared eminently corruptible, prey to both his appetites and his own bad judgment; each man could easily be portrayed as captive of his lusts.[27] Readers could find worrisome connections not only to Charles II but also to the Duke of York, his brother. York, the center of the firestorm over the succession, was a Catholic, a courtier, and a soldier. Readers might reasonably conclude that the 3rd Earl, who shared those characteristics, and who was represented in the pamphlet as avaricious and untrustworthy, was the sort of man upon whom York as Monarch would rely. The filial betrayal of the Catholic 3rd Earl readily suggested the fraternal betrayals possible from the Catholic York.

Like the pamphleteers, seventeenth-century historians also understood the value of Castlehaven's case as a commentary on Charles I.[28]

Bulstrode Whitelocke, whose father had been one of the assisting judges at the trial, considered the particulars too "infamous and beastly" to be remembered. Yet he still took note of them when he published his *Memorials* in 1682. So too did Lawrence Echard in 1707, despite wishing that "the laws of history would allow a veil to be drawn" over the incident. As the greatest scandal of the reign, Castlehaven's downfall was difficult for any historian writing about the age to ignore; only those who cast their work more specifically or much more generally could easily escape.[29] But in contrast with (perhaps even in answer to) pamphlets such as *The Arraignment and Conviction*, most of the historians who incorporated the trial did so to defend the former King, not to defame him. Castlehaven may have been a monster, but he was a monster slain by the judicious severity of the second Stuart Monarch. Set between retellings of inconclusive wars, controversial financial innovations, and religious dissension, royalist historians could make the resolution of Castlehaven's case (and of two other "remarkable" trials the same year) one of the reign's clearer accomplishments. Historians sympathetic to the Stuarts left no doubt that Castlehaven had indeed died for his crimes, and omitted or dismissed Charles I's mitigation of even the form of the Earl's punishment.[30]

Yet the small group of authors who gave extended attention to the trial were less unified in their understanding of it. Of the three men who published lengthy descriptions, two (Sir Hamon L'Estrange [1655] and Sir William Sanderson [1658]) were Royalists and one (John Rushworth [1680]) a Parliamentarian, but all were moderate enough to publish their histories under the eye of governments not particularly to their liking. L'Estrange was a theologian working at some distance from events; Sanderson had grown up in the Jacobean court; Rushworth had been at the heart of the parliamentary cause. All three claimed a special authority to report the trial—L'Estrange said that he had seen Castlehaven executed; Sanderson had been secretary to one of Castlehaven's jurors; Rushworth had begun in the early 1630s to attend and record notes on as many public events as possible.[31]

L'Estrange's account followed the pattern of the short notices in other royalist histories: the Earl was an evil man; the King who had him executed was a good one. L'Estrange slighted the attorneys' apocalyptic speeches for repetitions of the livelier testimony, but his edificatory purpose was clear: "offenses so prodigiously high as his [Castlehaven's], we may not stride over; contract they do a penalty too vital for one scaffold to determine, history must erect another." Not surprisingly, then, L'Estrange repeated no assertions of conspiracy, nothing of the complaints about questionable procedure. Moreover, in his most original contribution to the story, he insisted for the first time that the Earl had left this world neither confident nor mourned. At the ultimate moment, L'Estrange maintained, Castlehaven underwent "such a swarthy metamorphosis as near resembled smoke-dried bacon." The Earl died, L'Estrange insisted, "like a bad actor hissed off the stage."[32]

Sanderson's *History of the Life and Reign of King Charles* was an answer to what Sanderson believed were the inaccuracies and intemperance of L'Estrange's work, including the latter's account of the Earl of Castlehaven. Sanderson (whose deceased patron, Holland, had voted to acquit the Earl of buggery) considered Castlehaven's trial memorable not for the defendant's infamy, but as an administrative curiosity. This was "the first and last commission of this nature by this King," he wrote and its defendant "the only man of nobility of infamous note that suffered judicial execution by this King." In contrast to L'Estrange, who opened his account with the Earl's alleged crimes, Sanderson began with the fact that the accuser was Castlehaven's "son and heir." Sanderson's rendition reprised all Castlehaven's denials and complaints; the author confided that he thought Fitzpatrick might well have been tricked into confessing. Where L'Estrange had reported the buggery verdict by noting that fifteen peers had voted to convict, Sanderson recounted it by saying that twelve peers had voted to acquit. To him, hubris, not evil, was Castlehaven's downfall; assisted by the King's chaplains, the Earl, Sanderson believed, had ended his life "exceeding repentant." It "becomes an historian in dubious relations," he insisted, "to admit the most Christian and charitable [interpretation]." Sanderson's retelling was the closest thing to a redemptive narrative that ever appeared in print. The 1,149-page *History* of which it was only a minute part was a popular, but never a scholarly, success. Contemporary memoirists such as John Evelyn, Anthony Wood, and Richard Baxter dismissed Sanderson generally as unoriginal, unanalytical, and often inaccurate.[33]

The Parliamentarian John Rushworth shared neither the royalism of L'Estrange and Sanderson nor their interest in Castlehaven's character. Rushworth wanted to write objective history; one of his stated goals was to prove that a historian could be "of party and yet not partial." The obvious editorial intrusions of a L'Estrange or a Sanderson are missing in Rushworth. The report, like other accounts in his *Collections,* drew upon a personal archive that Rushworth had been amassing for decades, supplemented with materials copied, borrowed, or bought from others. It contained the sort of small errors typical of notes taken in haste, but added two items never before published: the questions and answers from the judicial consultations before the Earl's trial, and a judicial summary prepared for the King after the trials of Broadway and Fitzpatrick.[34] What he left out was also revealing. Rushworth emphasized the ceremonies, prosecutorial speeches, and official pronouncements of the trials rather than their drama. He compressed the testimonies (which form the bulk of most of the other narratives) into a single paragraph. He eliminated imputations against the chastity of either the Countess or her daughter, and suppressed all discussions of both heterosexual and homosexual penetration and emission. He sanitized all but the most necessary sexual allusions and dropped all references sympathetic to the Earl or in praise of Charles I. Despite the addenda on Broadway and Fitzpatrick, Castlehaven's execution is not reported. Readers would have had to strain to see a victory for either Castlehaven or the King in Rushworth's retelling or to find much affinity between the Earl and the Monarch. The story remained indeterminate.

CASTLEHAVEN AND ARISTOCRATIC VICE

As the seventeenth century ended, the Castlehaven saga came into print again, but its retelling now emphasized yet another arrangement of cultural priorities. Because the last principal in the story had died in 1684, the tale had less power as pure gossip; since the last son of Charles I had left the throne in 1688, it had less power as a direct critique of monarchy.[35] Yet the case still complemented the idea that the last male Stuarts had infected the nation with a moral weakness that it would be one of the obligations of William III to reverse. From the early 1690s into the second decade of the eighteenth century a loose private network of reformers pressed the church, the monarchy, and the law into action against "vice," which, it was alleged, had become "fashionable and brave."[36] Castlehaven became one of their cautionary examples.

Sodomy, with its associations to Catholics, foreignness, and contagion, was a particular target for reformers. They detested it as a wickedness "transplanted from hotter climates," something until recently rarely known in England, and "of late" increasingly in evidence. Yet despite superficial similarities, in 1700, the label of sodomite had quite a broader meaning than it had had a century or even a half a century before; it had become a specific weakness rather than a surrender to universal temptations. Male sodomites (at least in London) were less likely to be defined as those who committed sodomy, and increasingly as a "kind of people" who allegedly inhabited an elaborate culture of inversion, a world with discrete meeting-places, rituals, and language in which men could cross-dress, act as women, and even marry other men. Sodomy had become a vice of gender confusion rather than one of merely uncontrolled concupiscence. Perverse social relations accompanied perverse sexual ones; sodomites had no respect for the "natural" distinctions between sexes or between genders.[37]

Castlehaven's trial came to exemplify the dangers of a life given over to such indulgence, and of a particular elite type whose degradation resulted from his idleness and privilege. From the late 1690s into the mid-eighteenth century, the narrative's primary theme became sexual rather than monarchical morality: sodomy, aristocratic inadequacy, or (quite frequently) the combination and consequent intensification of the two. In an age of increasingly shrill moralism and increasingly visible sexual diversity, Castlehaven's story became part of a broader reconsideration by a reading public of the nature of both "vice" and class, an element of a literature that became part reformist, part philosophical, part exploitative.[38]

Between 1700 and 1750, Castlehaven's trial was reprinted more times than ever before or since. Its popularity derived in part from its fit with contemporary anxieties, but owed as much to commercial opportunism as to more high-minded motives. The end of formal licensing, the acceptance (however grudging) of the journalist as a permanent public figure, and the rapid growth of a diversified market of readers eager for material created a powerful incentive for the creation of new stories and the reprinting of old ones. As authors from at least the sixteenth century had realized, crime offered entertaining, even salacious, material, that could be sold with a claim to educate and to admonish. Probably no other printed material in the eighteenth century so efficiently informed, consoled, and enthralled readers, and probably no other century produced so many different types of anthologies of cases.[39] Publishers reprinted reports of old scandals and current trials; they sought out dying speeches and took advantage of new categories of legal material—for example, divorces by act of Parliament and suits for criminal conversation (by which accusations of heterosexual adultery became effectively grounds for divorce)—which exposed the intimate details (or alleged details) of elite discomfitures. If sex, aristocrats, and trials were each good business, combinations of the three were close to irresistible.[40]

The change in the presentation of the events of 1631 first became clear in *The Trial and Condemnation of Mervin Lord Audley* . . . (1699), a pamphlet inspired by the detention in 1698 of a group of men for buggery and attempted buggery. The arrests proved to be the first in a series of early-eighteenth-century prosecutions so extensive that one of today's leading historians of male homosexuality discusses them as "pogroms."[41] The alleged buggers were lead by one Captain Rigby. The heart of Rigby's degradation, according to *The Trial and Condemnation,* was not sodomy, but effeminacy; he represented a growing number of men whose "effeminate madness has banished all manly virtues." Tolerance of such behavior, the author of the pamphlet's preface maintained, would lead to the rape of children and the slander of virtuous women; even worse, it would lead to the contamination of other men. Neither effeminacy nor the concomitant love of luxury had played a discernible role in Castlehaven's original prosecution, but for the editor of *The Trial and Condemnation,* a conviction for sodomy was in itself evidence of womanishness. He or she remade Castlehaven into the quintessential fop whose downfall anticipated England's later moral crisis, and whose literary resurrection might prove the mechanism for its solution. Reviving Castlehaven's trial, the author of the preface hoped, would inspire sybarites either to reform or to leave the country.[42]

As if to reinforce the message, all of the speeches and testimony in *The Trial and Condemnation* appeared as dialogue, conveying a false exactitude usually reserved for eyewitness observations (for which this no doubt aspired to be taken), and creating a sense of dramatic immediacy belied by the case's date. In his opening statement to the court, *The Trial and Condemnation* had the Attorney-General characterize Castlehaven's crimes as an "infection." Fonthill became "a common brothel-house." A discussion of mitigation became a discussion of the Earl's "meditated mischiefs." Instead of assuming that the jury would be "curious" about pardoning the Earl, here Heath asked them to be "cautious." Broadway and Fitzpatrick appeared as heroes, men risking their lives for a greater good; their imperfections were added proofs of their veracity, for as the judges in *The Trial and Condemnation* explained, "no man of unstained credit could be witnesses [sic] of such monstrous inhumanities." After the presentation of the prosecution's case the pamphlet reported the Lord High Steward as having said, "I could not have believed there would have been such manifest proofs"; after the presentation of the Earl's defense, the same official allegedly commented that Castlehaven had proven very little. By repeating almost none of Castlehaven's procedural objections, *The Trial and Condemnation* made his case seem weaker; by acknowledging and then dismissing thorny issues of legal substance, it made the prosecution's case seem stronger. The uncertainties that had unsettled contemporaries in the early seventeenth century in this version became nothing more than easily resolvable technicalities.[43]

The next pamphlet version of the Castlehaven trial appeared in 1708, soon after another series of arrests. Published by John Morphew, this text (entitled *The Case of Sodomy . . .*) was the first to exploit the charge of buggery for commercial purposes in its title; earlier pamphlets, even the alarmist tract of 1699, had had titles emphasizing the identity of the defendant and giving priority to the rape accusation.[44] *The Case of Sodomy* was less condemnatory than the 1699 pamphlet. Printed without any preface and without editorial intrusions, it used a reportorial rather than a dialogic format.

It was more comprehensive than any previous printed narrative had been. *The Case of Sodomy* restored both the Earl's defense and his challenges to the court; it added sympathetic items available previously only in manuscript—copies of Castlehaven's alleged last letters to his family, his confession of faith, his sisters' petition, and reports of the trials and executions of Broadway and Fitzpatrick. Here were indications of Castlehaven's defiance and of his repentance. Although *The Case of Sodomy* eschewed the inflammatory style of *The Trial and Condemnation,* as well as its discussions of effeminacy, both the timing and the title of the new pamphlet affirmed a reprioritization of the case. For Morphew as for his predecessor, this was what Morphew entitled it, no longer a case including sodomy, but one primarily about it. *The Case of Sodomy* marked a critical moment in the publication history of the Castlehaven story. Moreover, this was the version of the trial adopted by later popular publishers, and it was the unacknowledged core of the retelling in *Cobbett's Complete Collection of State Trials.*

The comprehensiveness of Morphew's text restored malleability to the narrative; different editors could still understand and use the trial in distinctive and often contradictory ways. Between 1710 and 1720, for example, the story attracted the attention of two of the most intriguing figures of the eighteenth-century world of publishing, Edmund Curll and Thomas Salmon. The former reprinted the case as a vivid example of aristocratic vice; the latter as a vivid example of English justice. The ease with which the trial could appear concurrently and coherently as part of both a collection intended to mock the conventions of social status and a collection intended to preach the virtues of the Constitution reaffirms not only the story's continuing resonance, but also the folly of isolating "popular" from "elite" literature.

Edmund Curll, who "had knowledge and a ready pen, plenty of courage and more impudence," cared little for the niceties of polite society, and even less for those of journalistic convention.[45] Born poor and originally apprenticed to a London printer, Curll became a publisher and bookseller whose eclectic inventory included books denounced as obscene as well as a comprehensive stock of history, divinity, and literature. He freely appropriated texts from other publishers, manufactured scandals for publicity, and resold old material under new titles. Curll was a master of self-promotion, whether this meant manufacturing a false controversy over authorship, turning his own attempted poisoning into a marketable story, or convincing the crowd when he was pilloried that his only crime had been to defend the late Queen Anne. His outrage at pomposity, censorship, and the specter of his own poverty far surpassed his shock at any particular sexual behavior.

In 1710, Curll resurrected the story of the trial of Bishop Atherton and published it as a commentary on current clerical mores. Having either bought or simply taken Morphew's text, Curll then reprinted the trials of both Atherton and Castlehaven under the title *The Cases of Unnatural Lewdness.*[46] Within a month, he had added a third case, raised the price, and issued a second edition.[47] In response to the accusation that he was profiteering at the cost of public morality, Curll pleaded public service. These cases, he claimed disingenuously, were "the only ones ever proved criminal in this part of the world." Comparing Atherton, who after his condemnation "freely opened the inmost recesses of his soul" with Castlehaven, who "after the fairest trial and clearest conviction, retained such a spirit of obstinacy," would, Curll wrote, be a powerful deterrent to the "unnaturally vicious."[48]

In 1714, allegedly inspired by an impotency trial in France, Curll returned yet again to the Castlehaven text, this time for a publishing venture that subsumed the issue of sodomy under the broader umbrella of aristocratic weaknesses.[49] Castlehaven's story became part of *The Case of Impotency As Debated in England* . . . , which, despite its title, was an anthology. *The Case of Impotency as Debated in England* . . . appeared in a variety of formats (including individual units) and under a variety of titles, but Castlehaven's case was always included. Curll's biographer calls the collection "the first of the best sellers"; it went through numerous editions between 1714 and 1719, and appeared, in one form or another, in catalogs of Curll's wares for the next two decades. The collection grew ever more elaborate, from two to five "neat pocket volumes" and from four cases to almost a dozen.[50] The reprintings displayed ever grander claims of authority, first an "original" manuscript, then the imprimatur of the House of Lords, and finally the authorship of the just deceased Solicitor-General, Sir Clement Wearg.[51]

Curll's collections provided readers with a ready compendium of a century of scandals; every one concerned sex, the elite, and, in most instances, literal or figurative impotence. The accounts detailed the sexual travails of not only Castlehaven, but also an Earl of Essex, a Duke of Norfolk, Lord Roos (memorably described by his wife as a "bungling base blockheaded bedfellow"), and several knights and esquires. The legal narratives were long and esoteric, but the books also included briefer, more immediately accessible stories such as the account of a man granted a divorce after his testicles were pulled off by a horse. The volumes mingled instances of blatant cuckoldry with allegations of impotency with cases of actual physical disability.[52] Yet none of the cases other than Castlehaven's involved any hint of buggery or rape, even though Curll had examples of such trials on hand from the earlier *Cases of Unnatural Lewdness*.

What was Castlehaven's trial—manifestly not about physical impotency—doing in such company? What unified the pieces in these collections was not, in fact, sexual behavior, but class and gender. They all concerned highborn persons, the incompatibility of the sexes, and in most cases women's power to humiliate men.[53] The impotency implied was patriarchal as much as corporeal. Castlehaven's story in this guise was as meaningful for what he could not do—control his household and most particularly his wife—as for anything that he allegedly did. The message was closer to that of the early libels than to the intervening pamphlet literature—male honor was no match for female sexual desire. Set among so many other tales of aristocratic difficulty, Castlehaven's trial also helped to teach a more subversive lesson: England's ruling elite (not just one Earl, not just one King, not because of just one vice) could not effectively rule even their own households.

Thomas Salmon's background and interests were very different from Edmund Curll's. The son and younger brother of learned clerics, Salmon was a traveler, geographer, and historian; a writer and editor rather than a vendor of printed materials. As a young man, he had kept a coffeehouse in Cambridge, but by 1710, like so many others hoping for success, Salmon had moved to London.[54] Among his first editorial assignments there was an abridgment of Rushworth's *Historical Collections*. Some time before 1719, a syndicate of five publishers hired Salmon to edit a proposed collection of "state-trials." He considered the eventual results as "the greatest collection of fine speeches, and arguments, on the most important subjects, that have hitherto been exhibited to the world." But neither the syndicate nor Salmon felt that critical lessons in history, rhetoric, and politics precluded gripping drama. In announcing their design for the project in 1716, the consortium had advertised for copies of not just celebrated trials, but "any curious trial, either printed or M.S. [manuscript]."[55]

A Complete Collection of State Trials had three hundred subscribers before the first edition was published. Almost immediately, sales attracted additional investors, submissions for further editions, competitors who offered similar (and similarly titled) but cheaper installment collections, and enterprising editors who reprinted specific trials in provincial newspapers.[56] Salmon (who edited only the first edition) himself produced at least four complementary anthologies.[57] The collection went through five editions and five editors between 1719 and 1826; in its final form, it remains the most reliable and accessible comprehensive anthology of important public British trials.[58] Most of the hundreds of trials included concern either treason or freedom of speech or press.[59] Castlehaven, Broadway, and Fitzpatrick are the only defendants in thirty-three volumes to have been tried for rape or sodomy. The presence of their trials in these collections has been critical to both our awareness of the cases and our understanding of them. But apart from treason, no category of prosecutions is self-evidently a "state trial." In effect, the editors created (without ever attempting to articulate) the classification and did it so successfully that the term and the collection are now synonymous. The labeling of Castlehaven, Broadway, and Fitzpatrick as state criminals was initially a product of the case's meaning beyond rape and sodomy and eventually a product of the case's presence in an apparently official collection, and it was also a product of chance and of commercial acuity.

The element of chance began with Salmon, whose maternal grandfather was apparently the regicide John Bradshaw.[60] Among

Bradshaw's rewards for his services to the Commonwealth was Fonthill Gifford, the estate gained by Lord Cottington at Castlehaven's attainder. If Bradshaw was Salmon's grandfather, then the future editor would surely have known Fonthill. And having abridged Rushworth's work, Salmon would have been familiar with Rushworth's rendition of Castlehaven's story. Perhaps most important, since the proposal for *State Trials* appeared just after the first publication of Curll's *A Case of Impotency as Debated in England*, there was a popular printed version of the events available in the text used by John Morphew and then Edmund Curll.

Salmon might have known the case well, and still found it inappropriate, yet including the three trials in his collection made enormous financial sense. From the beginning, *State Trials* was a commercial venture, inspired by a desire not only to contribute to ongoing political debates, but also to exploit the vogue for dying confessions, scandalous stories, and criminal proceedings. The volumes were not, as they are today, the province of attorneys and academics; they were intended for and seemed to have reached a considerably broader public. The renditions of Castlehaven, Broadway, and Fitzpatrick used in the first and (with minor emendations) later editions of *State Trials* make it clear that the editors had no quarrel with practical success. From arraignment to sentence, the accounts were verbatim, unacknowledged, reprints of the best-selling *Case of Sodomy*. On issues unnoticed by that pamphlet, Salmon added material from Rushworth, the more reputable text perhaps, but the thinner and the duller one.[61] *State Trials* was a part of rather than apart from the worlds of Grub Street and Fleet Street. Curll's 1719 edition of *A Case of Impotency as Debated in England* . . . rounded the circle; it incorporated Salmon's borrowings from Rushworth.

Morphew's text and Rushworth's additions provided a version of the trials comprehensive enough to suit not only the commercial, but also the political requirements of different editors. Placed by the Tory Salmon between the cases of the Somersets and William Prynne, the story could represent royal determination to enforce the law and a litany of corruptness obstructed; set by the radical penultimate editor William Cobbett between two cases of scandalous accusation, the trials could illustrate the failings of the ruling elites and their vulnerability to public ridicule. Castlehaven's trial was complex enough to speak to the dangers of public life that worried Salmon, the inadequacies in public law that worried his successor Sollom Emlyn, and the corruption of power that worried Cobbett.[62]

CASTLEHAVEN UNDERGROUND

After 1730, sodomite-hunting on a large scale seems to have abated. Edmund Curll, who might have found ways to keep Castlehaven, Broadway, and Fitzpatrick before the public regardless of that change, died in 1747. The trials remained available to anyone who read older publications as well as in the editions of *State Trials,* but they seem temporarily to have disappeared from the popular press. When nearly a century later, Castlehaven's story found its way into the press again, it was once more as part of an anti-aristocratic topos, but with a slightly different flavor. Political repression and financial pressures in the 1790s and early 1800s laid waste to many presses; as a result, some radical publishers began to cater to the active market for graphic sexual publications. Taking advantage of a perpetual interest in the failings and hypocrisies of the ruling elites, they exploited a kind of "bawdy populism." Some periodicals reported various sexual escapades of the rich and titled; others specialized in narratives of specific sexual activities. The radical residue in these endeavors should not be exaggerated, but neither should we dismiss the political benefits for radicals of presenting aristocrats as lewd and lascivious.[63]

Between 1842 and 1844, one of the most prolific of these publishers, William Dugdale, produced "The Exquisite," a weekly collection of "tales, histories, and essays, funny, fanciful and facetious, interspersed with anecdotes, original and select, amorous adventures, piquant jests and spicy sayings." Unlike its competitors, most of which focused on recent scandals, "The Exquisite" generally eschewed the factual for the fantastical. The serial favored fiction (especially translated from French or Italian), memoirs, and epistolary discussions of sexual relationships. The paper never ran much history, yet Dugdale inaugurated his venture with a seven-week serialization of Castlehaven's trial.[64] Labeled as a case of "unnatural crimes and other offenses," the seven-part series included no indictments, no legal questions, no servants' trials, no tenets of belief, and no scaffold speeches. Many of the legal and religious passages disappeared, and the text tantalizingly substituted blanks for words such as "privities," "sodomy," and "thighs." The blanks gestured toward rather than enforced propriety; they neither consistently disguised nor obfuscated graphic descriptions. Here was the story drained of all but the most general political critique, flattened into a highly titillating narrative of aristocratic vice.

Outside of *State Trials* and the demiworld of projects such as "The Exquisite," Castlehaven virtually disappeared from direct public view after about 1750.[65] Yet his erasure was not complete. Victorian scholars put Herculean efforts into the compilation of comprehensive reference works, works that were intended to be definitive chronicles of England's great personages and great events. Eliminating Castlehaven, however personally inconsequential he might have been, was difficult; he became once more a ghostly presence, but one still found in footnotes and appendixes, added to or embedded within, other people's stories. The producers of these works preserved the case even as they wished it away. So the leading historian of Wiltshire forbore to "offend my readers by detailing all the particulars," then outlined the case, and referred readers to *State Trials* for further details. The author of the entry on the 3rd Earl of Castlehaven in the *Dictionary of National Biography* related the story of the trial as proof of his subject's precocious rectitude. The editor of the *Calendar of State Papers Domestic* as well as the historian Samuel Rawson Gardiner used Castlehaven's conviction as collateral evidence that his prophetic sister might well have been insane.[66] The distaste behind these asides is palpable, yet, even here there were differing interpretations of the truth. To the collector of *Pieces of Ancient Poetry from Unpublished Manuscripts and Scarce Books . . .*, Castlehaven's guilt was clear; he was a "wretched man." For the editor of the Fairfax correspondence "all the parties were grossly immoral." The compiler of *The Complete Peerage* thought the primary villain was the Countess; the Earl's death, he assured those who read his footnotes, "was certainly brought about by her means."[67]

That Castlehaven's trial has been retold is not surprising, nor is the fact that media, time, and audience have imposed changes upon the narrative. Yet this history is a caveat against treating any text too reverently, against forgetting that texts always reflect choices, for us as much as for their authors. More often than not, the choices are serendipitous and self-interested—the product of what is available, what will produce profits, what will help broader arguments. Castlehaven has always belonged to many stories, many readers, and many jumbled interpretations. Each rendition has had to find not only its audiences but also its place among the already existing stories: men and women who heard Castlehaven libels in the street, saw Milton's masque, or worshiped in St. Mary's Church in Harefield may have also owned or read histories, manuscripts, or pamphlets about the case. Each narrative also had to find a place among the cultural preoccupations of the day. Because it touched on issues of identity and law that have continued to be unstable, Castlehaven's trial always remained recognizable enough to be reconceived for new times, by new editors, and in new contexts. In its original circumstances, concerns about family, about good governance, and about salvation dominated the events. In the eighteenth century, the case became more narrowly focused upon sexuality and class. Even when it appeared to have been forgotten, in the nineteenth century, the trial remained available not only in older versions, but also as a newly used example of the lascivious, the mad, and the victimized. Castlehaven's has been and is a story about sodomy, rape, and property; about authority, resistance, and legal rights; about chastity, decadence, and honor. It has been about many things in many settings, but always about more than just one unhappy family.

CHAPTER 6

CONCLUSIONS

rimes and trials fascinate us; they show us, at a safe distance, passions unrestrained. Stories of crime and punishment remind us of our humanity; depending on the circumstances, they frighten, intrigue, comfort, and anger us. "When literature palls upon me," Sir Leslie Stephen wrote at the end of the nineteenth century, "I sometimes turn for relief to the great collection of State Trials."[1] Sir Leslie would be horrified at the comparison, but something of the same sentiment helps to explain why sensational trials sell books and newspapers, why the guilt or innocence of strangers elicits fierce debate, why at virtually any hour you can find on television fictional trials, actual trials, and trials staged specifically for the cameras.

Our sustained interest in historical trials draws partly upon their dramatic qualities, and partly upon their relationship to history. If at their most fantastical, stories of felons such as Castlehaven, Broadway, and Fitzpatrick make fact seem fictional, these tales also make history more immediate and more compelling. Crudely retold, such stories conflate the past and present, suggesting an essentialist psychology as deceptive as it is appealing. Retold more sensitively, however, trials can be superb illustrations of how past and present differ, of how distinctive meanings divide us from the past even as common forms connect us to it. Castlehaven's trial is an apt example. With its salacious and enigmatic narratives; its multiple and contradictory histories; its potential for integrating insights about sexuality, gender, and representation into more traditional analyses of crime and law, the story can be (and has been) easily retold through anachronous generalizations and stereotypes. The temptation to reduce the case to its sexual components has overshadowed much richer possibilities. The interplay among sexual accusations, legal process, and social values is what first drew me into this study.

My first objective here has been to reshape the accepted narrative of what happened in these trials as well as our understanding of why it happened. The mainstays of the case as traditionally told have been homosexual acts, Catholic identity, and Castlehaven's guilt. It has been all too simple to leap from the fact of indictments for buggery and rape to homosexuality and misogyny as motives for sodomy and rape; to interweave Castlehaven's religious wavering with general antipapist prejudice; and to work from legal condemnation to factual guilt to a contest between an apparently deranged man and the prescribed virtues of his society. Yet the facts belie this construction, muddying what superficially seems self-evident. This a story that looks, but is not, familiar; peopled by a confusing cast and made more convoluted still by adversarial maneuvering in the past and gaps of documentation in the present. The case has left a wealth of evidence, but none of it is entirely coherent and none of it is linked to any one cache of reliable materials. The narrative is labyrinthine and previous research thin enough that most modern renditions contain some errors of fact.[2] Not every error fatally distorts a reader's understanding, but accuracy matters, for getting the story "straight" in its essentials fundamentally transforms it. Neither Castlehaven's nor Fitzpatrick's actions fit the prior legal definition of sodomy and Broadway's may not have fit the technical threshold of rape. The critical proofs of the Earl's ignominy were nonsexual: his willingness to give away lands and goods, his inability to command his dependents, and his resolute defiance as a subject. Nor can the Earl's disrepute be explained as merely antipapist. The staunch Catholic in the family was not Castlehaven, but Lord Audley, the disaffected heir whose complaint the King and Castlehaven's peers eventually endorsed. In religion, as in much else, Castlehaven was unsettled; the fear that his devotional life inspired was a fear of faithlessness rather than of popery in particular. Equally influential were the facts that the

Touchets and the Stanleys had been publicly at odds for years, and that the relationship between the Touchets and the King was, at best, chilly.

Early modern men and women found the trial and its results more troubling than previous scholars have recognized. The witnesses were problematical, the judges' rulings were worrying, and the Earl's comportment was disquieting. Many early modern gentlemen (particularly aristocrats) were vulnerable to accusations such as sodomy or apostasy, and such charges were notoriously difficult to disprove. Splenetic wives and sons were hardly unusual: conspiracy on the part of a sexually demanding woman and an avaricious heir was at least as plausible to contemporary sensibilities as were sodomitical excesses and depraved Earls. In its time, Castlehaven's trial was neither foregone in its conclusions, nor universally sanctioned in its procedures. But that is not to say that early modern men and women necessarily considered the Earl innocent. Well before the spring of 1631, the household at Fonthill Gifford was rife with tensions—between spouses, between servants, and between generations. Castlehaven himself exhibited neither the stewardship of a proper ruler, the husbandry of a proper Englishman, nor the self-mastery of a proper man. In a society for which civic and sexual culpability went hand in hand, what damned Castlehaven was not what we would recognize as evidence (or lack thereof) of sexual or religious errancy, but allegations of immoderateness and ineffectualness. For contemporaries, these weaknesses would inevitably overflow into all spheres of behavior, including the sexual.

Excavating the archival remains of this case and disentangling what has documentary support from what does not makes it clear that a convincing interpretation of events demands the integration of their legal expression with the history of Castlehaven and his family, as well as with contemporary prescriptions of paternal governance, aristocratic purity, and national identity. This is a case about gender, law, and politics as well as about sex, religion, and culpability. The broader perspective makes sense out of what are otherwise discordant elements: among other things, it explains the emphasis on Castlehaven's relationships with Skipwith, Anktill, and Lady Audley; the tenor of the Earl's defiance; and the ambivalence of both peers and contemporary commentators. Rehearsing discussions about the distribution of power within society, the trial dramatically illustrates the unending need of early modern rulers to reiterate the organizing social principles of early modern English life: manhood, hierarchy, and English Protestantism.

Rethinking Castlehaven's story in this way allows us also to see beyond its central character; it makes more visible some of the temptations and vulnerabilities of servants in great establishments and some of the constraints and freedoms of aristocratic women. The centrality of the ideal of the well-ordered household to both the prosecution and the Earl's defense confirms the fragile mix of expectation and negotiation that constituted household management. The trial's testimony details the opportunities a large household offered, on the one hand, for men to intimidate women physically, verbally, and financially, and on the other hand, for women to orchestrate their sexual lives independently of male intentions or desires. Status, will, and changing circumstance shaped and reshaped life within each domestic arrangement. Ideologically, however, the prescriptive vision was inescapable; men ruled and women submitted. The expectation of patriarchal dominance was the standard that Lord Audley used when he complained against his father, it was the standard that the King's attorneys relied upon to condemn Castlehaven, and it was the standard that provided the language through which virtually every witness including the Earl explained his or her behavior.

The prosecutions of Castlehaven and Broadway for raping the Countess of Castlehaven are a powerful example of how difficult it was for early modern women, however privileged, to have an effective legal voice. Because they were understood to be fundamentally less reliable than men, none of the female servants at Fonthill Gifford seem ever to have been questioned (even though the investigators knew the women's names and whereabouts). Because neither the Countess nor her daughter could tell a sexual story publicly without losing face, neither appeared in court at Castlehaven's trial. The Countess's required appearance at the hearing of Giles Broadway was as brief as possible. Male surrogates controlled the presentation of complaints in a system that gauged credibility to some extent through a victim's active participation. Worse, absence deprived women of a forum in which to answer countercharges, in this instance leaving them vulnerable to new aspersions upon their characters. Despite the judges' admonition that a victim's reputation was irrelevant to the crime of rape, Castlehaven's defense rested upon the assumption that women were generally more sexually voracious, more unreasonable, and more devious than men; pace the verdict, the Countess and Lady Audley emerged from the trial with sullied reputations. Male jurors in early modern England routinely commiserated more easily with the vulnerabilities of defendants in charges of rape than with the vulnerabilities of victims, particularly when, as here, testimonies differed on the essential issue of carnal knowledge. In this case social prejudice overrode gender prejudice (Castlehaven allegedly having encouraged a servant to attack a woman who was the wife of one Earl and the daughter of another), but the conventions of the law still disempowered the women; their absences not only left the Countess susceptible to vilification, but also exposed the verdict in her favor to later procedural complaints.

The unfolding of Castlehaven's trial and execution refines our understanding of how at least one segment of early modern society believed that the common law should function. The depositions in the case offer a rare, albeit imperfect, glimpse into the way that arguments in court gained coherence by exploiting familiar anxieties. This perspective is critical to understanding why the attorneys could produce a successful prosecution that spoke so much about property, households, and religion and so relatively little about sex. The responses of the Earl and of those around him to his condemnation provide a peculiarly elaborate view of the exchanges (financial and/or emotional) associated with royal pardons. The Earl's behavior shows how fragile the association of royal and divine mercy was, how even someone so allegedly disreputable as Castlehaven could set the two against each other and trouble the confidence of observers about his guilt.

And the procedural challenges of the trial emphasize the value of seeing early modern law as process rather than product. Castlehaven's trial was significant for contemporaries not merely because its defendant was a peer, but also because of the pressure it placed upon familiar practices. In most criminal trials, principals were tried before accessories, defendants were allowed to confront the witnesses publicly, ambiguities in capital offenses were construed narrowly, and wives were not permitted to testify against their husbands. The meetings at the Sergeants' Inn before these trials suggest how uncertain the legal situation was; the jurors' disputations show how uncertain it remained. None of the decisions made in 1631 was demonstrably incorrect, but several, and particularly the construal of sodomy, were open to question. Common law, and especially criminal law, was in practice always a sort of scripted improvisation. Conventions dictated who spoke when, how, and with what likely impact; a skeletal text and audience acceptance limited the range of action. Yet the restrictions were directional, not determinative; new situations demanded responses that left considerable room for creativity.

Creativity, of course, is exceptionally personal; one person's resolution may be another's impropriety. Castlehaven's defense shows us a self-interested, but not incredible, understanding of procedural fairness: the opportunity to confront one's accusers, trial by a panel of uninterested and impartial jurors, respect for the integrity of the household, and judicial rulings that favored the letter of the law. The judicial view was equally convenient and justifiable, if diametrically different. The judges, believing that in this case, following convention would produce injustice, did what judges in common law routinely did and do; they adapted prior practice. The peers who voted against the Earl's conviction did not necessarily agree with him, but they certainly resisted the judges' claims to interpretative superiority, and they objected to a definition of statute that was expansive and retroactive. Such judicial grandiosity, it seemed to them, was both too independent and too servile: it respected the integrity of the law (and the peers) too little and the comfort of the King too much.

In addition to improving our factual knowledge, my intention in this book has been to understand the many lives of the Castlehaven story. The resilience of the trial seems, at first, to reflect a transhistorical fascination with sex and privilege, but its lasting appeal is more complicated than that. In addition to its sensationalness, these events have remained useful in part because they were ambiguous enough to absorb emendations easily. In a perverse way, the 2nd Earl of Castlehaven is a man for all seasons. He has belonged to a diversity of stories and a diversity of readers, and we would be mistaken to try too thoroughly to divide them from each other—those who owned and/or read formal histories may also have read and/or owned manuscripts, pamphlets, or ephemera; those who read or heard of the cuckolded Earl may also have read or heard of Castlehaven the victim and of Castlehaven the decadent. There need never have been a single dominant representation of the Earl; his dynamism is one of the most historically significant things about him. Over time, neither the central focus nor the perspective of the story has stayed the same: in the 1630s, retellings emphasized family and honor; in the 1680s, monarchy and vice; in the 1730s, corruption and the rule of law. Some editors have staged the trial as a sexual confrontation between spouses, others as an introspective religious struggle, still others as a conflict between the decrepitude of power and the robustness of the common law. Drained of its particulars, the story can be remolded to recall any generation's version of battles between husbands and wives, sin and conscience, privilege and responsibility. The retellings of the trial have traditionally been understood as attempts to tell the same story; they are better understood as attempts to tell different stories, each exploring a boundary between legitimacy and corruption, each cast from the same outline, but each framed for particular audiences and purposes.

Technology, commerce, and circumstance—fortuitous matches of text, editors, and timing—have also made a difference. The inclusion of Castlehaven's case in *Cobbett's Complete Collection of State Trials* as the single example indexed under either rape or sodomy has ensured the trial both continued visibility and a narrow construction. Yet the text is in *State Trials* not only for its rarity, but equally (or more so) because there was a burgeoning eighteenth-century market for stories that both detailed and condemned aristocratic vice. The trial fit a need to draw subscribers to an ambitious and precarious experiment in publishing. The established success of Edmund Curll's retellings, and Thomas Salmon's ability to augment Curll with details drawn from his own editorial work on Rushworth made its incorporation almost effortless. Curll, in turn, had appropriated the text from John Morphew, whose sources draw us back to the moral reform literature of the turn of the eighteenth century. The most readily used printed versions of the trial today, then, whether "serious" or "scurrilous," derive from similar commercial circumstances and similar sources.

Yet the legal peculiarities of the trial have ensured it a very different place in the professional sources of the common law. For lawyers, the plotting so necessary to commercial purposes is less important; except as the whos and hows might impinge upon the thinking behind legal oddities, they are of minimal importance to traditional scholarship on the law.[3] What most forcefully struck contemporaries—the novelty of the ruling defining sodomy—was fairly quickly set aside. The first printed legal report of the decision (Sir Richard Hutton's in 1656), explained it away as an interpretation intended not as "a general opinion that may be a rule in other cases," but one inspired by "the foulness and abominableness of this fact." Thus categorized, it almost immediately became, as the judges in 1631 had apparently intended, a dead letter.[4]

But if the trial had little direct influence on the law of buggery, it became a repeated point of reference in the law of spousal relations.[5] While in commercial form, Castlehaven's story over time became increasingly a tale of sodomy, as precedent, its lasting value has been as an unusual case of rape. The trial was "epoch-making" and immediately recognized as such, in its insistence that a wife could testify against her husband.[6] The civil autonomy implicit in this right has, in turn, been a crucial foundation for the development of the law of marital rape.[7] Yet, Castlehaven's case may also have been instrumental in creating the legal difficulty it has since helped to resolve. From the early eighteenth century, the definitive statement on the impossibility of rape within marriage has been Sir Matthew Hale's; virtually all later arguments return to him, refutations virtually always begin with him. Few sentences from legal treatises can have engendered as much controversy as Hale's comment that "a husband cannot be guilty of rape committed by himself upon his lawful wife, for by their mutual matrimonial consent and contract the wife has given herself in this kind to her husband which she cannot retract." Hale cited no earlier treatises for his view, and (outside the specific circumstances of abduction and concubinage) earlier authorities had been silent about the issue; why did he even discuss it?

The answer, at least in part, was Castlehaven. Directly following his statement about immunity, Hale retold the rape portion of the Castlehaven trial (using initials rather than names). He confirmed that the judgment therein established limits upon the indivisibility of marital contract, that it meant that a husband's marital rights were not transferable; that husbands acting as accomplices in assaults upon their wives were accountable as principals; and that a wife victimized by her spouse could both prosecute her husband and testify against him. The possible applications of these exceptions seems to have unnerved him; like later authorities, he apparently feared that such anomalies might encourage wives "to get rid of husbands that prove uneasy" (Castlehaven's own argument in 1631). Hale ended his chapter on rape not with Castlehaven, but with nonspousal examples emphasizing rape's peculiar susceptibility to "malicious contrivance."[8] Hale was no sexual egalitarian, but the Castlehaven precedent seems a more likely inspiration than misogyny for Hale's unusual concern with the possible ramifications of spousal autonomy.[9]

The variance between the ways that historians and lawyers have used this case points to my third goal for this book, to raise issues about how we write both legal and social histories. The last twenty years have seen a new appreciation of the interrelationship of history and law, from historians intrigued by the ethnographic potential of legal events and from legal theorists dismayed by what they see as the distortions of understanding law in terms of only its internal history. Trials, long a staple of an anecdotal scholarship, have become a staple of new sorts of cultural histories. Transforming occasions of individual concealment into moments of social disclosure, this type of work has pressed successfully to hear within legal records the voices of the usually voiceless.[10] Historians of early modern England, however, have played little substantial role in this move to micro-legal history.[11] With its plenitude of documentation, Castlehaven's case helps to end this silence, allowing us the opportunity to follow the negotiative processes of the early modern English law in action. This study broadens the ground usually traversed by such investigations: it concerns the elite as well as the humble, English rather than Continental law, and crimes that (however deceptively) seem too familiar to allow us a comfortable senses of distance.

My reconstruction, however, is intended to do more than simply provide some historiographical balance. Studies of legal cases often give either too much or too little consideration to the interrelationship of law and society. Sometimes, social and cultural influences appear as intrusions extrinsic to an otherwise self-referential law. More frequently, authors bring their broader cultural knowledge to bear in analyzing verdicts, but not in analyzing law and its procedures. The legal setting fades to background, to an occasion which happens to produce historically relevant materials. Yet this case exposes how completely interwoven are the legal and the cultural: ambiguities within the law allowed Castlehaven to build a defense directed at the foundations of the aristocracy; concerns about social stability underlay the prosecutors' insistence upon legal clarity. Disagreements about who could testify against whom and about what validated the accusations within the law exposed very real social differences; in turn, the resolutions of those disagreements provided legal clarifications that have long outlived the specifics of their origin. Concentrating on the trial rather than the verdict makes more obvious the commensurability of social, cultural, and legal forces. It highlights instead of masks the unpredictable twists and turns of this symbiosis. As the way that society's elites assure themselves of their connections to both the past and the future, common law is always both rules and choices, an inheritance and a creation. This does not make legal practice necessarily cynical any more than whiggishness would make it objective, but it does mean that separating the worlds within and beyond the courts wrenches both from important guides to understanding. And similarly, recognizing the verdict as an artificial conclusion rather than a truth inspires lines of inquiry that might otherwise be missed; making the verdict itself a question reaffirms law's place as a part of as well as apart from ordinary life.

Such an approach can also broaden the ways that as scholars we study the histories of sex. For traditional historians the notion that Castlehaven's trial contains sex has meant that it is only about sex; in their own way, historians of sexuality have been complicit in that view. The political power of that assessment has encouraged even scholars intrigued by the history of sex to disembody it. The sexual element in this story has guaranteed its popularity, but the case's graphic detail has made its serious study difficult. Yet only when we look at the trial's physical configurations and their legal status can we recognize the problems that this trial presented for contemporaries. What exactly constituted carnal knowledge? How were ideas of gender and sexual behaviors intertwined? What were the temptations and possibilities of physical relationships within ever-changing households? We will learn more about both sex and other aspects of culture when we learn to treat law less matter-of-factly and sexual practices more so.

The prosecution of the 2nd Earl of Castlehaven was both sui generis and revealing of its broader context, atypical and yet suggestive about familiar legal difficulties. However unpleasant we might find its details, the scandal has survived because it has repeatedly offered a platform from which to comment on matters that concern contemporary audiences. That durability of as well as the dynamics of the events of April 1631 deserve our attention. Castlehaven was a man of no importance, but the darkest moments of his family can and do shed light on his time, time since and time now.

THE JURORS

The vote on rape precedes the vote on sodomy under each juror's name below. Biographical details from CP and DNB.

Richard Weston, Lord Weston
guilty
guilty
> (1576/77–1634/35). Lord Treasurer. Student at the Middle Temple in 1593/94. Member of Parliament for Essex in 1614; privy councilor from 1621; Lord Treasurer from 1628 until his death. Male heir born 1605. Created Baron Weston in 1628 and 1st Earl of Portland in 1633.

Henry Montagu, 1st Earl of Manchester
guilty
guilty
> (ca. 1563–1642). Lord Privy Seal. In 1606 was a Reader at the Middle Temple. Member of Parliament for London, 1614; Sergeant-at-Law and King's Sergeant in 1611; Chief Justice of the King's Bench from 1616 to 1620; member of the Privy Council from 1620. Male heir born 1602. Close ally of the Countess of Castlehaven's mother; father-in-law to Warwick's daughter. Created Earl of Manchester, 1626.

Thomas Howard, Earl of Arundel
guilty
guilty
> (1585–1646). Earl Marshal. Privy councilor from 1616. Male heir born 1608. Restored to his father's earldom, 1604.

Philip Herbert, Earl of Pembroke
[KB8/63 lists his forename as John]
guilty
not guilty
> (1584–1649/50). Lord Chamberlain. Member of the Privy Chamber; Lord Chamberlain of the Household from 1626 to 1641. Lord Lieutenant of Wiltshire and several other counties from 1630. Married (1) 1604, Susan, daughter of Edward de Vere, 17th Earl of Oxford, and Anne Cecil and sister to Elizabeth,

Countess of Derby; (2) Anne, widow of Richard Sackville, Earl of Dorset, heir of George Clifford, Earl of Cumberland, and Margaret, daughter of Francis Russell, Earl of Bedford. Adulterous alliance with Berkshire's daughter. Male heir born 1619. Created Earl of Montgomery 1605 and succeeded his brother as Earl of Pembroke in 1630.

Henry Grey, Earl of Kent
guilty
not guilty
> (ca. 1583–1639). Member of Parliament for Bedfordshire 1614. Succeeded to the earldom, 1623.

Henry Somerset, Earl of Worcester
guilty
not guilty
> (1576/77–1646). Attended the Middle Temple 1598/99. Married in 1600 to Ann, daughter of Lord Russell; male heir born 1601. Brother-in-law of Petre. Succeeded to earldom, 1628.

Francis Russell, Earl of Bedford
guilty
not guilty
> (1593–1641). In 1608/9, married Catherine, daughter and co-heir of Giles Brydges, 3rd Baron of Chandos, and Frances, daughter of Edward Clinton, Earl of Lincoln. Male heir born 1616. Succeeded to the earldom, 1627.

Robert Devereux, Earl of Essex
guilty
not guilty
> (1590/91–1646). Married (1) 1605/6 to Frances Howard, daughter of Thomas Howard, Earl of Suffolk, and Katherine, daughter and co-heir of Sir Henry Knyvett; marriage dissolved in 1613; (2) 1630/31 to Elizabeth, daughter of Sir William Paulet of Eddington, Wiltshire. Former brother-in-law of Berkshire and of Howard. Restored to his father's earldom, 1604.

Edward Sackville, Earl of Dorset
guilty
not guilty
> (1590–1652). Chamberlain to the Queen from 1628. Member of the Privy Council from 1626. Married Mary, daughter and heir of Sir George Curzon, and governess to the children of Charles I. Male heir born 1622. Succeeded to the earldom, 1624.

William Cecil, Earl of Salisbury
guilty
not guilty
> (1591–1664/65). Member of the Privy Council from 1626. Brother-in-law of Clifford, Howard, and Berkshire; father-in-law of Percy; first cousin of Wimbledon. Succeeded to the earldom, 1612.

Robert Sydney, Earl of Leicester

guilty

not guilty

(1595–1677). Member of Parliament for Wilton in 1614. In 1615, married Dorothy, daughter of Henry Percy, Earl of Northumberland, and Dorothy, daughter of Walter Devereux, Earl of Essex; male heir born 1619. Brother-in-law of Percy and of Carlisle; related by marriage to Holland and Warwick. Succeeded to the earldom, 1626.

Robert Rich, Earl of Warwick

guilty

guilty

(1587–1658). Admitted to the Inner Temple in 1604; member of Parliament for Essex in 1614; burgess of Southampton, 1626. Male heir born 1611; older brother of Holland; related by marriage to Leicester and Carlisle. Succeeded to the earldom, 1619.

James Hay, Earl of Carlisle

guilty

guilty

(1580–1636). Born in Scotland, educated in France. Gentleman of the Bedchamber to James I 1603–15; member of the Privy Council from 1616/17. He married (1) in 1606/7, Honora, only child of Edward Denny, Earl of Norwich, and Mary, daughter of Thomas Cecil, Earl of Exeter; (2) in 1617 Lucy, daughter of Henry Percy, Earl of Northumberland, and Dorothy, daughter of Walter Devereux, Earl of Essex. Brother-in-law of Leicester and of Percy; related by marriage to Holland and Warwick. Created Lord Hay, 1606, Earl of Carlisle, 1622.

Henry Rich, 1st Earl of Holland

guilty

not guilty

(1590–1648/49). Steward of the Queen's Household from 1629; member of Parliament for Leicester, 1614; member of the Privy Council from 1625; Gentleman of the Bedchamber from 1626. Male heir born 1620. Brother of Warwick; related by marriage to Leicester and Carlisle. Created Earl of Holland, 1624.

Thomas Howard, Earl of Berkshire

guilty

not guilty

(ca. 1590–1669). Second son of Thomas, 1st Earl of Suffolk, and Catherine, daughter and co-heir of Sir Henry Knyvett of Charlton, Wiltshire. Member of Parliament for Wiltshire in 1614. Married Elizabeth, daughter and co-heir of William Cecil, 2nd Earl of Exeter, and niece of Viscount Wimbledon, in 1614. Designated in 1621/22 as the heir to his mother's Wiltshire estates and created Baron Howard of Charleton, Wiltshire. Male heir born 1615. Brother of Howard; brother-in-law of Salisbury; former brother-in-law of Essex; daughter was Pembroke's mistress. In 1625/26, created Earl of Berkshire.

Henry Danvers, 1st Earl of Danby

guilty
guilty

(1573–1643/44). Second son of Sir John Danvers of Dauntsey, Wiltshire. Fought as a soldier in Europe and in Ireland; Lord President of Munster, 1607–15; member of the Privy Council from 1628. Created Baron Danvers of Dantsey, Wiltshire, 1603, and Earl of Danby, Yorkshire, 1625/26.

Edward Cecil, Viscount Wimbledon

guilty
guilty

(1571/72–1638). Gentleman of the Privy Chamber for James I. Third son of Thomas Cecil, 1st Earl of Exeter. Married in 1601 to Theodosia, sister of Edward Noel, 2nd Viscount Campden, and of the 1st Dowager Countess of Castlehaven, Elizabeth Noel Touchet Crosby; first cousin of Salisbury. Created Viscount Wimbledon, 1625.

Edward Conway, Viscount Conway

guilty
guilty

(1594–1655). Son and heir of the former Secretary of State. Married 1621 to Frances, daughter of Sir Francis Popham of Littlecote, Wiltshire. Male heir born 1623. Succeeded to the viscountcy in January 1631.

Dudley Carleton, Viscount Dorchester

guilty
guilty

(1573/74–1631/32). Principal Secretary of State from 1628; member of the Privy Council from 1625. His second wife was Anne, daughter of Sir Henry Glenham, and Anne, daughter of Thomas Sackville, Earl of Dorset. Created Baron, 1626, Viscount, 1628.

Thomas, Viscount Wentworth

guilty
guilty

(1593–1641). Lord President of the North. Member of Parliament for Yorkshire, 1614; privy councilor from 1629. Male heir born 1626. Brother-in-law of Clifford. Created Baron in July 1628, Viscount in December 1628.

Henry Clifford, Lord Clifford

guilty
guilty

(ca. 1591/92–1643). Member of Parliament for Westmoreland, 1614. Son of the Earl of Cumberland (succeeded him 1641); brother-in-law of Salisbury and of Wentworth.

Algernon Percy, 4th Lord Percy

guilty

guilty

> (1602–68). Third but first-surviving son of the Earl of Northumberland. Son-in-law of Salisbury; brother-in-law of Leicester. Took his seat in the House of Lords as Lord Percy in 1626 and succeeded his father as Earl of Northumberland in 1632.

James Stanley, Lord Strange

guilty

guilty

> (1607–51). Son of William Stanley, Earl of Derby (succeeded in 1642). Summoned to Parliament as Lord Strange in 1627/28. Male heir born 1628. First cousin of Anne, Countess of Castlehaven.

Dudley North, 3rd Lord North

not guilty

not guilty

> (1582–1665/66). Male heir born 1602. Succeeded as Lord North, 1600.

William Petre, 2nd Lord Petre

guilty

guilty

> (1575–1637). Student at the Middle Temple in 1593. Married in 1596 to Katherine, 2nd daughter of Edward Somerset, 4th Earl of Worcester, and Elizabeth, daughter of Francis Hastings, 2nd Earl of Huntingdon. Male heir born 1599. Brother-in-law of Worcester. Succeeded 1613.

Edward Howard of Escrick

guilty

not guilty

> (b.?–1675). Youngest son of Thomas, 1st Earl of Suffolk, and Catherine, daughter and co-heir of Sir Henry Knyvett of Charleton, Wiltshire. Male heir born 1625. Married to Mary, daughter of Sir John Boteler and niece of the Duke of Buckingham. Brother of Berkshire; brother-in-law of Salisbury; former brother-in-law of Essex. Created Baron Howard of Escrick in 1628.

George Goring, Lord Goring

guilty

guilty

> (1585–1662/63). Master of the Queen's Horse since 1628; Gentleman of the Privy Chamber to the Prince of Wales in 1610 and to the King in 1611; Vice-Chamberlain of the Queen's Household, 1626–28. Married Lettice, third daughter of the 1st Earl of Cork and once the intended spouse of James, Lord Audley. Male heir born 1615. Created Baron Goring, 1628 (succeeded his Uncle as 2nd Earl of Norwich in 1644).

VERSES[1]

The Epitaph [from BL Add Ms 5832/222b]:
I need no trophies to adorn my hearse
My wife exalts my horns in every verse
And placed them so full upon my tomb
That for my arms there is no vacant room
Who will take such a Countess to his bed
That first gives horns and then cuts off the head?

Responsio [from CUL Add Ms 335/54r]:
Tis true you need no trophies to adorn your hearse
Your life being odious and below all verse
Nor was it your wife who came chaste to your bed
That did you horn; your own hands horned your head
Twas fit your head should of then most men censure
That you that lived so, should die a monster

The Lady's Answer [as in BL Add Ms 22, 591/89]:
Blame not your wife, for what yourself has wrought
You caused your horns in forcing me to nought
For had you been but human, not a beast
Your arms had been supporters to your crest
Nor need you yet have had a tomb or hearse
Besmeared with your sensual life in verse
Who then would take such a lord into her bed
That to gain horns himself, would lose his head.

The epitaph can be found (with minor variations) in several contexts. Starred references note copies that are followed by one of the two versions of the Countess's response:

Accompanying texts of the trial: *BL Add Ms 22,591/89; BL Harl Ms 738/328; *BL Lansdowne Ms 491/229v; Bod Rawlinson Ms A346/138; FSL Ms V.b.50; Yale Library Osborn Ms b.125; *Yale Library Osborn Ms b.126; *Trinity College Dublin Ms 731; *WRO Ms 413/401.

In miscellanies and commonplace books: BL Add Ms 5832/222b; BL Add Ms 22,118/29; BL Add Ms 44,963/38v; BL Sloane Ms 1446/64v; Bod Eng Poet Ms 14/87v; Corpus Christi College Mss 327/32v and 328/58; *Cambridge University Add Ms 335/54; Chester RO CR63/2/19; *Frye, *Pieces of Ancient Poetry from Unpublished Ms*, p. 11; FSL e.a.6/3; FSL v.a.124/18v–19 (titled The Earl of Newcastle on his Wife).

Bod Rawl Ms 26/21 makes a couplet of the epitaph's closing lines. NRO IL Ms 3337, p. 9 adds the verse to a discrete narrative of the Earl's scaffold speech; NRO IL Ms 3338/2v adds it to the satirical poem (NRO IL Ms 3338) below.

Lines added before the epitaph [from BL Lansdowne Ms 491/229v]:
My life is done my heart prepared for death
My trust in God who first did give me breath
My savior Christ has paid my debt and I
Am free from death and hell eternally.
And yet my heart from sorrow is not free
To think that my own flesh should injure me

My flesh and blood from flesh and blood is parted
We once were one but now are double hearted
My ill from evil sprang and malice wrought
My sinful action which was first in thought
And what remains in afterage to blame me
My flesh and blood did work my death to shame me
Ah whorish flesh what more is to be known
To thy disgrace more than to name mine own...

Lines added after the epitaph [from HEH Ms HM 116, p. 122]:
A proud cuckold tollit cornua
I would not have my wife exalt my horn
Keep on your mask and hide your eye
For with beholding it I die
For if your piercing eyes I see
They are worse than *basilikes to me.

*OED—a fantastic reptile classically believed to kill by its look and breath; also a large sixteenth-century cannon.

Upon the Lord Audleys Conviction April 1631 [from Bod Poet.e.97, pp. 67–68]:
Romes worst Philenis, and Pasiphaes dust
Are now chaste fictions and no longer lust
This colder age has monstered out a sin
That virtues them and saints an Aretine [?]

Scorning to owe a studied vice to times
Example, burns out with more noble crimes
*This blacker enigma is so hardly scanned
That virtue has no wit to understand
How sin should be so learned, that man should know
To rape himself and make one rape prove two
That lust should prove more barren than the grave
+That so high blood should prompt so base a spirit
To get an heir his blood to disinherit
If yet your chaste belief cannot discern
The monster know the King will make you learn
Whose justice thus the riddle can untie
#'Tis such a crime for which an Earl must die
And yet this sin above despair may sit
Since there's a higher King can pardon it

Bod. Ashm Ms47/88v adds:
*Such as weak Gibeahs air, or the loose flame
Lot darest not look at, a sin wants name
+It merits: or to wise a man a slave.
And how at once a strange incestuous love
Should both a father and an husband prove
#Twas such a crime for which an Earl must die
And yet this sin above despair may sit
Since there's a King can pardon it[2]

Bod Rawlinson A346/138 and Yale Library Osborn Ms b.125/38–38v add this
verse to copies of the text and epitaph.

NRO Isham Lamport Ms 3338 (each stanza after the first is numbered
    [2–14] in the margin.)
My Lord High Steward his grace
with many a rich mace
Came guarded into the Palace
And with a pair of scales did weigh
each word he did say
To keep his oration in ballace

To tell you no lie
He liked the canopy
so well, and the chair he sat in
that my lord high steward still
tis thought with a good will
he could have been contented to have been

The Red Flap of the Law, next
was to handle the text
and his part was to open the door
But mark the disaster
My lords grace his master
had taken up all before

The Attorney now began
upon his legs to stand
extolling the happiness of the King
That had lived so many years
and not one of his peers
had committed so vile a thing

And trust me twas strange
of all that great range
that sat it out that day
that not one of them all
should at some times fall
wander or go a stray

He used much scripture text
which many there perplexed
who did not think it possible
That a man of his trade
who so much profit had made
Should be so well read in the bible

But the oration was witty
and truly twas pity
He did no longer stand
for by the quotations in the Law
he showed he was not raw
in matters that then were at hand

The Solicitor most wise
did lift up his eyes
and to my Lord Steward his grace
And in spite of his Majesty
for and his great canopy
did look him full in face

Then he declared
what might have been spared
that the fault was abominandum

And was beholding many ways
to the old English phrase
Sir Reverence non nominandum

The prisoner now
had leave to show
concerning the rape of his wife
How that he did it not
but conceived it a plot
to take away him and his life

But alas twas in vain
himself for to strain
since the Judges delivered it Plano
that to know by the touch
was even just as much
as if it had been in Ano

It's thought their trunk hose
did also suppose
that in concubilu cum faeminis
there might be a rape
if lust made an escape
per ejectionem seminis

But sure in this case
no dishonor to the place
competent judges they were none
for by the closeness of their beards
twas more then to be feared
they were Eunuchs every one

Sir Thomas Fanshaw I'll swear
above all that were there
by no means must be left out
for he fasted twelve hours and more
and two days before
to be able to turn round about.

GENEALOGY OF MANUSCRIPTS AND PAMPHLETS[1]

REDACTION 1 (the earliest versions)[2]

NRO Isham Lamport Ms 3339
Discrete; seventeenth century. Listed in HMC 3rd Report in the collection of Sir Charles Isham of Lamport Hall. Trial only; probably the earliest text extant.

NRO Finch-Hatton Ms 2564
Discrete; seventeenth century. Listed in HMC 1st Report as part of the Hatton Mss. Trial only.

Bod Rawlinson Ms D859/144–55v
Miscellany of material from Elizabeth I to the 1670s, collected by Hannibal Baskerville, Buckinghamshire antiquary. Apparently eyewitness account of the execution.

NLW Chirk Castle Ms 1328F
Discrete, but badly damaged. Probably from the collection of the Myddleton family.

BL Harl Ms 6865/230–38
Miscellany of seventeenth- and eighteenth-century papers collected by H. Wanley from the library of Thomas Baker. Execution, letter to son, confession of faith.

Yale Library Osborn b126
Disbound; early seventeenth century. Execution, confession of faith, epitaph, and response.

Harvard Law School Ms 5043
Discrete; early seventeenth century. Probably belonged to H. R. Ashford, Stourbridge, Wilts. Execution, letter to son, confession of faith.

BL Stowe Ms 396/164–177
One of two texts in "Reports of State Trials 1521–1668"; bookplate of Arthur Capel, Earl of Essex, 1701. Execution. For the other, see below.

Bod Rawlinson Ms D911/398–403v
Fragment; miscellany of historical and legal notes, sixteenth to eighteenth centuries.

Variation 1a

FSL Ms V.b.50/pp. 519–47
Miscellany; early seventeenth century. Warwick version of execution, confession of faith, epitaph "found in the Earl's chamber."[3]

BL Sloane Ms 1709/63–83
Miscellany listed as part of the library of Sir Robert Cotton or his son. Notes rather than a narrative; Bohemia execution; confessions of Broadway and Fitzpatrick.[4] **BL Add Ms 45,124** is another copy.

BL Egerton Ms 2026/15–19v
"Political tracts, trials, etc chiefly early 17thc." Trial only.

BL Harl Ms 738/322–26
"A book in folio containing diverse law treatises promiscuously bound together." Bought 1707 from Bishop Edward Stillingfleet. Warwick execution, confession of faith, epitaph.

BL Lansdowne Ms 491/226–229v
Miscellany of parliamentary tracts seventeenth to early eighteenth centuries from the collection of a "Mr. Umfreville"; frontispiece of the Shelburne coat of arms. Warwick execution, letter to son, confession of faith, epitaph with added preface.

REDACTION 2

Trinity College Ms 731
Miscellany; late seventeenth century. Given to the College in 1674 by Sir Jerome Alexander, Judge of Common Pleas. Execution, epitaph, and answer.

Wiltshire RO Ms 413/401
Discrete; seventeenth century. Epitaph and answer (copies of two versions).

Variation 2a

BL Harl Ms 2194/78–90
"Lord Stewards of England and trials before them." William the Conqueror to 1631. Book plate of John, Duke of Newcastle. Execution, letters to son and sisters, confession of faith.

Bod Rawlinson Ms D719/329–49
Miscellany of historical tracts, 1590–1631. Execution, letters to son and sisters, confession of faith, confessions of Broadway and Fitzpatrick.

Bod Rawlinson Ms A346/124–42
Miscellany of materials, 1614–1714. Execution, letters, confession of faith, epitaph, and "Upon Lord Audley's Conviction."

Inner Temple Petyt Ms 538/8, pp. 351–92

Theatrum Criminalium "copied from the public records and other sources" by William Petyt, Keeper of the Records of the Tower, 1689–1707. Acquired from him, 1707. Trial only.

Bod Rawlinson Ms A135/579–601

Miscellany concerning the Popish Plot, once the property of R. Bridgman. Trial only.

Yale Osborn Ms b125

Discrete; early seventeenth century. Belonged to Andre de Copet. Perhaps the text noted in HMC Beaufort as part of the collection of Sir Henry Spelman. Execution, confession of faith, epitaph "Upon the Lord Audley's Conviction," confessions of Broadway and Fitzpatrick.

Bod Carte Ms 107/173–92v

"Office of the Earl Marshall etc. . . . " Acquired 1753 as part of the miscellany relating to the life of the Duke of Ormonde. Execution, letters to son and sisters, confession of faith.

Bod Rawlinson Ms D924/100–18v

"Historical Collections Elizabeth-George II." Independent pagination suggesting earlier binding. Execution, letters to son, confession of faith.

Variation 2b

Each of the texts below contains a version of the execution, letters of son and sisters, confession of faith, confessions of Broadway and Fitzpatrick, plus the petition of Castlehaven's sisters to Charles I, and a "mental description" of the Earl. All save the last are claimed to have been "set forth collected and composed" in 1631.

Folger Lib Ms V.b.328

Discrete. Likely source for all others in 2b.

PRO SP 16/207

Discrete. Identified in CSPD as "apparently prepared for the press."

Bod Tanner Ms 71/70–90v

Miscellany, mostly of correspondence, 1629–33. From the collections of Dr. Ward, Master of Sidney Sussex.

NLS Advocates Ms 2744

Discrete. Identified as a "contemporary document." Neilson Collection.

NLS Advocates Ms 23.7.12/52–85v

Miscellany. Acquired 1723 from the library of Sir Robert Sibbald.

BL Lansdowne Ms 213/182–202

Miscellany of tracts, sixteenth century to 1660.

University of Kansas Kenneth Spencer Research Library Ms D 153(4)/94–115

Star Chamber collection. 1583–1633 bound together in the seventeenth century. Apparently the text noted in HMC 3rd Report as part of the collection of the 2nd Duke of Westminster.

Natl Lib Ireland Ms. 16,999/14–40
Dated 1633 [sic].

Independent Texts

BL Stowe Ms 396/156–63
One of two texts in "Reports of State Trials 1521–1668"; bookplate of Arthur Capel, Earl of Essex, 1701. Trial only.

Bod Clarendon Ms 5/18–21
Clarendon State Papers. Notes rather than a narrative. Trial only.

Univ of Chicago Regenstein Library Ms249
"Trials before the Lord High Steward" to 1685. Labeled "collection Jos Smith", ca. 1800; perhaps the text noted in HMC, 5th Report as "Mr. Smith's account of the Lord Castlehaven", at that time part of the mss of the Catholic Chapter of London. Trial only.

BL Add Ms 22,591/81–93
Miscellany of sixteenth- and early-seventeenth-century pieces. Acquired 1857 from Rev. Philip Bliss. Execution, letters to son and sisters, confession of faith, epitaph, and response.

Bod Ashm Ms 824/21–5
Miscellany of speeches and trials, 1550s–1670s. Bequeathed by William Henry Black, one of the assistant keepers of the public records and described in the catalogue as "a report of the trial of that horrid wretch. . . . " Trial only, likely eyewitness.

BL Hargrave Ms 226/310v–313
Miscellany, 1600–1631. Notes rather than narrative. Trial only; likely eyewitness.

HEH Ellesmere Ms 7976/1–16
Miscellany of tracts; early seventeenth century. Notes rather than narrative (probably taken for Castlehaven's brother-in-law, John, Earl of Bridgewater). Confession of faith; likely eyewitness.

BL Hargrave Ms46/172–75
Law french reports 15 James–14 Charles. Notes only. Another copy at **BL Hargrave 22**

Lincolnshire Record Office, Worsley Ms 47/77–83
Miscellany of the Worsley family. Extensive fragment of the trial; likely eyewitness.

Untracked: Ms noted in HMC 9th Report as then part of the Mss of the Earl of Leicester, some of which originated in the library of Sir Edward Coke.

PARTIAL TEXTS

Executions

BL Add Ms 45,224/38–40b
BL Harleian Ms 791/51–2
 Unique burial information
NRO Isham Lamport Ms 3337

Trials of Broadway and Fitzpatrick
BL Harleian Ms 1330/61v–62

Various
BL Harleian Ms 6846/274–5
 Jurors; Castlehaven's questions

BL Harleian Ms 2067/18–18v
 Erroneous jury list; confession of faith

NRO Isham Lamport Ms 3484
 Confession of faith

Pamphlets

The Arraignment and Conviction of Mervin, Lord Audley, Earl of Castlehaven . . . 1643.[5] Allegedly printed in London for one Thomas Thomas.[6] From a version of Redaction 1.

The Trial of the Lord Audley . . . ,1679.[7] Source unknown, but someone with legal knowledge.

The Trial and Condemnation of Mervin Lord Audley Earl of Castlehaven . . . , 1699.[8] Claimed authority from "this trial lying by me [the prefacer] in an old manuscript which was never yet printed." Apparently drawn from a mix of Redaction 1a and already printed materials.

The Case of Sodomy . . . , 1708. Allegedly "printed from an original manuscript," perhaps BL Add Ms 22,591/81–93 or a version of Redaction 2.

Histories

L'Estrange: the core of information, but not the wording, comes from Redaction 1.

Sanderson: fits Redaction 2b, particularly BL Lansdowne Ms 213 almost exactly, adding only Fitzpatrick's claim that he had been entrapped.

Rushworth: apparently a mix of personally acquired information, a Redaction 2 text, and the 1679 pamphlet.

NOTES

Introduction

1. Chettle, "Successive Houses at Fonthill," p. 506.

2. See, for example, Stone, *Crisis*, p. 668; Underdown, *Revel, Riot and Rebellion*, p. 122; K. Sharpe, *Personal Rule*, p. 190; Hill, *Intellectual Origins Revisited*, p. 13. I owe this last reference to Scott Lucas.

3. *A Masque Presented at Ludlow Castle, 1634*, first published in 1637 and more commonly known by the name of its villain, Comus. On the connection to the trial, see Breasted, "'Comus' and the Castlehaven Scandal," pp. 201–24; *Milton Quarterly* 21 (1987), especially Creaser, "Milton's 'Comus,'" pp. 24–34; Brown, *Aristocratic Entertainments*. Creaser includes a survey of earlier critics; some of the most important are Mundhenk, "Dark Scandal," pp. 141–52; Hunter, *Milton's 'Comus': Family Piece*; Marcus, "Milieu of Milton's 'Comus,'" pp. 293–327; *Politics of Mirth*, ch. 6.

4. See Bingham's classic exploration of the trial, "Seventeenth-Century Attitudes Toward Deviant Sex," pp. 447–72, as well as the more popular and less reliable versions in Hyde, *Love That Dared Not Speak Its Name*, pp. 44–57; Davenport-Hines, *Sex, Death and Punishment*, pp. 63–64; R. Norton, *Mother Clap's Molly House*, pp. 26–31; Spencer, *Homosexuality*, pp. 166–68.

5. PRO C66/2578m6; C66/2578m13.

6. *ST*, 3: cols. 401–26.

7. Both names can be found in contemporary materials; hereafter, I have used Florence, the name on the indictment, PRO KB9/795.

8. Herrup, "The Patriarch at Home," first presented in 1990 to the Women's History Seminar, Institute for Historical Research (London), and to the 8th Berkshire Conference on the History of Women (Douglass College); the views below reflect a more complex understanding of the case.

9. See the works cited above as well as Hitchcock, *English Sexualities*, p. 66.

10. The methodological issues raised below are at the center of vigorous exchanges in several disciplines. The works cited here are only a few of those most useful for historians. On history and evidence, see Finley, "Refashioning of Martin Guerre," and Davis, "On the Lame," pp. 553–603; Schama, *Dead Cer-*

tainties; Chandler, Davidson, and Harootunian, eds., *Questions of Evidence;* Eley, "Is All the World a Text?", pp. 193–244; Spiegel, "History, Historicism, and the Social Logic of the Text in the Middle Ages," pp. 59–86; Shapin, *Social History of Truth;* Dening, *Performances.*

11. On history and narrative, see H. White, *Content of the Form;* Kellner, *Language and Historical Representation;* Somers, "Narrativity, Narrative Identity and Social Action," pp. 591–630. On law and narrative, a good start can be made with J. B. White, *Heracles' Bow;* Davis, *Fiction in the Archives;* "Legal Storytelling"; Brooks and Gewirtz, eds., *Law's Stories.*

12. Law's relationship to its surroundings is the focus of what has come to be known in the United States as critical legal studies. Kelman, *Guide to Critical Legal Studies Reader,* and Williams, *Alchemy of Race and Rights,* offer good introductions; cf. Farber and Sherry, "Telling Stories Out of School," pp. 807–57.

Chapter 1

1. For the sake of clarity, throughout this book, Touchet normally refers to George Touchet, 11th Baron Audley and 1st Earl Castlehaven (1551–1617); Castlehaven refers to Mervin Touchet, 12th Baron and 2nd Earl (1593–1631); and Audley refers to James, 13th Baron and 3rd Earl (1612–84).

2. Dodd, *Church History,* 3:167. Rutter, *Delineations of Fonthill,* appendix A, pp. 103–7; Chettle, "Successive Houses of Fonthill"; *VCH Wiltshire,* 13:160. Gifford was the family name of the earliest recorded possessors of the manor.

3. Except as noted, genealogical information here and below comes from *CP* or Burke, *Burke's Extinct Peerages.* . . . On the Touchets, see also Drake, *Fasciculus Mervinensis* [hereafter *Fasc Merv*]; Courteaux, *Histoire Genealogique;* Stone, *Crisis,* appendix VIII; *VCH Staffordshire,* 3:236–37; *VCH Somerset,* 5:190–94; Hutchins, *History and Antiquities of the County of Dorset,* 3:670–71.

4. *CSPI 1603–6,* pp. 258–59; records of Touchet's pleas for reward are scattered through *CSPI,* the *Calendar of the Carew Mss . . . 1575–1624* and *HMC: Salisbury* from the mid-1580s until 1611; for the grants, *Irish Patent Rolls of James I,* pp. 47, 222, 304; Hill, *Historical Account of the Plantation in Ulster,* pp. 268–71.

5. *CSPD 1608–11,* p. 583; PRO-Northern Ireland DOD#294 (I want to thank Anthony Malcolmson for a copy of this deed); *CSPI 1611–14,* pp. 102, 162–63; *CSPI 1615–25,* p. 24; *HMC: Hastings,* 4:14; cf. *Two Elizabethan Women* on the family's residential patterns.

6. *CP* dates the marriage as 1584, but Wall, "For Love, Money or Politics?", pp. 511–33, believes that the couple's eldest daughter, Maria, was born about 1580; *History of Parliament,* 3:26–27, 508; *Fasc Merv,* pp. iv–v, 17–19, appendix 1.

7. The exact date of the Barham/Touchet marriage is unknown, but the earliest record of one of their children was a baptism in the summer of 1612 (DRO Mic/R/79); *Inquisitones Post Mortem for London,* pp. 257–63; *History of Parliament,* 1:398; PRO C54/2495pt7m25; Stone, *Crisis,* pp. 628–32, appendix XXXI;

Fasc Merv, p. 18n; HLRO Parchments Box 7a. Richard Grassby was kind enough to provide me with information about Elizabeth Barnham's portion.

8. WRO 132/3/7 is a lease signed by Elizabeth Barnham Touchet in October 1622. On the Stanleys: *CP;* Stone, *Crisis,* pp. 253, 305–6, 760–61; HEH EL784, 938, 957; *Stanley Papers;* Fogle, *Patronage in Late Renaissance England,* pp. 10–19, 25.

9. Coward, *Stanleys,* ch. 4; Brydges, *Memoirs of the Peers,* pp. 383–93; PRO SP16/198/18; Falk, *Bridgewater Millions,* p. 59.

10. Braithwait as cited in Amussen, *Ordered Society,* p. 37; on privacy, see Pollock, "Living on the Stage of the World," pp. 78–95; LRO DE 3128/171; /174/2.

11. NLS Ms 2678/3v, 4, 7, 15; PRO SP16/192/11; PRO PROB11/174 (70 Goare); LRO DE 3128/184. The household included at least a page, a footman, two lady's maids, two coachmen, a cook, and ten others whose duties were unspecified; Castlehaven said that he rarely slept with fewer than four servants in his chamber. Giles Broadway came from near the Brydges' estates at Winchcome (Sudeley); John Anktill from near Stalbridge; Henry Skipwith from near the Touchet lands in County Cork; LRO DE 3128/173, 174/2, 179, 183, 185; PRO SP16/247/63, PRO SP16/222/6; Hutchins, *Dorset,* 3:62–63.

12. On the court and Parliament: BL Add Ms 38, 857, pp. 50, 62, 69; BL Egerton Ms 2816; *HMC: Ancaster,* pp. 393–94; *Proceedings in Parliament 1614,* pp. 75, 81–82, 145, 322, 395, 484, 496; *HMC: Hastings,* 4:285; PRO SO3/7–9. On local office: Wall, "Wiltshire Commission of the Peace," p. 28, appendix 1; PRO C231/4; *Wiltshire County Records,* 4:14, 131, 139, 140; *HMC: Various,* 1:78; WRO A1/150/4–6; WRO A1/110/1630; WRO d1/39/2/11; PRO C181/3. Compare references to Castlehaven with those to Chandos and Derby in Nichols, *Progresses Elizabeth I;* Nichols, *Progresses James I; Letters of John Chamberlain.*

13. Quotes from *CSPI 1608–10,* p. 297, and LRO DE3128/185. On the family's reputation, see *HMC: Hastings,* 4:14, 176, 180–81; "Annals of the Reign of James I," p. 646; BL Cotton Ms Titus B, x, 12/205; *CSPI 1611–14,* p. 102; *CSPI 1615–25,* pp. 24, 92–93, 221–26; *CSPI 1625–32,* p. 252; *Cal. Carew Ms 1603–24,* pp. 224, 229, 410–11, 132–34.

14. Dodd, *Church History,* 3:167; *Records of the English Province of the Society of Jesus,* 3:520ff.; *Diary of Walter Yonge,* p. 64; LRO DE 3128/185; *Journals of the House of Commons,* 1:776, *APC 1625–26,* pp. 227–29; *CSPD 1625–26,* pp. 170, 182, 184, 217; *HMC: Buccleugh,* 3:267. On Castlehaven's statements in 1631, see ch. 3 below.

15. Oliver, *Collections Illustrating the History of the Catholic Religion,* p. 68; *Cal Carew Ms 1603–24,* p. 148; Boyle, *Lismore Papers,* ser. 1, 2:205, 207, 210, 212; *CP.* On Castlehaven's siblings and children, see also ch. 4 below.

16. See, for example, the descriptions reprinted in *Illustrations of Irish History* and the secondary sources cited in the bibliography to Spenser, *View of the State of Ireland.*

17. *CSPI 1608–10,* p. 256; *1615–25,* pp. 92–93; LRO DE3128/172, /176.

18. LRO DE 3128/184; 174/2, /176; WRO 130/18b.

19. HEH EL 938; LRO DE 3128/176, 180–82; *ST*, 3: cols. 411, 424.

20. On Anktill: LRO DE 3128/173, 176, 184, 185; Hutchins, *Dorset*, 3:62–63; *VCH Wiltshire*, 5:122, 130; "List of Representatives," p. 216. Anktill's brothers were also Touchet family retainers. On Skipwith: PRO C54/2916; LRO DE3128/172, 174/2, 178, 185. On Broadway: Bod Ashm Ms 824/23; LRO DE 3128/183; *ST*, 3: cols. 423–24.

21. LRO DE 3128/174/2; *ST*, 3: cols. 422, 424.

22. Osborne, "Secret History of the Court of James," p. 274; see also *Diary of Sir Simonds D'Ewes*, p. 93; Bergeron, *Royal Family, Royal Lovers*; Somerset, *Unnatural Murder*; Bellany, "Poisoning of Legitimacy?"

23. K. Sharpe, *Personal Rule*, chs. 2–7; K. Sharpe, "Private Conscience and Public Duty," pp. 643–65; Richards, "'His Nowe Majestie' and the English Monarchy," pp. 70–96; Smuts, *Court Culture*.

24. These were also years in which regional economic distress prompted concern: Kerridge, "Revolts"; Cust, *Forced Loan*; Reeve, *Charles I and the Road to Personal Rule*; Cust and Hughes, eds., *Conflict in Early Stuart England*; Sharp, *In Contempt of All Authority*; Bellany, "Poisoning of Legitimacy?"

25. On Ferdinando: PRO SP16/161/171; SP16/162/65; SP16/165/5; *APC 1629–30*, pp. 281, 290, 294–95, 358. On Lady Eleanor: Cope, *Handmaid of the Holy Spirit*, chs. 1–2.

26. *CSPI 1625–32*, pp. 381, 493–94; *CSPI 1628–29*, p. 126; Clarke, "Sir Piers Crosby, 1590–1646," pp. 142–60; Robinson, "British Settlement in County Tyrone," pp. 5–26; *Irish Patent Rolls, James I*, pp. 47, 454; *Calendar of the Patent & Close Rolls of Chancery in Ireland 1–8 Charles I*, pp. 358–60, 557; HEH HAL Box 3(1); PRO SP16/120/15; *APC 1628–29*, p. 220; *1629–30*, p. 29; PRO SP16/388/47. Castlehaven still held scattered parcels in Wexford, Kildare, Cork, Tipperary, Carlow, and Munster; Dunlop, "Unpublished Survey of the Plantation of Munster in 1622," pp. 128–46.

27. To complicate matters further, in 1628, Sir Piers abandoned the Dowager Countess of Castlehaven. She lost her wits and set fire to her house in Drury Lane, endangering (among other things) the houses of the Dowager Duchess of Lennox and the Countess of Livingston. In the spring of 1629, her care was given to three trustees (excluding her husband); PRO SP16/120/15; *APC 1628–29*, p. 220; *APC 1629–30*, p. 29.

Chapter 2

1. Birch, *Court and Times of Charles I*, 2:106–7. Bridgewater was Castlehaven's brother-in-law; Exeter was both openly Roman Catholic, and, at sixty-five, older than any of those chosen to be jurors except for Manchester, the Lord Privy Seal, who was both an experienced attorney and a close associate of Castlehaven's in-laws.

2. See BL Harl Ms 390/529–30; cf. PRO C115/m31 #8133.

3. See J. A. Sharpe, "Domestic Homicide in Early Modern England,"

pp. 29–48; Ingram, *Church Courts, Sex and Marriage*, pt. 2; Gowing, *Domestic Dangers*, ch. 6; Amussen, "'Being Stirred to Much Unquietness,'" pp. 70–89; Pollack, "Domestic Dissidence"; Foyster, "A Laughing Matter?", pp. 5–21.

4. Fitzherbert, *New Boke of Justices of the Peas*, /19; James VI/I, *Basilikon Doron*, book 2, p. 31.

5. T. E., *Lawes Resolutions of Womens Rights*, p. 377; *Memorials of Father Augustine Baker*, pp. 34–35; D'Ewes, *Diary*, pp. 92–93; Stone, *Crisis*, pp. 666–67; Bray, *Homosexuality*, pp. 54–55, *HMC: Salisbury*, 11:93–94; see also Shepard, *God's Plot*, pp. 39–40, 72; BL Add Ms 35, 331/76.

6. This overview relies upon J. A. Sharpe, *Crime in Early Modern England*, p. 55; Bashar, "Rape in England," pp. 33–40; *Calendar of Assize Records*.

7. Bray, *Homosexuality*, pp. 51–53; Pittenger, "'To Serve the Queere,'" pp. 162–89; *Memorials of Father Augustine Baker*, p. 35; *God's Plot*, p. 39; *Statutes of the Realm*, vols. 3–5, passim; Gossett, "'Best Men Are Molded out of Faults,'" pp. 305–27; Goldberg, *Sodometries*; Smith, *Homosexual Desire*.

8. Coke, *3rd Part of the Institutes*, ch. 11; Jacob, *New Law Dictionary*; 18 Elizabeth I c.7. As opposed to crimes created by legislation, common law crimes were those so obviously capital that they required no enabling legislation. Statutes might clarify the process of their prosecution, but could neither establish nor abolish them as crimes.

9. 25 Henry VIII c.6; 5 Elizabeth I c.17; Coke, *3rd Part of the Institutes*, ch. 10; Jacob, *New Law Dictionary*; cf. Smith, *Homosexual Desire*, pp. 51–522, which mistakes Coke's repetition of an example for definition. *Puerum* was not standard in indictments for sodomy, and the phrase suggesting the use of force [*insultum fecit*] was a legal fiction. Coke's repeated use of the same example (in the *3rd Part of the Institutes*, p. 59; the *Book of Entries*, pp. 351–52; and the *Twelfth Part of the Reports*, pp. 36–37) most likely reflects his familiarity with the case and the small number of relevant precedents; cf. the indictments against Castlehaven in *ST*, 3: col. 407.

10. *Calendar of Assize Records*: thirty of the 134 relevant entries involve defendants identified as gentlemen, yeomen, or clerics; forty-seven identify victims as age twelve or younger; eighteen more call victims daughters, servants, or boys. The pattern elsewhere in England seems to have been broadly similar; see Bray, *Homosexuality*, pp. 71–75; Smith, *Homosexual Desire*, pp. 194–96; Chaytor, "Husband(ry)," pp. 381, 385; Bashar, "Rape in England," pp. 37–38. Because status identifications were necessary to legitimate indictments, the labels may say more about clerical ingenuity than social reality, but at the least they suggest the sorts of persons clerks thought most credibly associated with specific crimes. The identification of victim status, which was voluntary, is more reliable.

11. On the credibility of women, see Hawarde, *Les Reportes del Cases*, pp. 39, 161; Lindley, *Trials of Francis Howard*, ch. 3, pp. 184–86.

12. Bashar, "Rape in England," p. 38; Walker, "Rereading Rape and Sexual Violence in Early Modern England," pp. 1–25; cf. Chaytor, "Husband(ry)." Car-

nal knowledge implied both penetration and emission; Coke, *3rd Part of the Institutes*, pp. 59, 60.

13. Hale, *History of the Pleas of the Crown*, 1:635 and more generally pp. 628–36; *Lawes Resolutions*, pp. 389–90. Baines, "Effacing Rape in Early Modern Representations," pp. 69–98.

14. Bray, "Homosexuality and the Signs of Male Friendship," pp. 40–61; Stewart, *Close Readers*; see also Smith, *Homosexual Desire*; Jeff Masten, "My Two Dads," pp. 228–309.

15. Gossett, "'Best Men Are Molded out of Faults'"; Coke, *3rd Part of the Institutes*, ch. 10; Kyrkham, *Of the Horrible and Woeful Destruction of Sodom and Gomorrah*; A. Hill, *Crie of England*; Milles, *Abraham's Sute for Sodom*; J. Harris, *Destruction of Sodom*.

16. Pollock and Maitland, *History of the English Law before the Time of Edward I*, 2:490–91; 3 Edward I c.13; 13 Edward I c.34; 6 Richard II c.6; *Lawes Resolution*, for example, devotes most of its twenty-five-page explanation of the crimes of rape and abduction to abduction; Coke's brief discussion in the *3rd Part of the Institutes*, ch. 11, does the same.

17. Judges 19–20.

18. The literature on Lucretia is considerable; in general, I have followed Donaldson, *Rapes of Lucretia*; Baines, "Effacing Rape."

19. What follows focuses on sodomy, not homosexuality, following Jonathan Goldberg's contention that treating the two as synonymous reifies categories that are socially created: *Sodometries*, ch. 1. The notion that sexual identity is a social product rather than something more transcendent is a matter of heated disagreement; compare, for example, Boswell, "Revolutions, Universals and Sexual Categories," pp. 17–36, and David M. Halperin, "Is There a History of Sexuality?," pp. 416–30.

20. Bruce Smith and Nora Johnson are doing interesting work on this aspect of sodomy; Trumbach, "Birth of the Queen," pp. 129–40, and "Sodomy Transformed," pp. 105–24.

21. The most famous (and extreme) examples from the antitheatrical literature are Stubbes, *Anatomy of Abuses*, and Prynne, *Historio-matrix*. On Castlehaven and drink, see LRO DE 3128/178; /184; /185; FSL Ms V.b.328/37v.

22. Cf. Smith, *Homosexual Desire*, who argues for the concomitant presence of an egalitarian sodomitical ideal. Despite the literature idealizing equality between male friends, I am skeptical that, given the nuances of social status and the obsessive concern with precedence among the upper classes in England, any relationship escaped the implications of imbalance in age, riches, and/or power.

23. Coke, *3rd Part of the Institutes*, p. 58; Marston cited in Bray, *Homosexuality*, p. 20; *Memorials of Father Augustine Baker*, pp. 34–35.

24. 25 Henry VIII c.6; Pollock and Maitland, *History*, 2:556–57, on the crime's prelegislative history. The law itself was not amended until the nineteenth century, and not repealed in England until 1967. It is frequently cited as the grounding for antisodomy legislation in the United States, although modern U.S.

laws are, in fact, framed very differently; see Goldberg, *Sodometries,* ch. 1, and the sources cited there.

25. Elton, *Policy and Police,* pp. 124–27, 153–55, 200–201, 205, 341; 28 Henry VIII c.6; 31 Henry VIII c.7; 32 Henry VIII c.3. On the legislative history of specific bills, see Lehmberg, *Reformation Parliament,* p. 185; Mager, "John Bale and Early Tudor Sodomy Discourse," pp. 141–61.

26. 2&3 Edward VI c.29; 1 Mary I; Jordan, *Edward VI,* 1:172–75, 305–8; Loach, *Parliament and the Crown,* pp. 75–77.

27. 5 Elizabeth I c.17; Elton, *Parliament of England,* pp. 110, 299; D'Ewes, *Journal of All the Parliaments,* pp. 51, 55.

28. See also the ancillary complaints of peculation, treason, and murder in less well-documented suspicions. An exception to this pattern may be the slurs against the 4th Earl of Bath, but the gossip surrounding him is also exceptionally indirect. BL Add Ms 35, 331/76; *HMC: Salisbury,* 11:93–94; BL Add Ms 32, 464; Stone, *Crisis,* pp. 666–67; Strafford, *Letters and Dispatches,* 2:57; Lisa Jardine and Alan Stewart, *Hostage to Fortune;* cf., for example, *Calendars of Assize Records;* Quaife, *Wanton Wenches and Wayward Wives,* p. 175.

29. *Letters and Papers Foreign and Domestic of the Reign of Henry VIII,* xv, #498, 926, 1029; xvi, #578; BL Cotton Titus B1/397; *LJ,* 1, passim.

30. This account relies upon the transcriptions of state papers made by Alan Nelson for his forthcoming work on the Earl. I owe much to Nelson for this kindness and for discussing the case with me.

31. PRO SP16/175/2; LRO DE 3128/183; /173; /174/1, 2; /178.

32. LRO DE 3128/178.

33. The following construction of the case relies primarily upon the depositions in the Braye Collection on deposit in the Leicestershire Record Office [LRO DE 3128], the orders of the Privy Council [APC], and miscellaneous materials in State Papers Domestic [PRO SP16]. The depositions of the Countess, Giles Broadway, and at least one interrogation of Florence Fitzpatrick are now missing; where necessary, I have supplemented from Bod Ashm Ms 824/21–25, one of the earliest versions of the case, but such renditions contain only what the prosecution deemed critical to the case. See *LJ,* 4:140–42, for a description of what existed in 1640.

34. PRO 11/174 [70 Goare]; Cope, *Handmaid of the Holy Spirit,* ch. 3; Strafford, *Letters and Dispatches,* 1:155–56; HEH HA Legal Box 5, folder 2(1).

35. Audley, Wroughton, and Skipwith each told the council that Anne Hunt and Jane Trapp, the maidservants of Lady Audley and the Countess of Castlehaven, respectively, had valuable information, and given the nature of the charges, they likely did.

36. Early modern terms for sexual unions are varied and ambiguous; those used in materials associated with this case range from explicit phrases such as "carnal knowledge" or "use of her body" to the much more common and indeterminate "lay with"; see *Dictionary of Sexual Language and Imagery.*

37. LRO DE 3128/171; /172; /183; *Winthrop Papers,* 6:32a–b; cf. Bod Ashm 824/22v, 24.

38. LRO DE 3128/173; /184; cf. the servant Scott's alleged comment in Bod Ashm Ms 824 that the affair with Skipwith was the cause rather than the result of estrangement between Lord and Lady Audley. Lord Audley's report of his night with "the sweetest bedfellow I could wish between a pair of sheets (excepting some three or four ladies in England and two or three in Ireland)" can be found in *Crown Servants. Series One,* 20 September 1633.

39. LRO DE 3128/174/2.

40. LRO DE 3128/174/1; /175; Bod Ashm Ms 824/23. LRO DE 3128/174/1 is an undated, untitled, and incomplete set of signed answers from Skipwith. The marginal key to the now missing questions suggests that this may be a continuation of LRO DE 3128/174/2, but the fact that both sheets are signed makes that unlikely. Since the Earl's examination on the 8th refers to information from Skipwith not recorded in the extant examinations, 174/1 appears to be the last page of a now lost deposition discussing the attempted rape. Despite the current references, internal evidence suggests that 174/1 must have come after 174/2 and no later than 8 December.

41. LRO DE 3128/176; NLS 2678/21; PRO SP16/189/72. The parson was William Mervyn, rector of Fonthill Gifford since 1611; he had been appointed by Castlehaven's grandfather, Sir James Mervyn, but the relationship between the two Mervyns is unknown.

42. LRO DE 3128/177; /178; PRO SP16/177/30; SP16/185/89; *APC 1630–31,* pp. 147, 148, 150, 151, 156, 165, 166, 167, 168. Coke believed that inventorying goods before the return of an indictment made a prosecution seem inappropriately "precipitate, violent and undue"; *3rd Part of the Institutes,* ch. 103.

43. *ST,* 3: cols. 411, 413; Bod. Ashm Ms 824/22–23.

44. LRO DE 3128/182; *APC 1630–31,* p. 220. Anktill's examination is dated 4 March, but the order from the Council to commit him is dated 4 February; it is impossible to know if this is an error or a coincidence.

45. LRO DE 3128/178; /179; /181; *APC 1630–31,* p. 197; cf. Bod. Ashm Ms 824/22–23; *ST,* 3: cols. 413, 419, 423–25. Broadway's drinking companion was identified by the son of Castlehaven's steward as "Lord Coke." The only Lord Coke in England in 1631 was the jurist Edward. As wonderful as such a connection would be, Coke's infirmity, past rivalry with the Countess's stepfather, and omission of the Castlehaven case from his corpus make it more likely that the informant mistook the privy councilor Sir John Coke for a Lord.

46. LRO DE 3128/181. It is uncertain if Castlehaven meant that the Countess was not credible because she lacked integrity or because she lacked independence or both; he later made both arguments in court; see below, ch. 3.

47. *Winthrop Papers,* ibid.; Bod Ashm Ms 824/22–23; *ST,* 3: cols. 412, 413; LRO DE 3128/171; /182; *APC 1630–31,* pp. 291, 295. None of the extant depositions except Lady Audley's mention Fitzpatrick at all, not even the examinations of the Earl.

48. NRO IL Ms 3339, p. 11.

49. BL Harl Ms 390/529–30.

50. *APC 1630–31,* pp. 156, 160, 161, 165, 171, 172, 178, 183, 196, 197, 226, 237, 238, 245, 248, 258, 287–88, 302; PRO SP 16/182/62; SP16/185/98.

51. PRO C181/4; PRO KB8/63/13–16, 18, 20; *APC 1630–31,* p. 291; PRO C115/m31; Wall, "Commission of the Peace"; *VCH Wiltshire; Register of Admissions to the Honorable Society of the Middle Temple 1500–1944,* 1. These sources plus a reading of the extant wills for both jurors and defaulters suggest no discernible patterns of religious or political allegiance.

52. *Royal Commission on Historical Monuments: The Monuments of West London,* 2:120ff.; Rushworth, *Historical Collections,* 2:96; FSL Ms V.b.328/2–2v; HEH HA Legal Box 5, folder 2(1). I can find no other record of this proclamation.

53. PRO KB8/63/m9, 17; Prob11/174 [70 Goare]; BL Sloane Ms 3075.

54. LRO DE 3128/174/1; /176; /185.

55. PRO SP16/189/19; Lowell, "Trial of Peers in Great Britain," p. 75. Wiltshire's other great peer, the Earl of Pembroke, who was the Lord Chamberlain and a privy councilor, was on the jury.

56. BL Harl Ms 700/326. "My lord of D" could refer to Dorset, Danby, or Dorchester; Dorset did vote to acquit Castlehaven of buggery, although according to Fitzpatrick, he was also instrumental in bringing the Earl to trial.

57. PRO SP16/189/19; HEH HA Legal, Box 5, folder 2(1). The Earl of Worcester, Viscount Conway, Lord Petre, and Lord Howard of Escrick were the substitutes. The 23 April roster also miscounts twenty-six peers as twenty-seven, omitting Lord Goring.

58. BL Add Ms 17017/1; Mayes, "Sale of Peerages in Early Stuart England," pp. 21–37; "Early Stuarts and the Irish Peerage," pp. 227–51; Stone, *Crisis,* esp. ch. 3. I want to thank Paul Hardacre for making me aware of this very important letter and Tom Cogswell for suggesting the implications of Hyde's comment. See appendix A for a full list of the jury.

59. *CP;* see also ch. 1 above.

60. Rushworth, *Historical Collections,* 2:94–95; HLRO Parchments /60. Heath also posed a series of more mechanical questions. Despite complaints about their fairness, pretrial consultations with judges were used by James I and Charles I; see Coke, *3rd Part of the Institutes,* ch. 2; *4th Part of the Institutes,* ch. 64; Jones, *Politics and the Bench,* especially pp. 50–52, 58–60; Reeve, *Road to Personal Rule,* p. 120n. 8, 131, 137ff.; cf. K. Sharpe, *Personal Rule,* pp. 659, 661.

61. NRO IL Ms 3339, pp. 3–4; FSL Ms V.b.328/24; *Middle Temple* 1 (5 January 1611); PRO SP16/189/56; *APC 1630–31,* p. 196; LRO DE 3128/178; HEH HA Legal Box 5, folder 2(1); Rushworth, *Historical Collections,* 2:94. Bacon (d. 1626) and Davies (d. 1626) had both been the Earl's brothers-in-law.

62. Boyer, "Sir Edward Coke, Ciceronianus," pp. 10–16.

63. J. F. Stephen, *History of the Criminal Law of England,* 1:397.

64. The trials of the Duke of Norfolk (*ST,* 1: cols. 957–1050), the Earl of Essex (*ST,* 1: cols. 1333–69), and the Earl of Somerset (*ST,* 2: cols. 951–1022) are the most apt comparisons. See also, Lowell, "Trial of Peers" and Phillipps, *State Trials,* 2: Appendix.

65. *ST,* 1: col. 407n, on the 1535 acquittal of Lord Dacre; 1: cols. 967–1027; 2: col. 968, for privileges granted in other cases.

66. HEH HA Legal Box 6, folder 1; Bod Clarendon Ms5/18–18v, is the most elaborate description of these ceremonies. The only substantial disagreement among the texts is over whether the peers recognized the honor of the Earl by returning his salute; cf. FSL Ms V.b.328/2v–4v; Rushworth, *Historical Collections,* 2:96–97. The five earliest detailed texts of the trial's proceedings (in no particular order) are Bod Clarendon Ms 5/16–21; HEH EL Ms 7976/1–16; BL Hargrave Ms 226/310v–313; Bod Ashm Ms 824/21–25; and NRO IL Ms 3339, pp. 1–12. Each favors different sorts of information: the first is fullest on the ceremonies of the court, the second on legal detail, the third on legal strategy, the fourth on specific testimonies, and the last on the trial as a whole; whenever possible I have relied on these manuscripts. On occasion I have added language from one of the first of the extended narratives circulating after the Earl's execution, FSL Ms V.b.328. On the differences between these and other texts, see appendix C.

67. Except where noted below, the details and statements of the prosecution come from HEH EL Ms 7976/5–5v[Crew], 5v–11 [Heath], 11v–12 [Sheldon], the fullest versions of the attorney's speeches. The fourth legal officer present, the Queen's Attorney-General, seems to have taken no active part in the prosecution. When it does not change the meaning, I have on occasion preferred and noted language from another account. I have cited occasions where early accounts diverge, but not each overlapping reference.

68. FSL Ms V.b.328/9v–10.

69. HEH EL Ms 7976/6v says since the reign of Athelred (1014–16); NRO IL Ms 3339, p. 6 says since the reign of Aethelstan (927–939).

70. BL Hargrave Ms 226/313 has Sheldon rather than Heath deal with the issue of the Countess's prior reputation; NRO IL Ms 3339, p. 7, alone has Heath's statement on sodomy.

71. Only in NRO IL Ms 3339, pp. 5, 7.

72. BL Hargrave Ms 226/312.

73. NRO IL Ms 3339, p. 7, omits Broadway's denial of penetration.

Chapter 3

1. The notion that as a matter of fairness, jurors should have as little knowledge as possible of the case to be put before them was an innovation of the eighteenth century. See Langbein, "Criminal Trial before the Lawyers," pp. 263–316; Green, *Verdict According to Conscience;* Herrup, *Common Peace,* esp. ch. 6.

2. The only important omission was witchcraft.

3. PRO SP16/175/2; HEH EL Ms 7976/3v.

4. As in the preceding chapter, information on the prosecution and defense rely upon the earliest sources wherever possible. Quotes here from HEH EL Ms 7976/2v–3; Bod Clarendon Ms5/20v.

5. HEH EL Ms 7976/4–4v.

6. NRO IL Ms 3339, p. 7; Michael Hunter, "Problem of 'Atheism' in Early Modern England," pp. 135–57; quote from p. 137. On the Earl's religion, see above, ch. 1.

7. NRO IL Ms 3339, pp. 7, 8, 10; Bod Ashm Ms 824/22–23; HEH EL Ms 7976/11. Ashm Ms 824 mentions only a single wedding for Lord and Lady Audley. Tom Cogswell alerted me to the strategic advantages of religious ambiguity for an Irish Earl.

8. See Walsham, *Church Papists.*

9. For a more detailed, but more mono-causal version of what follows here, see Herrup, "Patriarch at Home."

10. The most reliable brief introduction to this view of the household is Houlbrooke, *English Family,* but one cannot ignore Lawrence Stone's ambitious and hugely controversial *Family, Sex and Marriage.* On the implications of such forms, the most extensive discussions are Schochet, *Authoritarian Family and Political Attitudes;* Amussen, *Ordered Society;* and Orlin, *Private Matters and Public Culture;* but see also Norton, *Founding Mothers and Fathers;* Mendelson and Crawford, *Women;* and Weil, *Gender, the Family and Political Argument.*

11. On the constitution of early modern women and men, see Maclean, *Renaissance Notion of Woman;* Paster, *Body Embarrassed,* pp. 1–22; Fletcher, *Gender, Sex and Subordination,* pt. 1; Amussen, "'Part of a Christian Man,'" pp. 213–32; Bray, "To Be a Man in Early Modern Society," pp. 155–66.

12. Davies, "Continuity and Change in Literary Advice in Marriage," pp. 58–80; Powell, *English Domestic Relations.*

13. Kowaleski, "Singlewomen in Medieval and Early Modern Europe"; Wrigley and Schofield, *Population History of England.*

14. Pollock, "'Teach Her to Live under Obedience,'" pp. 231–58; Hodgkin, "Thomas Whythorne and the Problems of Mastery," pp. 20–41.

15. For some examples, see Fletcher, *Gender, Sex and Subordination,* pt. 2; Pollock, "Rethinking Patriarchy and the Family in Seventeenth-Century England," pp. 3–27; Pollock, "Domestic Dissidence"; Gowing, *Domestic Dangers,* ch. 6; J. A. Sharpe, "Domestic Homicide"; Dolan, *Domestic Familiars,* chs. 1–3.

16. In addition to the sources just above, see Woodbridge, *Women and the English Renaissance;* Foyster, "A Laughing Matter?", pp. 5–21; Dolan, *Domestic Familiars;* Lindley, *Trials of Frances Howard;* Burnett, *Masters and Servants in English Renaissance Drama and Culture,* chs. 3–5; Jardine, "Companionate Marriage versus Male Friendship," pp. 114–31. Although it has been suggested that these decades saw a particular "crisis" in gender relations, to date, the evidence for such particularity is thin; see Underdown, "Taming of the Scold," pp. 116–36; cf. Ingram, "'Scolding Women Cucked or Washed,'" pp. 48–80.

17. BL Hargrave Ms 226/312. As earlier, I have cited specific texts only for quotations or to note factual differences.

18. Quotes from BL Hargrave Ms 226/312; Bod Ashm Ms 824/22–22v, 24v; NRO IL Ms 3339, pp. 10–11. I have used the sentiments and details most often corroborated, but no two versions of the testimonies are identical; compare, for

example, Bod Ashm Ms 824/22 and NRO IL Ms 3339, p. 8, on the servants' prosperity.

19. NRO IL Ms 3339, pp. 9–11; LRO DE 3128/173. Bod Ashm Ms 824/22–23, for the statement on Lady Audley, which is nowhere else confirmed.

20. NRO IL Ms 3339, p. 12.

21. A fuller discussion of these issues in this case can be found in Herrup, "'To Pluck Bright Honour from the Pale-Faced Moon,'" pp. 137–59; see also Fletcher, *Gender, Sex and Subordination,* ch. 7; Cust, "Honour and Politics."

22. NRO IL Ms 3339, pp. 5, 6.

23. HEH EL Ms 7976/5v, 14v.

24. NRO IL Ms 3339, p. 12; cf *ST,* 1: cols. 1252–53; 2: col. 970. For the general concern, see Mayes, cited above, ch. 2.

25. FSL Ms v.b.328/11; Bod Ashm Ms 824/21v–22; BL Hargrave Ms 226/311–312v; LRO DE 3128/176. On the added dishonor of making elite private business public, see Pollock, "'Living on the Stage of the World,'" pp. 88–89.

26. BL Hargrave Ms 226/312v; NRO IL Ms 3339, p. 12; LRO DE 3128/184; Bod Ashm Ms 824/23v; see also Yale Osborn Ms 125/50v–51; LRO DE 3128/174/2.

27. Lindley, *Trials of Frances Howard;* Bellany, "Poisoning of Legitimacy," and the sources above, ch. 1.

28. Feltham, *Resolves,* p. 86. As it happened, Feltham had dedicated this edition of his work to Coventry.

29. PRO SP16/175/2.

30. HEH EL Ms 7976/6, for quotes; BL Hargrave Ms 226/311–311v, for the reference to the Benjaminites.

31. He was marginally more successful after the trial when he had the leverage of control over forfeited property; see below, ch. 4.

32. NRO Ms 3339, pp. 4, 6; HEH EL Ms 7976/2v, 11. Saying was not the same as doing; see below.

33. HEH EL Ms 7976/3v–4, 10–10v, /12–12v; quote from FSL Ms V.b.328/8v.

34. Blackstone, *Commentaries on the Laws of England,* 4:28–29, 349, 352; Coke, *3rd Part of the Institutes,* ch. 2; Reeve, *Road to Personal Rule,* ch. 5.

35. BL Hargrave Ms 226/312v.

36. NRO IL Ms 3339, p. 12; FSL Ms V.b.328/21.

37. HEH HAL Box 5, folder 2(1); KB8/63m10; North, *Lives of the Norths,* 1:5; 3:67, 282. Sources vary on the length of the deliberations, most saying two hours; cf. BL Hargrave Ms 226/313, which says only "above a half an hour."

38. The three near-contemporaries of the Earl who did not dissent were Conway, Wentworth, and Clifford, all of whom who were particularly dependent upon the King. Worcester, at fifty-five, was the oldest of the Earl's supporters. The jury included two men in their twenties (no votes for acquittal), four in their thirties (two votes to acquit), thirteen in their forties (nine votes to acquit), and eight older than fifty (one vote to acquit).

39. Essex and Kent were the two peers without sons who voted to acquit.

Berkshire and Howard were both younger sons of the Earl of Suffolk and Holland was a younger son of the deceased Earl of Warwick.

40. Among the known Catholics, Berkshire and Worcester voted to acquit; Petre and Weston to convict; among Wiltshire men, Pembroke, Berkshire, and Howard voted to acquit; Danby and Conway on the other side.

41. Among the dissenting group, only Holland was a favorite; Holland and Dorset were members of the Queen's household, Pembroke of the King's, but not even they were Charles's men in the same way as those named in the text.

42. HEH HA Legal box 5, folder 2(1); Reeve, *Road to Personal Rule*, p. 119. Bedford, Essex, and North had opposed the King in the earlier 1620s; so too had Warwick.

43. Percy and Warwick were the two peers who had voted to convict and later fought against the King; Dorset, Berkshire, and Worcester were the dissenters who supported Charles. For allegiances: *DNB*; Russell, *Fall of the British Monarchies*; Newman, *Royalist Officers in England and Wales*. Adamson, "Baronial Context of the English Civil War," pp. 93–120, offers a more radical explanation of these allegiances. By 1642, Carlisle, Wimbledon, Dorchester, Petre, Wentworth, Weston, Bedford, and Kent were dead and Manchester was dying.

44. Although Robert Creighton, a Scottish peer, had been hanged in England in 1612 for procuring a murder, the last English peer executed for felony was Charles, Lord Stourton, condemned for murder in 1557.

45. BL Hargrave Ms 226/312v; HEH HM 55603 (25 December 1632). I want to thank David Cressy for alerting me to this reference, and Mary Robertson for background information about Drake and his diary.

46. *HMC: Gawdy*, appendix ii, #625; BL Add Ms 17,017/1–1v; Birch, *Charles I*, 2:111–17; BL Harl Ms 7010/155v.

47. PRO SP16/190/41; PRO SO3/10; PRO SP16/189/69 (second copy at SP16/207/36v–37). The sisters petitioning were the Ladies Amy Blount, Elizabeth Griffin, and Christian Mervyn. Maria Touchet was dead. The absence of the Earl's more colorful siblings, Ferdinando and Eleanor, and his adult daughters, Lucy Anktill and Dorothy Butler, remains unexplained. Ferdinando and Castlehaven's daughters were all in Ireland, but the silence might also have been strategic or the product of estrangement; see below and Cope, *Handmaid of the Holy Spirit*, pp. 54–55.

48. BL Harl Ms 7010/155v; PRO SP16/190/68; *HMC: Portland*, 2:121–22. The presence of two of the Queen's favorites, Dorset and Holland, among the dissenters suggests how her sympathy might have been engaged.

49. PRO SP16/190/60; BL Harl Ms 1330/62. Douglas's witnesses were Guy Hopkins, "free mason," and one Brian Gray.

50. BL Harl Ms 390/550v; Sharpe, *Personal Rule*, pp. 189–90; *APC 1630–31*, pp. 322, 383; cf. FSL Ms V.b.328/30–30v, which suggests that Douglas was ordered to prison for the "presumption" of delivering the sisters' petition, but that his confinement was deferred "by reason of a suit he had depending before their lordships." The Council's warrant to release Douglas is dated 12 June.

51. HEH EL Ms 7976/13v–14; BL Hargrave 226/313–313v, has him ask to be "for ever banished or sent into Virginia . . ." Most later texts omit any plea, see below, ch. 5. The most common intangible incentive for a pardon was the hope that it would encourage a restoration of one's estates to the proper heirs; obviously, this was unlikely to motivate Castlehaven.

52. *HMC: Portland*, 2: appendix, pt. 2, p. 122; BL Harl Ms 590/550v; PRO E371/818m.7–8; Bod Rawlinson Ms D859/153; cf. Yale Osborn Ms 126/19 and BL Stowe Ms 396/176, where Castlehaven declared his innocence more conditionally as "according to the laws of the realm."

53. The desire to die a "good death" and to be known as having done so sustained a minor literary industry. Cressy, *Birth, Marriage and Death,* chs. 17–20, and the sources cited there are the best introduction to the topic. On the complex uses of English executions, see J. A. Sharpe, "'Last Dying Speeches,'" pp. 144–67; Laqueur, "Crowds, Carnivals and the State in English Executions," pp. 305–55; Lake and Questier, "Agency, Appropriation and Rhetoric under the Gallows," pp. 65–107.

54. *HMC: Portland*, 2:121–22; FSL Ms V.b.328/28–28v, 30, 33v; *Barrington Family Letters 1628–1632,* p. 189; BL Add Ms 17017/1v; cf. BL Harleian Ms 7010/155v, which claims that he would have no confessor but a "mass priest." The information of this letter's author, John Beaulieu, is often at odds with that of other correspondents.

55. For what follows, I have mostly relied on Bod Rawlinson Ms D859/151–56, which claims to be an eyewitness account, and three other exceptionally early texts: Yale Osborn Ms 126/17v–22v; Harvard Law School Ms 5043, pp. 13–15; and BL Stowe Ms 396/175–177v. The Rawlinson text is fuller on the scaffold speeches; the others on the description of the ceremony. I have only cited quotations or substantial disagreements between texts.

56. Yale Osborn Ms 126/18; Rawlinson Ms D859/152–152v is the only text to mention the urging by the ministers and the only one explicitly to mention popery.

57. BL Harl Ms 390/550v; Bod Rawlinson Ms D859/155; Birch, *Charles I,* 2:118. The comments on the Palsgrave also appear in some later texts (most importantly in the printed *ST* version), but not in most.

58. Bod Rawlinson Ms D859/155–56; on the later texts, see below, ch. 5. Neither the *Royal Commission on Historical Monuments* nor the records of the Warder of the Tower (personal communication) can confirm the burial, but the records are incomplete, and the chapel was the graveyard of many executed nobles whose graves have since been disturbed and reused.

59. *Fairfax Correspondence,* 1:231–33; BL Harl Ms 390/550v; Essex RO d/d By C21#42; BL Add Ms 17017/1v. I would like to thank Christopher Thompson for sending me the Randolph-Bacon reference.

60. The earliest extant versions of these trials are Yale Osborn Ms 125/39–55v; and Bod Rawlinson Ms D719/343–49, virtually identical in content. BL Harl Ms 1330/61v–62, is an early law French summary; Rushworth,

Historical Collections, pt. 2, pp. 102–3, adds information about judicial reaction. I have only cited quotations.

61. Rushworth, *Historical Collections,* ibid. Broadway had been indicted in March with Castlehaven; Fitzpatrick's indictment was returned on 10 June; PRO KB9/795m68–70; cf. Birch, *Charles I,* 2:123–26. Thanks to Christopher Whittick for tracking down Fitzpatrick's indictment.

62. Rushworth, *Historical Collections,* p. 102; BL Harl Ms 1330/61v–62, says that Fitzpatrick also argued from an Irish practice of special treatment for those whose testimony convicted others.

63. Yale Osborn Ms 125/42v–43, 46, 49, 51, 50v; *Fairfax,* 1:235–36, also reports the speeches, but confuses the one for the other; see also the report in PRO C115/m30 #8082.

Chapter 4

1. PRO SP16/175/2; LRO DE 3128/178.

2. PRO SP16/192/11; SP16/189/70; SP16/198/18. John Creaser's suggestion that the Countess's complaints were strategic may be correct, but that would not necessarily have made the situation any less troublesome; in "Milton's 'Comus,'" p. 30.

3. PRO SP16/195/36; PRO C66/2619m7. The annuity, set for life, was to be £300 per year from her husband, £200 per year from her grandmother and mother.

4. PRO SP16/203/100; PRO C66/2578m6; C66/2578m13; cf. Brown, *Aristocratic Entertainments,* pp. 20–22.

5. PRO SP16/192/11; SP16/189/25; SP16/247/63; NLS Ms 2678; *APC 1630–31,* pp. 340, 366; *CSPD 1630–31,* p. 171; HEH HA Misc Box 11; HEH EL Ms 6524.

6. BL Harl Ms 390/551; BL Add Ms 35,331/39v; PRO SP16/198/16; HEH HA Legal Box 5, folder 2(1).

7. PRO E401/2450; NLS 2678/2,8; LRO DE 3128/172, /178, /183, /185; PRO SP16/194/24; PRO PC2/41/16–16v; PRO C66/2600m5; HEH HAL Box 5, folder 2(1).

8. PRO SO3/10; Stone, *Crisis,* pp. 412–13.

9. PRO SP16/182/62; SP16/189/47; SP16/201/17; SP16/192/100; PRO PC2/43/2v suggests that the Bishop's claim was still under review in 1633.

10. Quoted in Havran, *Caroline Courtier,* p. 107; PRO C66/2600m5; PRO E403/2591, pp. 34B–35; PRO SO 3/10. That Cottington paid the 3rd Earl, despite the forfeiture, provided grounds for a later attempt to invalidate the transfer; see below.

11. PRO SO3/10; PRO PC2/43/2v; PC2/43/27v; *Crown Servants* (20 September 1633). The King's right to regrant a forfeited barony without an Act of Parliament was unclear; in 1679, Parliament passed an Act confirming the 3rd Earl's rank and status, HLRO Original Acts 29/30 Charles II #17; Palmer, *Peerage Law in England,* p. 198.

12. *HMC: Buccleuch,* 3:398; HLRO Main Papers Parchments/10 December 1640, 17 February 1641; HLRO Braye Ms18/114v, 116v–117; HLRO Original Journals, xv–xvi; Manuscript Minutes, vii–viii; PRO SP16/482/92; *LJ,* 4:107, 123, 139, 140, 148, 164, 169, 172, 181, 257, 263, 264, 276, 279. The most dramatic of these events were the trial and execution of the Earl of Strafford, almost exactly coincident with Castlehaven's business; on the political climate of these months, see Russell, *Fall of the British Monarchies,* chs. 5–7, p. 289, for Cottington's resignation.

13. *Crown Servants* (20 September 1633); *Lismore Papers,* ser. 1, 3:202–3; 4:190, 192, 194, 199, 202, 203, 206, 224; 5:11, 12–17, 75, 88, 113, 118, 122, 126, 155; PRO SO3/11; *Calendar of the Committee for Compounding,* p. 2859; BL Add Ms 38,847, vol.2/46–70; *HMC: Fifteenth Report,* appendix, pt. 2, pp. 98, 115. *CSPD 1679–80,* pp. 335, 347; CP. Cork cleared his title to Stalbridge only in 1639 after an appeal to Chancery; PRO C2/Charles I/C66/24.

14. *Lismore Papers,* ser. 1, 3:202–3; *Journal of the House of Lords in Ireland,* 1; *Crown Servants* (20 September 33; 14 August year unknown; 18 June 1634; 22 September 1635); *CSPD 1635–36,* p. 151; WRO 132/2/10–13; 132/3/7; DRO D/ANG uncatalogued; PRO SO3/11; PRO C54/2916; *VCH Wiltshire,* 6:82; 8:6; Touchet, *Remonstrance,* p. 14; *Bibliotheca Topographica,* 4:74–75; PRO SP16/415/80; PRO SP16/423/17. I owe the *Bibliotheca* reference to the kindness of Michael Mendle.

15. *Proceedings of the Short Parliament,* pp. 61, 98; *LJ,* 4. *HMC: Buccleuch,* pp. 397, 398, 399, 401, 411, 412; PRO SO3/12.

16. *Remonstrance,* pp. 7–23, quotations from pp. 8, 14; *Earl of Castlehaven's Review,* passim; Ohlmeyer, *Civil War and Restoration,* chs. 4–5.

17. See also DR0 D/FSI series boxes 268, 270, 273; PRO SO3/13, 16, 17; *Diary of Samuel Pepys,* 5:239; *Diary of John Evelyn,* 4:296, 318; BL Stowe Ms 205/3–3v, 39–40; 207/398; 208/57, 326; 210/325; 211/312; 212/147; Simington, *Civil Survey; CSPI 1660–62,* pp. 118, 187, 373, 443, 570; *CSPI 1663–65,* pp. 57, 63, 201, 606, 657; *CSPI 1666–69,* pp. 15, 17, 84; *CSPI 1669–70,* p. 252; *CSPD 1660–61,* p. 289; *CSPD 1668,* p. 234; *CSPD 1672,* p. 50.

18. Quotations from BL Stowe Ms 210/159; BL Add Ms 34,345/45; *Memoirs of the Verney Family,* 2:378; William Salt Library SMS 490; *CSPI 1663–65,* p. 652; *CSPI 1669–70,* pp. 151, 328–29; *CSPD 1670,* p. 308; *CSPD 1671,* p. 77; *CSPD 1673–75,* pp. 198–99, 218, 223, 260, 575; *CSPD 1675–76,* pp. 533–34; *CSPD 1678,* pp. 34, 564–65; *CSPD 1683,* pp. 260–61; *CSPD 1684,* p. 213.

19. BL Add Ms 34,345/15; Add Ms 33,589/112, 114; Add Ms 22,548/96; BL Stowe Ms 211/22, 67; *Pepys,* 4:349; 8:246; *CSP Venetian 1661–64,* pp. 127–29, 136–37, 142, 148, 188, 193; *CSP Venetian 1675–76,* p. 399; *CSPI 1663–65,* p. 86; *CSPI 1666–69,* p. 15; *CSPD 1667,* pp. 163, 533; *CSPD 1671,* p. 116; *CSPD 1678,* p. 29; *Castlehaven's Review,* appendix; *HMC: Seventh Report* (Graham), p. 363; Foley, *Society of Jesus,* 5:379; as well as the citations above.

20. *HMC: Ormonde,* n.s., 4:408–10, 414–15 (quote from 414); *LJ,* 13:141, 142, 151, 162, 163, 211, 212, 219; *Journals of the House of Commons,* 9:447, 458, 472, 474, 475; HLRO Main Papers 7 February 1678; HLRO Original Acts

29 & 30 Chas II#17; HLRO Minutes of Committees, book 3/21–25 February 1678; HLRO Original Journals, lvi–lvii; HLRO Manuscript Minutes, xix–xx.

21. *HMC: Ormonde*, n.s., 4:486; BL Add Ms 33,589/114; *LJ*, 13:341, 362, 365, 373, 374, 378, 384, 394, 395–96, 402–9; cf. HLRO Manuscript Minutes 20 (30 November), where it is suggested that the tribute arose from Lord Audley's "resentment" of his condition. *Trial of the Lord Audley* is discussed in ch. 5 below. On the Catholics in Restoration politics, see Miller, *Popery and Politics*, pp. 14–32, 67–90, 124–82.

22. BL Add Ms 22, 548/93; *CSPD 1682*, pp. 332, 359–61; *HMC: Seventh Report* (Ormonde), pp. 743–44; n.s., 5:445–46, 581, 586, 599, 602–3, 608–9; 6:258–60, 310–11, 323–25. The argument can be followed in Borlase, *Reduction of Ireland to the Crown of England*, reprinted in expurgated form as *History of the Execrable Irish Rebellion*; Castlehaven, *Memoirs*; *Review*; Annesley, *Letter from a Person of Honour in the Country*; Ormonde, *A letter . . . in answer to the . . . Earl of Anglesey*; B[orlase], *Brief Reflections on the Earl of Castlehaven's Memoirs*. Toby Barnard is undoubtedly right that Ormonde rather than Audley was the primary target of the controversy; Barnard, "Crises of Identity Among Irish Protestants," pp. 79–80.

23. *Evelyn*, 4:296; references to his hunting routines are scattered through his *Review*; May, *Accomplisht Cook*, pp. 7–8.

24. A new agreement with her husband in 1644 raised his contribution to her annuity from £300 to £400, but it is unclear whether the total sum increased from £500 to £600; *Calendar of the Committee for Compounding*, p. 2859; Stone, *Crisis*, appendix xxiii.

25. *Lismore Papers*, ser. 1, 5:11; PRO SP23/72/704–13 [*Calendar of the Committee for Compounding*, p. 2859]; PRO C9/235/48; PRO SP29/48/51, i; SP29/53/59; *CSPD 1661–62*, pp. 423, 436, 458; PRO PSO5/9; *HMC: Hodgkin*, pp. 301–2; *HMC: Fourth Report*, p. 279; *Pepys*, 5:109, 133; Aveling, *Handle and the Axe*, pp. 184–85.

26. *Calendar Committee for the Advancement of Money*, pp. 709–10; *Calendar Committee for Compounding*, pp. 846–47; PRO PROB 11/174 [70 Goare]; HEH EL Ms 6524; HEH EL Ms 827, 956, 957; HEH HAF Box 15, item 30.

27. For the testimony and execution speeches, see above, ch. 3; for the libel and contemporary versions of the trial, see below, ch. 5; BL Add Ms 69,919; *Woe to the House*, *The Word of God to the City of London*; HLRO Parchment 179/21; Main Papers Parchments/60.

28. Pevsner, *Middlesex: Buildings of England*, 3. I thank Nigel Llewellyn for encouraging me to consider further the meaning of the Derby monument; cf. Brown, *Aristocratic Entertainments*.

29. PRO SP16/371/66; Gillow, *Literary History or Bibliographical Dictionary of English Catholics*; Oliver, *Collections Illustrating the History of the Catholic Religion*, pp. 422–23 (under Somerset rather than Wiltshire); *Registers of the Catholic Chapels*, passim.

30. *Review*, pp. 39, 43–50; PRO SO3/14; PRO PC2/69, p. 19; *LJ*, 13:503;

HMC: Dartmouth, 1, appendix, p. 121; *HMC: Ormonde* n.s., 7:288, 291, 348; *CSPD 1684*, pp. 213–14.

31. *CP*; of the two remaining Touchet daughters, Dorothy, already married before 1631 and dead by 1634, had also wed a Butler (Edmund, Viscount Mountgarret); Anne seems to have died young and unmarried; cf. George, Lord Chandos, who married the daughter of Henry Montague, Earl of Manchester; William Brydges, who married Susan, co-heir of Garrett Kerr or Carr of London; and Frances Brydges who married Edward Fortescue, esq.

32. Hutchins, *Dorset*, 3:62–63; *Lismore Papers*, ser. 1, 4:190, 203; NLS Ms2678/1, 4v; PRO C2/Charles I/R21/41; PRO PC2/41/177v; PRO C54/2916.

Chapter 5

1. Bod Rawlinson Ms D859/155v [labeled /156]. I'd like to thank Laetita Yeandle for help deciphering this document.

2. Dolan, *Dangerous Familiars*; Wiltenburg, *Disorderly Women*; Lake, "Deeds against Nature"; Gaskill, "Reporting Murder."

3. Cf. the aftermath of the trial of the Earl of Somerset; Bellany, "Poisoning of Legitimacy?", pt. 1.

4. Lady Eleanor's pamphlets are discussed below.

5. The English Short Title Catalogue lists no other year in this period with a comparable concentration.

6. Prynne, *Historio-Matrix*, p. 214; Wotton, *Panegyrick*, pp. 74–75; *Journal of the House of Lords of Ireland, 1634*, pp. 30–48; *Strafford*, 1:345–53.

7. Fletcher, *Maske*, line 580. The family tie between Castlehaven and the audience was important, but the trial was a specter that floated across all aristocratic families. For critical appraisals of the masque's link to Castlehaven, see the works cited above in the Introduction. Although my conclusions differ, my argument owes much here to Brown, *Aristocratic Entertainments*.

8. Cust, "News and Politics in Early Seventeenth-Century England," pp. 60–90; Powell, *John Pory*, esp. pp. 51–59; Levy, "How Information Spread among the Gentry 1550–1640," pp. 11–34; Sharpe, *Personal Rule*, pp. 683–90. An equally vigorous, but harder to track, oral network existed as well; see Fox, "Rumor, News and Popular Political Opinion," pp. 597–620; Freist, *Governed by Opinion*.

9. Fairfax, *Letters*, 1:231–33. Comments on the case survive in collections representing virtually every part of England, but with the exception of the Hyde letters, there are none from the shires most closely associated with either the Touchet or the Stanley families.

10. BL Harl Ms 390/529, 550v; BL Add Ms 17,017/1–2; HEH HA Legal, Box 5, folder 2(3); Bod Rawlinson Ms D859/151–56. Immediacy did not always mean accuracy. The correspondent of HEH HA Ms Legal tells us quite plausible things unreported elsewhere, but calls Fonthill, Fountain Bleu; Broadway, Skipwith; and the 26/1 verdict, unanimous.

11. PRO C115/m31 #8133; BL Harl Ms 390/529; above, ch. 3. Although contemporary diarists reveal a similar ambivalence, since they rarely editorialize, I have tended to find them less quotable: however, see BL Add Ms 35, 331/39v, 42v; BL Egerton Ms 784/162; *Diary of John Rous,* p. 60.

12. *Clarendon State Papers,* 2:315–17.

13. Compared to other scandals, Castlehaven's seems to have produced relatively few mocking verses. The casual scurrilousness of libellers may have faltered before the details of the case, but more likely, an unknown peer whom the King had clearly repudiated was just not worth the trouble of lampooning; cf. Marotti, *Manuscript, Print and the English Renaissance Lyric;* Croft, "Reputation of Robert Cecil," pp. 43–69; Bellany, "'Rayling Rymes and Vaunting Verse,'" pp. 285–310; Cogswell, *Blessed Revolution.* I find Marotti's equation of status and political conservatism as well as his interpretation of the verses on this trial unpersuasive.

14. Chester RO CR63/2/19; Frye, comp., *Pieces of Ancient Poetry,* p. 11; HEH Ms HM116, p. 122; FLS Ms V.b.50/547. By tomb, Davenport probably meant the wooden frame around the coffin or perhaps the grave itself.

15. The Stanley arms included three antlered stags, further adding to the play upon the traditional association of horns and cuckoldry. I have followed the most common versions of each line; the variations between texts are inconsequential. See appendix B for the texts and locations of all poems discussed below.

16. See Marotti, *Renaissance Lyric,* ch. 1, on the nature of different verse collections; FSL Ms V.a.124/18v–19, for the Newcastle reference. Margaret, Countess, and later Duchess of Newcastle was an opinionated and prolific author.

17. The two versions, one titled the "Responsio" and one "The Lady's Answer," are different in language, but the same in content; see appendix B.

18. NRO IL Ms 3338, a separate sheet paired with a copy of the epitaph, is the only copy of this text of which I am aware. I want to thank Alastair Bellany for first alerting me to the survival of this text.

19. What follows about the nature of these manuscripts relies upon Marotti, *Renaissance Lyric;* Love, *Scribal Publication in Seventeenth-Century England;* Woudhuysen, *Sir Philip Sidney and the Circulation of Manuscripts.* The texts are more fully discussed in appendix C.

20. University of Chicago Regenstein Lib. Ms 249/51.

21. BL Lansdowne Ms 213/202 is one of many versions of this redaction; see appendix C.

22. Hibbard, *Charles I and the Popish Plot;* Noonan, "'Cruel Pressure of an Enraged, Barbarous People,'" pp. 151–77; Shagan, "Constructing Discord," pp. 4–34; Underdown, *Freeborn People,* ch. 5. I owe this last reference to Michael Mendle.

23. *Arraignment and Conviction.* My sense of the possibilities of this literature has been helped enormously by conversations with Rachel Weil and Alastair Bellany and particularly by Weil's comments on a paper that I gave at the

American Historical Association in 1994. The pamphlets are discussed more fully in appendix C below.

24. *Life and Death of John Atherton;* Bernard, *Penitent Death of a Woeful Sinner;* see also Bernard, *Sermon Preached at the Burial of John Atherton; Arraignment and Conviction,* p. 3.

25. *Word of God to the City of London,* p. 7; *Crying Charge; The Restitution of Prophecy.* Lady Eleanor inscribed her copy of the last as a gift for the 3rd Countess of Castlehaven; FSL Bd.w.2010.

26. *Trials of the Lord Audley,* pp. 1, 2, 9–10, 13; Miller, *Popery and Politics,* pp. 124–82.

27. Zwicker, *Lines of Authority,* chs. 4–5; Harris, *London Crowds in the Reign of Charles II,* pp. 84–85; Weil, "Sometimes a Scepter Is Only a Scepter," pp. 125–53.

28. In addition to works cited specifically below, what follows draws upon Baker, *Chronicle,* p. 450; Wood, *Life and Reign of King Charles,* pp. 26–27; Howell, *Medulla History,* p. 299; Seller, *History of England,* p. 588; Kennett, *Complete History of England,* 3:59. I want to thank Esther Cope for the reference that opened up this line of inquiry.

29. Whitelocke, *Memorials of the English Affairs,* 1:46; Echard, *History of England,* p. 451. Cf. Wood, *Florus Anglicus;* Meriton, *Brief History of England;* H. C., *Plain Englishman's History.* On these and the histories discussed below, see Macgillivray, *Restoration Historians.*

30. The other trials were those of Sir Giles Allington for incest and of Donald, Lord Rea v. David Ramsey for treason; cf. Whitelocke, *Memorials,* 1:46, and Rushworth, *Historical Collections,* pt. 2, pp. 93–102, both of whom had served in the Cromwellian governments.

31. L'Estrange, *Reign of King Charles I,* pp. 115–19; Sanderson, *History of the Life and Reign of King Charles,* pp. 154–60; Rushworth, *Historical Collections,* pt. 2, preface, pp. 93–103. Frankland, *Annals of King James and King Charles the First,* pp. 391–95, is omitted here because it was lifted entirely (including its errors) from Rushworth.

32. L'Estrange, *Reign of King Charles,* pp. 115, 117–18; possible sources for these texts are discussed in appendix C below.

33. Sanderson, *History of the Life and Reign,* pp. 154, 155, 160; Macgillivray, *Restoration Historians,* p. 22. The complaints were not particularly directed at Sanderson's discussion of Castlehaven.

34. Rushworth's method is described in the prefaces to both parts of *Historical Collections.* Among his errors in pt. 2, pp. 93–103 are conflating the opening speeches of Crew and Heath, misciting both Biblical verses and statutes, reporting a verdict that did not match the size of the jury, and misaligning the questions and answers in the pretrial conference (although this may be the source's error rather than Rushworth's). The most likely source for the added documents was Whitelocke, whose father James had been a judge present on

both occasions; the younger Whitelocke is known to have helped with Rush-worth's first volume; see Macgillivray, *Restoration Historians*, pp. 99–100, 103–4.

35. Virtually all of the major eighteenth-century histories save the vehe-mently anti-Stuart Sir John Oldmixon (*History of England during the Reigns of the Royal House of Stuart*, 1:113) and the vehemently royalist Thomas Carte (*General History of England*, 4:212) ignored Castlehaven. See Okie, *Augustan Historical Writing*; Hicks, *Neoclassical History and English Culture*, on changing scholarly interests.

36. William Tong (1704), cited in Bahlman, *Moral Revolution of 1688*; see also Claydon, *William III and the Godly Revolution*; Rose, "Providence, Protestant Union and Godly Reformation," pp. 151–69; Hayton, "Moral Reform and Country Politics," pp. 48–91.

37. Trumbach, "Birth of the Queen," as well as his *Sex and the Gender Revolution*; Hitchcock, *English Sexualities*, ch. 5. Richard Smallbroke and Sir John Gonson (1728), cited in Bahlman, *Moral Revolution of 1688*, p. 4; see pp. 2–5 on sodomy's particular threat.

38. Barker-Benfield, *Culture of Sensibility*, esp. chs. 2, 5; Andrew, "'Adultery a-la-Mode,'" pp. 5–23; cf. Porter, "Mixed Feelings," pp. 1–27.

39. Devereux, "City and the Sessions Paper," pp. 466–503; Linebaugh, "Ordinary of Newgate and His *Account*," pp. 246–69; Faller, *Turned to Account*; Faller, *Crime and Defoe*; Brewer, *Pleasures*, chs. 3–4, 11.

40. Harris, "Trials and Criminal Biographies," pp. 1–36; Wagner, "Pornographer in the Courtroom," pp. 120–40.

41. *Trial and Condemnation*; Bray, *Homosexuality*, p. 91; see also *Account of the Proceedings against Captain Edward Rigby*; *Trial and Condemnation of Several Reputed Sodomites*; *Full and True Account of the Discovery and Apprehending of a Notorious Gang of Sodomites in St. James*; *Select Trials for Murders, Robberies, Rapes, Sodomies, Coinings, Frauds and other Offences*. Simpson, "Masculinity and Control," table 11, suggests that after 1730, such prosecutions were quite rare; cf. vol. 4 of *Select Trials* (1733–41) with its earlier counterparts.

42. *Trial and Condemnation*, preface. Reviving Castlehaven's story may have had more commercial appeal than retelling Rigby's because by 1699, one version of Rigby's case was already in print; it may have had more moral appeal because the Earl was both of higher status and having been convicted of buggery rather than of attempted buggery, much more severely punished.

43. *Trial and Condemnation*, pp. 9, 11, 12, 14–15, 19, 20, 22, 23–24.

44. See Appendix C.

45. Strauss, *Unspeakable Curll*; Curll, *Curlicism Displayed*; Swift, "Full and True Account," and "Further Account of the Deplorable Condition of Mr Edmund Curll," pp. 205–22.

46. Cf. Strauss, who working from Curll's advertisements, identifies a 1708 Castlehaven pamphlet which I have been unable to locate (but which may be Morphew's); three issues in 1710 (two in February under the *Lewdness* title and one in March as a discrete "second" edition), and a 1711 text of Castlehaven,

Atherton, and two Scottish sex scandals previously published as *The Spirit of Fanaticism*; Strauss, *Unspeakable Curll*, pp. 211–12; see also FSL 184–525q. I have been more conservative than Strauss, but it is difficult to be exact about Curll's reprints and editions because he altered titles and sometimes dates, repackaged older pamphlets under new titles, and often labeled texts as second editions when he had had no part in their earlier publications.

47. Morphew's 1708 pamphlet had sold for 6d, as did Curll's Castlehaven "separate." *The Cases of Unnatural Lewdness* sold first for 1/6 stitched, then for 3/. The rises correspond roughly to the increased number of pages, although one attack on Curll took the "very high" price of his tracts as evidence that he reprinted for profit rather than (as he claimed) for his readers' moral education; *Case Of John Atherton . . . Fairly Represented*, p. 8.

48. *The Case of John Atherton*, advertisement printed after the title page. The attack on Curll had come in John King's anonymous *Case of John Atherton . . . Fairly Represented*, pp. 7–8.

49. Curll's alleged inspiration was the trial between the Marquis de Gesvres and Mlle de Mascranny; he issued two versions of this trial "done from the Paris edition" by the Marquis: *Case of Impotency Debated in the Late Famous Trial at Paris*.

50. The first set of two volumes appeared in 1714 for 5/; it included the trials of Gesvres and Castlehaven and the divorce trials of the Jacobean Earl and Countess of Essex, and of the Williamite Duke and Duchess of Norfolk. By the end of 1715, Curll was advertising four volumes for 10/. In 1719, there was a third edition in five volumes sold for 12/6. Curll also published a parallel collection called *Cases of Impotency and Divorce* with more divorce trials; see Strauss, *Unspeakable Curll*, and the catalogues at FSL Bd.w.QB54F71715 Cage (1715); Bd.w.HQ449A5 Cage (1718); Bd.w.PR3403.H55 1728 Cage (1728); Bd.w.PR3633 A3 1735a.v.Cage (1735).

51. Strauss, *Unspeakable Curll*, p. 228. *Case of Sodomy; Trial of Mervin, Lord Audley; Cases of Impotency and Divorce as Debated in England. . . .* Although the first edition of the text had been signed from the Inner Temple, where Wearg was a member, Curll "revealed" Wearg's involvement only after the Solicitor-General's death. When a contributor to the *London Journal* attacked Curll's claim, he swore an extremely general affidavit to its truth. Wearg's involvement remains unclear; see *DNB* on Wearg.

52. *Cases of Impotency and Divorce*, 3:125. Several of the divorce cases are discussed at length in Stone, *Road to Divorce*, ch. 10.

53. The exceptions were Barbara Villiers, Duchess of Cleveland where the Duchess was the primary victim and John Dormer whose troubles began in his refusal to consummate his marriage.

54. *DNB*; Salmon's most lasting fame is as a geographer, but he also wrote political commentaries and a treatise on marriage.

55. *Complete Collection of State Trials*, 1:xix–xx; *London Gazette*, 12–16 June 1716 [#5442]; 6–9 July 1717 [#5553]. On the printers, Plomer, *Dictionary of the Booksellers and Printers*.

56. Wiles, *Serial Publication,* pp. 66–67, appendix B; Cranfield, *Development of the Provincial Newspaper,* p. 72; Wiles, *Freshest Advices. Felix Farley's Bristol Journal,* 29 August–16 September, 1752, 1, n.s contains a reprint of Castlehaven's trial. I owe this reference to my former student Julie Sikkink.

57. *Trials for High Treasons and other Crimes; Characters of the Several Noblemen and Gentlemen. . . . ; New Abridgement and Critical Review of the State Trials; Collection of Proceedings and Trials against State Prisoners.*

58. The later editions, printed under slightly varying titles, appeared in 1730 (edited anonymously by Sollom Emlyn in six volumes with two more published in 1735), 1742 (with an additional two volumes in 1766), 1776–81 (edited by Francis Hargrave, with one additional volume), 1793 (available only in Ireland), and 1809–26 (in thirty-three volumes, the first ten volumes edited by William Cobbett and Thomas B. Howell, the remainder by Howell and his son, Thomas Jones Howell. For the trials studied here, the major changes between editions are matters of detail more than substance.

59. Muddiman, *State Trials,* is the most sustained examination to date of the political background to the series, but his essay needs correction in both tone and detail; for more reliable summaries of the collection's origins, see *State Trials,* ed. David Thomas, pp. 2–14; Langbein "Criminal Trial before the Lawyers," pp. 264–65; Clark, *Critical Historian,* pp. 92ff.; Plucknett, "Rise of the English State Trial," pp. 542–59. Even the best of these analyses underestimates the differences between the editors.

60. *DNB* entries on Salmon, his father, and his brother; cf. entry for Bradshaw.

61. The 1719 *State Trials* acknowledges no sources. Where Rushworth and *The Case of Sodomy* deviate, Salmon follows the pamphlet, as he also does where the pamphlet and its probable source deviate; when the editor of the 1730 edition, Emlyn, added citations to the trials, he noted Rushworth and *The Reports of that Reverend and Learned Judge, Sir Richard Hutton,* pp. 115–17, but together these do not account for all of the provided information.

62. The introductions to each edition are the best guide to their concerns; all are reprinted at *ST,* 1:xix–liv.

63. McCalman, *Radical Underworld,* pp. 204–25; Rogers, "Piggot's Private Eye," pp. 247–63. I want to thank James Epstein for suggesting these sources to me.

64. "The Exquisite," #1–7 (1842). On the paper and its competitors, see Ashbee [Pisanus Fraxi], *Index Librorum Prohibitorum,* reprinted as the *Encyclopedia of Erotic Literature,* 3, *Catena Libero,* pp. 323ff.

65. This is true even of the many small collections of "state trials" published after *ST:* see George Burrow, *Celebrated Trials;* Phillipps, *State Trials;* Jardine, *Criminal Trials;* Burke, *Celebrated Trials Connected with the Aristocracy.*

66. *Hoare's History of Modern Wiltshire,* p. 15 (see also pp. 16–20); *DNB* entry by Robert Dunlop; *CSPD 1633–34,* pp. xviii–xix; Gardiner, *History of England,* 7:302–3.

67. Frye, *Ancient Poetry,* p. 77n; *Fairfax Correspondence,* 1:233n; *CP.* See also

Rymer, *Foedera*, 19:284, 319; Oliver, *Collections Illustrating the History of the Catholic Religion*, p. 68; Brydges, *Memoirs of the Peers*, p. 86; *VCH Wiltshire*, 13:160.

Chapter 6

1. Stephen, *Hours in a Library*, 3:308. See also the intriguing comments of Wendy Lesser, *Pictures at an Execution*.

2. The errors range from mistakes of minor detail to confusions in the narrative to presentist rewritings; see, for example, Otten, ed., *English Women's Voices*, pp. 19, 33–40; Norton, *Mother Clap's Molly House*, pp. 26–31. Differences between my rendition and others can be assumed to be deliberate.

3. The cost of this method of reasoning is the heart of the critiques associated with critical legal studies; see the references cited in the Introduction above.

4. *Reports of Sir Richard Hutton*, p. 116. Jacob, *New Law-Dictionary*, seems the only later legal exception to Hutton's dismissal. Contrary to what most renditions of the trial suggest, Hutton was likely not one of the judges at the trial; see his own report at BL Add Ms 50,116/141v. I am grateful to Wilf Prest for help on this point.

5. The case has also been authoritative regarding the special rights of peers on trial; see Hale, *Pleas*, 2:275, 319; *Digest*, case 11,667.

6. 1979 A.C. 474 (Hoskyn v. Metropolitan Police) quote at p. 501; see also *English Reports* 43 (1909) (R. v. Azire [1726]); Hale, *Pleas*, 2:301; Hawkins, *Treatise of the Pleas of the Crown*, 2:432; Blackstone, *Commentaries*, book 1, ch. 15; Peake, *Compendium of the Law of Evidence*, pp. 121–22; East, *Treatise of Pleas of the Crown*, 1:ch. 10; Archbold, *Summary of the Laws*, pp. 97–98; Warburton, *Selection of Leading Cases in the Criminal Law*, pp. 228–29; Wigmore, *Evidence in Trials at Common Law*, 8 Wigmore 2227, 2239. Since 1898 (Criminal Evidence Act ss 1,4), spousal privilege has been a matter of statutory rather than common law.

7. Since Castlehaven did not physically rape his wife, his case was germane only in the early stages of this process, in establishing that a husband could be an accessory to his wife's rape; see, for example, 1976 Q.B.217 (R. v. Cogan); 1976 A.C. 182 (DPP v. Morgan); *Digest*, case 1100; cf. Brooks, "Marital Consent in Rape," p. 878; *Law Commission: Criminal Law: Rape within Marriage*.

8. Hale, *Pleas*, 1: ch. 58 (quotes from pp. 629, 635); Gilbert, *Law of Evidence*, pp. 96–97; see also *English Reports* 83 (1908) (Mary Grigg's case); Nelson, *Law of Evidence* (1717) pp. 35–38; (1739), pp. 55–56; Jacob, *Everyman His Own Lawyer*, p. 317.

9. Cf. Geis, "Rape-in-Marriage," pp. 285–86; "Lord Hale, Witches and Rape," pp. 26, 43, refuted on other grounds by Lanham, "Hale, Misogyny and Rape," pp. 148–66, and Prest, "Hale as Husband," pp. 142–44.

10. The "classics" of the early modern genre are Ginzburg, *Cheese and the Worms*, and Davis, *Return of Martin Guerre*.

11. There have been excellent brief studies of individual crimes (especially cases of witchcraft), but only the murder charges against the Earl and Countess of Somerset have received sustained attention, none of it focused on the law; White, *Cast of Ravens;* Lindley, *Trials of Francis Howard;* and Somerset, *Unnatural Murder.* See, however, Macfarlane, *The Justice and the Mare's Ale* and now Geis and Bunn, *A Trial of Witches.*

Appendix B

1. I am extremely grateful to Alastair Bellany for help in both the discovery and the analysis of these verses.

2. The verse is sometimes attributed to Jo: R:; but I have been unable to identify the author; see Crum, *First Line Index.*

Appendix C

1. The taxonomy here is based upon the work of my former research assistant, Scott Lucas. Without his carefulness and diligence, it would have been impossible. I am extremely grateful for his efforts. Dates and provenances below generally rely upon information provided by the relevant repositories and John Baker's *Index to English Legal Manuscripts.* I would also like to thank Clive Holmes for alerting me to the presence of Worsley MS 47.

2. Within redaction versions, I have clustered together texts that have the closest relationship.

3. This version of the execution speech includes a request from Castlehaven that the Earl of Warwick convey a message of gratitude and good wishes to the King.

4. This version of the execution includes a specific wish for the success and happiness for Charles's beleaguered daughter and son-in-law, the King and Queen of Bohemia.

5. Wing #A3743. The revised Wing lists eight known copies of the tract, housed at BL, Bod, the Clark Library, the now dispersed Fairfax Collection, FSL, HEH, Yale, and Worcester College, Oxford.

6. Despite the London imprint, this was most likely Thomas Thomas, the Bristol bookseller who is noted on the title page of a handful of extant works (but no other reprised legal cases) linked to issues of moral and political reform.

7. Wing #T2227. Wing lists six extant copies: John Rylands Library, HEH, Library of Congress, Harvard, FSL, and Yale. My former student Colleen Seguin discovered another copy in Downside Abbey Tracts 211: Acc 28329, a collection of pamphlets relating to the Popish Plot.

8. Wing #T2144. Wing lists 3 extant copies: BL, Bod, Haigh Hall.

BIBLIOGRAPHY OF SOURCES CITED

Manuscripts*

*For references to manuscript texts and poems describing the trials and/or executions of the 2nd Earl of Castlehaven, Giles Broadway, and Florence Fitzpatrick, see appendices B and C.

British Library (London)
  Additional Mss
  Cotton Mss
  Egerton Mss
  Hargrave Mss
  Harleian Mss
  Sloane Mss
  Stowe Mss
Dorset Record Office
  D/ANG uncatalogued (Stalbridge Deeds)
  D/FSI series boxes 268, 270, 273 (Household Accounts of the King in Exile)
  Mic/r/79 (Abbotsbury Parish Register)
Essex Record Office
  ERO d/d By C21#42 (Correspondence)
Henry E. Huntington Library (San Marino, Calif.)
  Ellesmere Mss
  Hastings Mss
  HM 55603 (Diary of Sir William Drake)
House of Lords Record Office (London)
  Braye Mss
  Main Papers
  Manuscript Minutes
  Minutes of Committees
  Original Acts
  Original Journals
  Parchment Collection
Leicestershire Record Office
  Braye Mss (Depositions relating to the trial of the 2nd Earl of Castlehaven)
National Library of Scotland (Edinburgh)
  Ms 2678 (Accounts, Receipts, etc. of the 2nd Earl of Castlehaven's Forfeited Estates . . .)
Public Record Office (London)

C2, 9 (Chancery proceedings)
C54 (Close Rolls)
C66 (Patent Rolls)
C115 (Scudamore Letters)
C181 (Crown Office Entry Books)
C231 (Crown Office Docquet Books)
E371 (Exchequer, Originalia Rolls)
E401 (Exchequer, Auditor's Receipt Books)
E403 (Exchequer, Auditor's Books of Entries)
KB8 Baga de Secretis
KB9 Ancient Indictments
PC2 Privy Council Registers
PROB11 Prerogative Court of Canterbury
PSO Privy Seal Docquet Books
SO3 Signet Office Docquet Books
SP16 State Papers, Charles I
SP23 Committee for Compounding
SP29 State Papers, Charles II
Public Record Office, Northern Ireland (Belfast)
  PRO-NI DOD#294 (Family Papers)
William Salt Library (Stafford)
  SMS 490 (Correspondence)
Wiltshire Record Office
  130 (Family Papers)
  132 (Temple Mss)
  A1/150 (Sessions Minute Books)
  A1/110 (Sessions Great Rolls)
  D1/39 (Instance and Office Books)

Printed Sources

Note: Unless otherwise stated, all books were published in London.

Abbott, George. *The Case of Impotency as Debated in England . . .* (1715), 2 vols.
An Account of the Proceedings against Captain Edward Rigby . . . (1698).
Acts of the Privy Council of England (1890–1964), 46 vols.
Annesley, Arthur. Earl of Anglesey, *A Letter from a Person of Honour in the Country* (1681).
Archbold, J. F. *A Summary of the Laws Relative to Pleading and Evidence in Criminal Cases* (1822).
The Arraignment and Conviction of Mervin, Lord Audley, Earl of Castlehaven, (who was by 26 (sic) Peers of the Realm Found Guilty for Committing Rapine and Sodomy) at Westminster, on Monday, April 25, 1631 (1643).
Baker, J. H. *English Legal Manuscripts in the United States of America: A Descriptive List* (1985).
Baker, Richard. *A Chronicle of All the Kings of England* (7th ed., 1679).
Barrington Family Letters 1628–1632, ed. Arthur Searle, Camden Society, 4th ser., 28 (1983).
Bernard, N. *The Penitent Death of a Woeful Sinner* (Dublin, 1641).

Bernard, N. *A Sermon Preached at the Burial of John Atherton* . . . (1641).

Bibliotheca Topographica Britannica . . . (1783), vol. 4.

Birch, Thomas. *The Court and Times of Charles I* (1848), 2 vols.

Blackstone, William. *Commentaries on the Laws of England* (Chicago, 1979 fasc. repr. of 1769), 4 vols.

Borlase, Edmund. *Reduction of Ireland to the Crown of England* . . . (1675), reprinted in expurgated form as *History of the Execrable Irish Rebellion* (1680).

B[orlase], E[dmund]. *Brief Reflections on the Earl of Castlehaven's Memoirs* (1682).

Boyle, Richard. *The Lismore Papers: Autobiographical Notes, Remembrances and Diaries of Sir Richard Boyle* . . ., ed. Alexander B. Grosart; ser. 1 (1886), 5 vols.; ser. 2 (1887), 5 vols.

Brydges, Samuel Egerton. *Memoirs of the Peers of England during the Reign of James I* (1802), 2 vols.

Burke, Sir Bernard. *Burke's Extinct Peerages* . . . (1866), 3 vols.

C., H. *Plain Englishman's History* (1679).

Calendar of Assize Records: Home Circuit Indictments Elizabeth I and James I, ed. J. S. Cockburn (1975–85), 11 vols.

Calendar of the Carew Mss . . . *1575–1624*, ed. J. S. Brewer and William Bullen (1873), vol. 6.

Calendar of the Committee for the Advance of Money, ed. M. A. E. Green (1888), 3 parts.

Calendar of the Committee for Compounding with Delinquents, ed. M. A. E. Green (1889–93), 5 parts.

Calendar of the Patent & Close Rolls of Chancery in Ireland 1–8 Charles I, ed. James Morrin (Dublin, 1863).

Calendars of State Papers:

    Calendar of State Papers, Domestic, Edward VI, Mary, Elizabeth I and James I, ed. R. Lemon and M. A. E. Green (1856–72), 12 vols.

    Calendar of State Papers, Domestic, Charles I, ed. John Bruce, W. D. Hamilton, and S. C. Lomas (1858–97), 23 vols.

    Calendar of State Papers, Domestic, The Commonwealth, ed. M. A. E. Green (1878–84), 13 vols.

    Calendar of State Papers, Domestic, Charles II, ed. M. A. E. Green, F. H. B. Daniell, and F. Bickley (1860–1947), 28 vols.

    Calendar of State Papers Relating to Ireland, Henry VIII, Edward VI, Mary and Elizabeth I, ed. H. C. Hamilton, E. G. Atkinson, and R. P. Mahaffy (1880–1912), 11 vols.

    Calendar of State Papers Relating to Ireland, James I, ed. Rev. C. W. Russell and J. P. Prendergast (1872–80), 5 vols.

    Calendar of State Papers Relating to Ireland, Charles I and Commonwealth, ed. R. P. Mahaffy (1900–1903), 4 vols.

    Calendar of State Papers Relating to Ireland, Charles II, ed. R. P. Mahaffy (1905–11), 4 vols.

    Calendar of State Papers, Venice. State Papers and Manuscripts Relating to English Affairs, Existing in the Archives and Collections of Venice . . ., ed. A. B. Hinds (1907–47), vols. 13–38.

Camden, William. "Annals of the Reign of James I," in *A Complete History of England*, vol. 2 (1706).

Carte, Thomas. *A General History of England* . . . (1747–55), 4 vols.

The Case of Impotency Debated in the Late Famous Trial at Paris (1714; 2nd ed., 1715).

The Case of John Atherton . . . (1640).

The Case Of John Atherton Bishop of Waterford in Ireland Fairly Represented Against a Late Partial Edition . . . (1710).

The Case of Sodomy, in the Trial of Mervin, Lord Audley, Earl of Castlehaven, for Committing a Rape and Sodomy with Two of His Servants . . . (1708).

Cases of Impotency and Divorce (1726, 1737).

Cases of Unnatural Lewdness (1715).

Celebrated Trials and Remarkable Cases of Criminal Jurisprudence from the Earliest Records to the Year 1825, comp. George Burrow (1825), 6 vols.

Celebrated Trials Connected with the Aristocracy in the Relations of Private Life, comp. Peter Burke (1849).

Chamberlain, John. *The Letters of John Chamberlain,* ed. N. E. McClure (Philadelphia, 1939), 2 vols.

The Civil Survey 1654–56, ed. Robert C. Simington (Dublin, 1937).

Cobbett's Complete Collection of State Trials . . ., ed. W. Cobbett and T. B. Howell (1809–26), 33 vols.

Cokayne, G. E. C. *The Complete Peerage of England, Scotland, Ireland, Great Britain and the United Kingdom,* rev. Vicary Gibbs (1913), 13 vols.

Coke, Sir Edward. *3rd Part of the Institutes of the Laws of England* (6th ed., 1680); *4th Part* (1681).

Coke, Sir Edward. *Book of Entries* (1614).

Coke, Sir Edward. *The Twelfth Part of the Reports of Sir Edward Coke* (1656).

A Collection of Proceedings and Trials against State Prisoners . . . (1741).

Collections Illustrating the History of the Catholic Religion in the Counties of Cornwall, Devon, Dorset, Somerset, Wiltshire and Gloucestershire, comp. Rev. George Oliver (1857), 2 parts.

Complete Collection of State Trials, printed for Timothy Goodwin, John Walthoe, John Darby, Jacob Tonson, and John Walthoe Sr. (1719), 4 vols.

Complete Collection of State Trials . . ., ed. Sollom Emlyn (2nd ed., 1730), 6 vols.; (1735), 2 suppl. vols.

Complete Collection of State Trials . . ., ed. Francis Hargrave (4th ed., 1775), 10 vols.; (1781), vol. 11.

Crown Servants. Series One: The Papers of Thomas Wentworth, 1st Earl of Strafford 1593–1641 (Marlborough, 1994), 20 reels.

Crum, Margaret. *First Line Index of English Poetry, 1500–1800 in Manuscripts of the Bodleian Library.* (Oxford, 1969).

Curll, Edmund. Sales Catalogues, bound with various printed texts. Folger Shakespeare Library Bd.w.2010, Bd.w.QB54F71715 Cage (1715), Bd.w.HQ449A5 Cage (1718), Bd.w.PR3403.H55 1728 Cage (1728), Bd.w.PR3633 A3 1735a.v.Cage (1735), FSL 184–525q.

Curll, Edmund. *Curlicism Displayed* . . . (1718).

Davies, Lady Eleanor. *Woe to the House* (1633).

Davies, Lady Eleanor. *The Word of God to the City of London from the Lady Eleanor* (1645).

Davies, Lady Eleanor. *The Crying Charge* (1649).

Davies, Lady Eleanor. *The Restitution of Prophecy* (1651).

D'Ewes, Sir Simonds. *The Diary of Sir Simonds D'Ewes,* ed. Elizabeth Bourcier (Paris, 1974).

D'Ewes, Sir Simonds. *Journal of All the Parliaments During the Reign of Queen Eliza-*

beth, revised and published by Paul Bowes (1682; repr. Irish University Press, 1973).

de Thoyras, Paul Rapin. *History of England written in French and translated into English with additional notes by N. Tindal* (2nd ed., 1726–31), 12 vols.

A Dictionary of the Booksellers and Printers Who Were at Work in England, Scotland, and Ireland 1688–1725, comp. Henry Plomer (Oxford, 1922).

Dictionary of National Biography, ed. Leslie Stephen (& Sidney Lee) (1885–1901), 66 vols.

A Dictionary of Sexual Language and Imagery in Shakespearean and Stuart Literature, comp. Gordon Williams (1994), 3 vols.

The Digest: Annotated British, Commonwealth and European Cases (2nd reissue, 1993).

E., T. *Lawes Resolutions of Womens Rights: or the Lawes Provision for Women* (1632; fasc. repr., 1979).

East, E. H . *A Treatise of Pleas of the Crown* (1806), 2 vols.

Echard, Lawrence. *History of England . . .* (1707; 3rd ed., 1720), 2 vols.

English Reports.

English Women's Voices 1540–1700, ed. Charlotte F. Otten (Miami, 1992).

Evelyn, John. *Diary of John Evelyn,* ed. E. S. de Beer (Oxford, 1955), 6 vols.

"The Exquisite," ## 1–7 (1842).

The Fairfax Correspondence: Memoirs of the Reign of Charles I, ed. George W. Johnson (1848), 2 vols.

"Felix Farley's Bristol Journal," 1, n.s. (29 August–16 September 1752).

Feltham, Owen. *Resolves: a duple century one new an other of second edition* (1628).

Fitzherbert, Anthony. *The New Boke of Justices of the Peas* (1538; fasc. repr., 1969).

Frankland, Thomas. *Annals of King James and King Charles the First Both of Happy Memory . . .* (1681).

A Full and True Account of the Discovery and Apprehending of a Notorious Gang of Sodomites in St. James . . . (1709).

Gilbert, G. *The Law of Evidence . . .* (1754; fasc. repr., 1979).

Gillow, Joseph. *Literary History or Bibliographical Dictionary of English Catholics* (1885), 5 vols.

Hale, Sir Matthew. *Historia Placitorum Coronae. . . . History of the Pleas of the Crown,* ed. Sollom Emlyn (Dublin, 1778), 2 vols.

Harris, John. *The Destruction of Sodom* (1628).

Hasler, P. W., ed. *History of Parliament: The House of Commons 1558–1603* (1981), 3 vols.

Hawarde, John. *Les Reportes del Cases in Camera Stellata 1593–1609,* ed. W. P. Baildon (1894).

Hawkins, William. *Treatise of the Pleas of the Crown* (fasc. repr. 1975), 2 vols.

Hill, Adam. *The Crie of England* (1593).

Historical Manuscripts Commission volumes:
> *Fourth Report* (1874).
> *Seventh Report* (1879).
> *Fifteenth Report* (1899).
> *Report on the Manuscripts of the Earl of Ancaster, preserved at Grimsthorpe* (1907).
> *Report on the Manuscripts of His Grace the Duke of Buccleugh . . .* (1899–1926), 3 vols.
> *Manuscripts of the Earl of Dartmouth* (1887–96), 3 vols.

Report on the Manuscripts of the Family of Gawdy . . . (1885).

Report on the Manuscripts of the Late Reginald Rawdon Hastings . . . (1947), 4 vols.

Manuscripts of J. Eliot Hodgkin (1897).

Manuscripts of the Marquis of Ormonde, n.s. (1902–20), 8 vols.

Report on the Manuscripts of His Grace the Duke of Portland (1891–97), 4 vols.

Calendar of the Manuscripts of the Most Hon. the Marquis of Salisbury . . . (1883–1940), 18 vols.

Report on Manuscripts in Various Collections (1901–14), 8 vols.

Howell, William. *Medulla History* (4th ed., 1694).

Hutton, Sir Richard. *The Reports of that Reverend and Learned Judge, Sir Richard Hutton . . .* (1656).

Hyde, Edward, Earl of Clarendon. *State Papers Collected by Edward, Earl of Clarendon Commencing from the Year 1621 . . .* (Oxford, 1767–86), 3 vols.

Illustrations of Irish History and Topography . . ., ed. C. Litton Falkiner (1904).

Inquisitones Post Mortem for London, ed. Edward Alexendar Fry, British Record Society Index Library, vol. 36 (1908).

Irish Patent Rolls of James I (facsimile of the Irish Record Commission's Calendar, Dublin, 1966).

Jacob, Giles. *New Law Dictionary* (3rd ed., 1736).

Jacob, Giles. *Everyman His Own Lawyer* (1737).

James VI/I. *Basilikon Doron or His Majesties Instructions to His Dearest Son Henry the Prince* (1603).

Jardine, David. *Criminal Trials* (1832, 1835), 2 vols.

Journal of the House of Lords of Ireland (Dublin, 1779), 8 vols.

Journals of the House of Commons (1803–ongoing).

Journals of the House of Lords (1809–ongoing).

Kennett, White. *Complete History of England . . .* (1706), 3 vols.

Kyrkham, H. *Of the Horrible and Woeful Destruction of Sodom and Gomorrah* (1570).

The Law Commission: Criminal Law: Rape within Marriage (1992).

The Law Reports.

L'Estrange, Hamon. *The Reign of King Charles I . . .* (1655).

Letters and Papers Foreign and Domestic of the Reign of Henry VIII, arranged by James Gairdner and R. H. Brodie vols. 15–16 (1897–98).

The Life and Death of John Atherton, Lord Bishop of Waterford and Lismore within the Kingdom of Ireland, born near Bridgewater in Somersetshire (1641).

"List of Representatives in Parliament from 1295–1832 for the County and Boroughs of Wiltshire . . ." transcribed by Canon F. H. Manley, *Wiltshire Archeological and Natural History Magazine* 47 (1935), pp. 177–264.

The London Gazette #5442, #5553.

May, Robert. *The Accomplisht Cook . . .* (1665).

Memorials of Father Augustine Baker and Other Documents Relating to the English Benedictines, ed. Dom Justin McCann and Dom Hugh Connelly, Catholic Record Society, vol. 33 (1933).

Meriton, George. *Brief History of England* (1658).

Milles, Robert. *Abraham's Sute for Sodom* (1611).

Milton, John. *A Masque at Ludlow Castle,* trans. Harris Fletcher in John S. Diekhoff, ed., *A Maske at Ludlow: Essays on Milton's Comus* (Cleveland: The Press of Case Western Reserve University, 1968), pp. 207–40.

Milton, John. *John Milton's Complete Poetical Works reproduced in photographic facsimile,* comp. and ed. Harris Francis Fletcher (Urbana: University of Ilinois Press, 1943), 4 vols.

Nelson, William. *The Law of Evidence* (1717, 1739).

Nichols, John. *The Progresses, Public Processions of Queen Elizabeth I* (1823).

Nichols, John. *The Progresses, Processions and Magnificent Festivities of King James I* (1828).

North, Roger. *The Lives of the Norths,* ed. A. Jessup (1890; repr., 1972), 3 vols.

Oldmixon, Sir John. *History of England during the Reigns of the Royal House of Stuart* (1730), 3 vols.

Ormonde, James, Duke of. *A letter . . . in answer to the . . . Earl of Anglesey . . . His Observations and Reflections upon the Earl of Castlehaven's Memoirs* (1681).

Osborne, Francis. "Secret History of the Court of James," in *Historical Memoirs of the Reigns of Elizabeth and King James* (Edinburgh, 1811), 2 vols.

Peake, Thomas. *A Compendium of the Law of Evidence* (1801; fasc. repr., 1979).

Pepys, Samuel. *The Diary of Samuel Pepys,* ed. Robert Latham and William Matthews (Berkeley, 1970–83), 11 vols.

Pieces of Ancient Poetry from Unpublished Manuscripts and Scarce Books, comp. John Frye (Bristol, 1814).

Proceedings in Parliament 1614, ed. Maija Jansson (Philadelphia, 1988).

Proceedings of the Short Parliament of 1646, ed. Esther Cope in collaboration with Willson Coates, Camden Society 4th Series, vol. 19 (1977).

Prynne, William. *Histrio-matrix: The Players' Scourge or the Actor's Tragedy* (1633).

Records of the English Province of the Society of Jesus, ed. Henry Foley (1877–83), 7 vols.

Register of Admissions to the Honorable Society of the Middle Temple 1500–1944, comp. H. A. C. Sturgess (1949), 3 vols.

Registers of the Catholic Chapels Royal and of the Portuguese Embassy Chapel 1662–1829, ed. J. Cyril and M. Weale, Catholic Record Society, vol. 38 (1941).

Rous, John. *Diary of John Rous . . .,* ed. Mary Anne Everett Green, Camden Society, vol. 66 (1856).

Royal Commission on Historical Monuments: An Inventory of the Historical Monuments of West London (1924–30), 5 vols.

Rushworth, John. *Historical Collections* (1680), 2 vols.

Salmon, Thomas. *Characters of the Several Noblemen and Gentlemen that have died in the Defence of their Respective Princes or the Liberties of Their Country . . .* (1724).

Salmon, Thomas. *New Abridgement and Critical Review of the State Trials . . .* (1738).

Salmon, Thomas, ed. *Trials for High Treasons and other Crimes . . .* (1720).

Sanderson, Sir William. *History of the Life and Reign of King Charles from His Cradle to His Grave* (1658).

Select Trials for Murders, Robberies, Rapes, Sodomies, Coinings, Frauds and other Offences . . . (1734; 2nd expanded ed., 1742), 4 vols.

Seller, John. *History of England . . .* (1696).

Shepard, Thomas. *God's Plot: the Paradoxes of Puritan Piety, Being the Autobiography and Journal of Thomas Shepard,* ed. Michael McGiffert (Amherst, 1992).

Spenser, Edmund. *A View of the State of Ireland,* ed. Andrew Hadfield and Willy Maley (Oxford, 1997).

The Spirit of Fanaticism . . . (1711).

The Stanley Papers, part one, ed. Thomas Heywood, Chetham Society, vol. 29 (1853); *part two,* ed. Rev. F. R. Raines, Chetham Society, vol. 30 (1853).

State Trials or a Collection of the Most Interesting Trials Prior to the Revolution of 1688, ed. Samuel March Phillipps (1826), 2 vols.

State Trials, ed. David Thomas (1972), 2 vols.

Statutes of the Realm (1810–28), 11 vols.

Strafford, Thomas Wentworth, Earl of. *Letters and Dispatches of the Earl of Strafford,* ed. William Knowler (1739), 2 vols.

Strauss, Ralph. *The Unspeakable Curll Being Some Account of Edmund Curll, Bookseller, to which is added a full list of his books* (1927).

Stubbes, Phillip. *The Anatomy of Abuses . . .* (1583).

Swift, Jonathan. *The Works of Jonathan Swift . . .,* notes and introduction by Sir Walter Scott, (2nd ed., 1883), 19 vols.

Touchet, James. *The Memoirs of James Lord Audley, Earl of Castlehaven His Engagement and Carriage in the Wars of Ireland . . .* (1680; repr. 1684 as *The Earl of Castlehaven's Review*).

Touchet, James. *A Remonstrance of the Right Hon. James, Earl of Castlehaven and Lord Audley Concerning His Imprisonment in Dublin and Escape from Thence* (Waterford, 1643).

The Trial and Condemnation of Mervin Lord Audley Earl of Castle-haven at Westminster, April the 5th (sic). *For Abetting a Rape upon His Countess, Committing Sodomy with His Servants, and Commanding and Countenancing the Debauching His Daughter . . .* (1699).

The Trial and Condemnation of Several Reputed Sodomites . . . (1707).

The Trial of Mervin Lord Audley, Earl of Castlehaven for a Rape and Sodomy . . . (1719).

The Trial of the Lord Audley, Earl of Castlehaven for Inhumanely Causing His Own Wife to be Ravished and for Buggery (1679).

Two Elizabethan Women, ed. Alison Wall, Wiltshire Record Society, vol. 34 (1983).

Verney, Frances P., and Margaret M. *Memoirs of the Verney Family during the Seventeenth Century* (1907), 2 vols.

Warburton, H. P. I. *A Selection of Leading Cases in the Criminal Law* (1897).

Whitelocke, Bulstrode. *Memorials of the English Affairs* (Oxford, 1853), 4 vols.

Wigmore, John Henry. *Evidence in Trials at Common Law,* rev. James H. Chadbourn (4th ed., 1979), 10 vols.

Wiltshire County Records: Minutes of the Proceedings in Sessions . . ., ed. H. C. Johnson, Wiltshire Archaeological and Natural History Society Record Branch, vol. 4 (1948).

The Winthrop Papers Collections of the Massachusetts Historical Society, 1863, 4th ser., vol. 6 (1863).

Wood, Lambert. *Florus Anglicus or an Exact History of England* (1658).

Wood, Lambert. *Life and Reign of King Charles . . .* (1659).

Wotton, Sir Henry. *A Panegyrick of King Charles, being observations upon the inclination, life and government of our Sovereign Lord the King* (1633; first trans., 1649).

Yonge, Walter. *Diary of Walter Yonge,* ed. George Roberts (1848).

Secondary Sources

Adamson, J. S. A. "The Baronial Context of the English Civil War." *Transactions of the Royal Historical Society,* 5th ser., vol. 40 (1990): 93–120.

Amussen, Susan Dwyer. *An Ordered Society: Gender and Class in Early Modern England* (Oxford, 1988).

Amussen, Susan Dwyer. "'Being Stirred to Much Unquietness': Violence and Domestic Violence in Early Modern England." *Journal of Women's History* 6, no. 2 (1994): 70–89.

Amussen, Susan Dwyer. "'The Part of a Christian Man': The Cultural Politics of Manhood in Early Modern England." In Susan Dwyer Amussen and Mark A. Kishlansky, eds., *Political Culture and the Culture of Politics: Essays Presented to David Underdown* (Manchester, 1995), pp. 213–32.

Andrew, Donna T. "'Adultery a-la-Mode': Privilege, the Law and Attitudes to Adultery 1770–1809." *History* 72 (1997): 5–23.

Ashbee, Henry S. [Pisanus Fraxi], *Index Librorum Prohibitorum being Notes Biographical Bibiliographical Iconographical and Critical on Curious and Uncommon Books*, reprinted as the *Encyclopedia of Erotic Literature* (New York, 1962), 3 vols.

Aveling, J. C. H. *The Handle and the Axe: Catholic Recusants in England from the Reformation to the Emancipation* (1976).

Bahlman, W. R. Dudley. *The Moral Revolution of 1688* (New Haven, 1957).

Baines, Barbara J. "Effacing Rape in Early Modern Representations." *English Literary History* 65 (1998): 69–98.

Barker-Benfield, G. J. *The Culture of Sensibility: Sex and Society in Eighteenth-Century Britain* (Chicago, 1992).

Barnard, T. C. "Crises of Identity Among Irish Protestants 1641–1685." *Past and Present* 127 (1990): 39–83.

Bashar, Nazife. "Rape in England between 1550 and 1700." In London Feminist History Group, ed., *The Sexual Dynamics of History* (1983), pp. 33–40.

Bellany, Alastair. "'Rayling Rymes and Vaunting Verse': Libellous Politics in Early Stuart England." In Kevin Sharpe and Peter Lake, eds., *Culture and Politics in Early Stuart England* (Stanford, 1993), pp. 285–310.

Bellany, Alastair. "The Poisoning of Legitimacy? Court Scandal, News Culture and Politics in England, 1603–1660." Unpublished Ph.D. diss. (Princeton University, 1995).

Bergeron, David. *Royal Family, Royal Lovers: King James of England and Scotland* (Columbia, Mo., 1991).

Bingham, Caroline. "Seventeenth-Century Attitudes Toward Deviant Sex," with comment by Bruce Mazlish. *Journal of Interdisciplinary History* 1 (1971): 447–72.

Boswell, John. "Revolutions, Universals and Sexual Categories." In Martin Bauml Duberman, Martha Vicinus, and George Chauncey Jr., eds. *Hidden from History: Reclaiming the Gay and Lesbian Past* (New York, 1989), pp. 17–36.

Boyer, Allen D. "Sir Edward Coke, Ciceronianus: Classical Rhetoric and the Common Law Tradition." *International Journal for the Semiotics of Law* 10, no. 28 (1997): 3–36.

Bray, Alan. *Homosexuality in Renaissance England* (1982).

Bray, Alan. "Homosexuality and the Signs of Male Friendship in Elizabethan England." In Jonathan Goldberg, ed., *Queering the Renaissance* (Durham, N.C., 1994), pp. 40–61.

Bray, Alan. "To Be a Man in Early Modern Society: The Curious Case of Michael Wigglesworth." *History Workshop Journal* 41 (1996): 155–66.

Breasted, Barbara. "'Comus' and the Castlehaven Scandal." *Milton Studies* 3 (1971): 201–24.

Brewer, John. *The Pleasures of the Imagination: English Culture in the Eighteenth Century.* (New York, 1997).

Brooks, Peter, and Paul Gewirtz, eds. *Law's Stories: Narrative and Rhetoric in the Law* (New Haven, 1996).

Brooks, Richard. "Marital Consent in Rape." *Criminal Law Review* (December 1989): 877–87.

Brown, Cedric C. *John Milton's Aristocratic Entertainments* (Cambridge, 1985).

Burnett, Mark Thornton. *Masters and Servants in English Renaissance Drama and Culture: Authority and Obedience* (1997).

Chandler, James, Arnold I. Davidson, and Harry Harootunian, eds. *Questions of Evidence: Proof, Practice and Persuasion across the Disciplines* (Chicago, 1994).

Chaytor, Miranda. "Husband(ry): Narratives of Rape in the Seventeenth Century." *Gender & History* 7, no. 3 (1995): 378–407.

Chettle, Lt. Col. H. F. "The Successive Houses at Fonthill." In *Wiltshire Archeological & Natural History Magazine* 49 (1942): 505–12.

Clark, G. Kitson. *The Critical Historian* (New York, 1967).

Clarke, Aidan. "Sir Piers Crosby, 1590–1646: Wentworth's 'tawney ribbon.'" *Irish Historical Studies* 26, no. 102 (1988): 142–60.

Claydon, Tony. *William III and the Godly Revolution* (Cambridge, 1996).

Cogswell, Thomas. *The Blessed Revolution: English Politics and the Coming of War, 1621–24* (Cambridge, 1989).

Cope, Esther S. *Handmaid of the Holy Spirit: Dame Eleanor Davies, Never Soe Mad a Ladie* (Ann Arbor, 1992).

Courteaux, Theodore. *Histoire Genealogique de la Maison de Touchet . . .* (Paris, 1910).

Coward, Barry. *The Stanleys, Lords Stanley and Earls of Derby 1385–1672: The Origins, Wealth and Power of a Landowning Family* (Manchester for the Chetham Society, 1983).

Cranfield, G. A. *The Development of the Provincial Newspaper 1700–1760* (Oxford, 1962).

Creaser, John. "Milton's 'Comus': The Irrelevance of the Castlehaven Scandal." *Milton Quarterly* 21 (1987): 24–34; reprinted from *Notes & Queries,* n.s. 31 (1984): 307–17.

Cressy, David. *Birth, Marriage and Death: Ritual, Religion and the Life-Cycle in Tudor and Stuart England* (Oxford, 1997).

Croft, Pauline. "The Reputation of Robert Cecil: Libels, Political Opinion and Popular Awareness in the Early Seventeenth Century." *Transactions of the Royal Historical Society,* 6th ser., 1 (1991): 43–69.

Cust, Richard. "Honour and Politics in Early Stuart England: The case of Beaumont vs. Hastings," *Past & Present* 149 (1995):57–94.

Cust, Richard. "News and Politics in Early Seventeenth-Century England." *Past & Present* 112 (1986): 60–90.

Cust, Richard. *The Forced Loan and English Politics 1626–1628* (Oxford, 1987).

Cust, Richard, and Ann Hughes, eds. *Conflict in Early Stuart England: Studies in Religion and Politics 1603–1642* (1989).

Davenport-Hines, Richard. *Sex, Death and Punishment: Attitudes to Sex and Sexuality in Britain Since the Renaissance* (1990).

Davies, Kathleen M. "Continuity and Change in Literary Advice in Marriage." In R. B. Outhwaite, ed., *Marriage and Society* (1981), pp. 58–80.

Davis, Natalie Zemon. *The Return of Martin Guerre* (1983).

Davis, Natalie Zemon. *Fiction in the Archives: Pardon Tales and Their Tellers in Sixteenth-Century France* (Stanford, 1987).

Davis, Natalie Zemon. "On the Lame." *American Historical Review* 93, no. 3 (1988): 572–603.

Dening, Greg. *Performances* (Chicago, 1996).

Devereux, Simon. "The City and the Sessions Paper: 'Public Justice' in London, 1770–1800." *Journal of British Studies* 35, no. 4 (1996): 466–503.

Diekhoff, John S., ed. *A Maske at Ludlow: Essays on Milton's Comus* (Cleveland: The Press of Case Western Reserve University, 1968).

Dodd, Rev. Charles. *Dodd's Church History of England from the Commencement of the Sixteenth Century to the Revolution of 1688* (fasc. repr., New York, 1971), 5 vols.

Dolan, Frances. *Domestic Familiars: Representations of Domestic Crime in England 1550–1700* (Ithaca, 1994).

Donaldson, Ian. *The Rapes of Lucretia: A Myth and Its Transformation* (Oxford, 1982).

Drake, Sir William. *Fasciculus Mervinensis being notes Historical Geneological and Hearaldic of the Family of Mervyn* (1873).

Dunlop, Robert. "An Unpublished Survey of the Plantation of Munster in 1622." *Journal of the Royal Society of Antiquaries of Ireland* 54 (1924): 128–46.

Eley, Geoff. "Is All the World a Text?" In Terrence J. McDonald, ed., *The Historic Turn in the Human Sciences* (Ann Arbor, 1996), pp. 193–244.

Elton, G. R. *Policy and Police: The Enforcement of the Reformation in the Age of Thomas Cromwell* (Cambridge, 1972).

Elton, G. R. *The Parliament of England 1559–1581* (Cambridge, 1986).

Falk, Bernard. *The Bridgewater Millions: A Candid Family History* (1942).

Faller, Lincoln. *Turned to Account: The Forms and Functions of Criminal Biography in Late Seventeenth and Early Eighteenth Century England* (Cambridge, 1987).

Faller, Lincoln. *Crime and Defoe: A New Kind of Writing* (Cambridge, 1993).

Farber, Daniel A., and Suzanna Sherry, "Telling Stories Out of School: An Essay on Legal Narratives." *Stanford Law Review* 65, no. 4 (1993): 807–57.

Finley, Robert. "The Refashioning of Martin Guerre." *American Historical Review* 93, no. 3 (1988): 553–71.

Fletcher, Anthony. *Gender, Sex and Subordination in England 1500–1800* (1995).

Fogle, French R. *Patronage in Late Renaissance England* (William Andrews Clark Memorial Library, 1983).

Fox, Adam. "Rumor, News and Popular Political Opinion in Elizabethan and Early Stuart England." *The Historical Journal* 40, no. 3 (1997): 597–620.

Foyster, Elizabeth. "A Laughing Matter? Marital Discord and Gender Control in Seventeenth-Century England." *Rural History* 4, no. 1 (1993): 5–21.

Freist, Dagmar. *Governed by Opinion: Politics, Religion and the Dynamics of Communication in Stuart London 1637–1645* (1997).

Gardiner, Samuel Rawson. *A History of England from the Accession of James I to the Outbreak of the Civil War* (1893), 10 vols.

Gaskill, Malcolm. "Reporting Murder: Fiction in the Archives in Early Modern England." *Social History* 23, no. 1 (1998): 1–30.

Geis, Gilbert. "Rape-in-Marriage: Law and Law Reform in England, the United States and Sweden." *Adelaide Law Review* 6 (1977/78): 284–303.

Geis, Gilbert. "Lord Hale, Witches and Rape." *British Journal of Law and Society* 5 (1978): 26–44.

Geis, Gilbert and Ivan Bunn. *A Trial of Witches: A Seventeenth-Century Witchcraft Prosecution* (1997).

Ginzburg, Carlo. *The Cheese and the Worms: The Cosmos of a Sixteenth-Century Miller* (Baltimore, 1980).

Goldberg, Jonathan. *Sodometries* (Stanford, 1992).

Gossett, Suzanne. "'Best Men Are Molded out of Faults': Marrying the Rapist in Jacobean Drama." *English Literary Renaissance* 14, no. 3 (1984): 305–27.

Gowing, Laura. *Domestic Dangers: Women, Words and Sex in Early Modern London* (Oxford, 1996).

Green, Thomas Andrew. *Verdict According to Conscience* (Chicago, 1985).

Halperin, David M. "Is There a History of Sexuality?" In Henry Abelove, Michele Barale, and David M. Halperin, eds., *The Lesbian and Gay Studies Reader* (1992), pp. 416–30.

Harris, Michael. "Trials and Criminal Biographies: A Case Study in Distribution." In Robin Myers and Michael Harris, eds., *Sale and Distribution of Books from 1700* (Oxford, 1982), pp. 1–36.

Harris, Tim. *London Crowds in the Reign of Charles II: Propaganda and Politics from the Restoration to the Exclusion Crisis* (Cambridge, 1987).

Havran, Martin J. *Caroline Courtier: The Life of Lord Cottington* (1973).

Hayton, D. "Moral Reform and Country Politics in the Late Seventeenth Century House of Commons." *Past and Present* 128 (1990): 48–91.

Herrup, Cynthia. *The Common Peace: Participation and the Criminal Law in Seventeenth-Century England* (Cambridge, 1987).

Herrup, Cynthia. "The Patriarch at Home: The Trial of the Second Earl of Castlehaven for Rape and Sodomy." *History Workshop Journal* 41 (1996): 1–19.

Herrup, Cynthia. "'To Pluck Bright Honour from the Pale-Faced Moon': Gender and Honour in the Castlehaven Story." *Transactions of the Royal Historical Society*, 6th ser., 6 (1996): 137–59.

Hibbard, Caroline. *Charles I and the Popish Plot* (Chapel Hill, 1983).

Hicks, Philip. *Neoclassical History and English Culture: From Clarendon to Hume* (1996).

Hill, Christopher. *Intellectual Origins of the English Revolution Revisited* (Oxford, 1997).

Hill, George. *An Historical Account of the Plantation in Ulster at the Commencement of the Seventeenth Century 1608–1620* (Belfast, 1877; repr. Shannon, 1970).

Hitchcock, Tim. *English Sexualities 1700–1800* (New York, 1997).

Hoare, Sir Richard Colt. *History of Modern Wiltshire* (1822–43), 6 vols.

Hodgkin, Katharine. "Thomas Whythorne and the Problems of Mastery." *History Workshop Journal* 29 (1990): 20–41.

Houlbrooke, Ralph. *The English Family 1450–1700* (1984).

Hunter, Michael. "The Problem of 'Atheism' in Early Modern England." *Transactions of the Royal Historical Society*, 5th ser., 35 (1985): 135–57.

Hunter, William B. *Milton's 'Comus': Family Piece* (Troy, N.Y.: Whitston, 1983).

Hutchins, John. *History and Antiquities of the County of Dorset*. 3rd ed. revised by Rev. William Shipp and James Whitworth Hodson (1861–70), 4 vols.

Hyde, H. Montgomery. *The Love That Dared Not Speak Its Name: A Candid History of Homosexuality in Britain* (Boston, 1970).

Ingram, Martin. *Church Courts, Sex and Marriage in England 1570–1640* (Cambridge, 1987).

Ingram, Martin. "Scolding Women Cucked or Washed: A Crisis in Gender Relations in Early Modern England." In J. Kermode and Garthine Walker, eds., *Women, Crime and the Courts in Early Modern England* (1994), pp. 48–80.

Jardine, Lisa. "Companionate Marriage versus Male Friendship: Anxiety for the Lineal Family in Jacobean Drama." In *Reading Shakespeare Historically* (1996), pp. 114–31.

Jardine, Lisa, and Alan Stewart. *Hostage to Fortune: The Troubled Life of Francis Bacon* (1998).

Jones, W. J. *Politics and the Bench: The Judges and the Origins of the English Civil War* (1971).

Jordan, W. K. *Edward VI: The Young King* (Cambridge, Mass., 1968–70), 2 vols.

Kellner, Hans. *Language and Historical Representation: Getting the Story Crooked* (Madison, Wis., 1989).

Kelman, Mark. *A Guide to Critical Legal Studies Reader* (Cambridge, Mass., 1987).

Kerridge, Eric. "The Revolts in Wiltshire against Charles I." *Wiltshire Archaeological & Natural History Magazine* 57 (1958–60): 64–75.

Kowaleski, Maryanne. "Singlewomen in Medieval and Early Modern Europe: The Demographic Perspective." Ch. 2 in Judith M. Bennett and Amy M. Froide, eds., *Singlewomen in the European Past 1250–1800* (Philadelphia, 1999).

Lake, Peter. "Deeds against Nature: Cheap Print, Protestantism and Murder in Early Seventeenth-Century England." In Kevin Sharpe and Peter Lake, eds., *Culture and Politics in Early Stuart England* (Stanford, 1993), pp. 257–84.

Lake, Peter, and Michael Questier. "Agency, Appropriation and Rhetoric under the Gallows: Puritans, Romanists and the State in Early Modern England." *Past & Present* 153 (1996): 65–107.

Langbein, J. H. "The Criminal Trial before the Lawyers." *University of Chicago Law Review* 45 (1978): 263–316.

Lanham, David. "Hale, Misogyny and Rape." *Criminal Law Journal* 7 (1983): 148–66.

Laqueur, T. "Crowds, Carnivals and the State in English Executions, 1604–1878." In A. L. Beier, D. Cannadine, and J. Rosenheim, eds., *The First Modern Society* (Cambridge, 1989), pp. 305–55.

"Legal Storytelling." Special issue, *Michigan Law Review* 87 (1989).

Lehmberg, Stanford. *The Reformation Parliament 1529–1536* (Cambridge, 1970).

Lesser, Wendy. *Pictures at an Execution: An Inquiry into the Subject of Murder* (Cambridge, Mass., 1993).

Levy, F. J. "How Information Spread among the Gentry 1550–1640." *Journal of British Studies* 21 (1992): 11–34.

Lindley, David. *The Trials of Frances Howard: Fact and Fiction in the Court of King James* (1993).

Linebaugh, Peter. "The Ordinary of Newgate and His Account." In J. S. Cockburn, ed., *Crime in England 1550–1800* (1977), pp. 246–69.

Loach, Jennifer. *Parliament and the Crown in the Reign of Mary Tudor* (Oxford, 1986).

Love, Harold. *Scribal Publication in Seventeenth-Century England* (Oxford, 1995).

Lowell, Colin Rhys. "The Trial of Peers in Great Britain." *American Historical Review* 55 (1949): 69–81.

Macfarlane, Alan. *The Justice and the Mare's Ale* (Cambridge, 1981).

Macgillivray, Royce. *Restoration Historians and the English Civil War* (The Hague, 1974).

Maclean, Ian. *The Renaissance Notion of Woman* (Cambridge, 1980).

Mager, Donald. "John Bale and Early Tudor Sodomy Discourse." In Jonathan Goldberg, ed., *Queering the Renaissance* (Durham, N.C., 1994), pp. 141–61.

Marcus, Leah Sinanoglou. "The Milieu of Milton's 'Comus': Judicial Reform at Ludlow and the Problem of Sexual Assault." *Criticism* 25 (1983): 293–327.

Marcus, Leah Sinanoglou. "Milton's Anti-Laudian Masque." Ch. 6 in *The Politics of Mirth* (Chicago, 1986).

Marotti, Arthur. *Manuscript, Print and the English Renaissance Lyric* (Ithaca, 1995).

Masten, Jeff. "My Two Dads: Collaboration and the Reproduction of Beaumont and Fletcher." In Jonathan Goldberg, ed., *Queering the Renaissance* (Durham, N.C., 1994), pp. 228–309.

Mayes, Charles R. "The Sale of Peerages in Early Stuart England." *Journal of Modern History* 29 (1959): 21–37.

Mayes, Charles R. "The Early Stuarts and the Irish Peerage." *English Historical Review* 73 (1958): 227–51.

McCalman, Ian. *Radical Underworld: Prophets and Pornographers in London 1795–1840* (Cambridge, 1988).

Mendelson, Sara & Crawford, Patricia. *Women in Early Modern England 1550–1720* (Oxford, 1998).

Miller, John. *Popery and Politics in England 1660–1688* (Cambridge, 1973).

Muddiman, J. G. *State Trials: The Need for a New and Revised Edition of "State Trials"* (Edinburgh, 1930).

Mundhenk, Rosemary Karmelich. "Dark Scandal and the Sun-Clad Power of Chastity: The Historical Milieu of Milton's 'Comus.'" *Studies in English Literature 1500–1900* 15 (1975): 141–52.

Newman, Peter. *Royalist Officers in England and Wales 1642–1660* (1981).

Noonan, Kathleen M. "'The Cruel Pressure of an Enraged, Barbarous People': Irish and English Identity in Seventeenth-Century Policy and Propaganda." *The Historical Journal* 41, no. 1 (1998): 151–77.

Norton, Mary Beth. *Founding Mothers and Fathers: Gendered Power and the Forming of American Society* (New York, 1996).

Norton, Rictor. *Mother Clap's Molly House: The Gay Subculture in England 1700–1830* (1992).

Ohlmeyer, Jane H. *Civil War and Restoration in the Three Stuart Kingdoms* (Cambridge, 1993).

Okie, Laird. *Augustan Historical Writing: Histories of England in the English Enlightenment* (Lanham, Md., 1991).

Orlin, Lena Cowan. *Private Matters and Public Culture in Post-Reformation England* (Ithaca, 1994).

Palmer, Francis Beaufort. *Peerage Law in England* (1907; fasc. repr., 1978).

Paster, Gail Kern. *The Body Embarrassed: Drama and the Disciplines of Shame in Early Modern England* (Ithaca, 1993).

Pevsner, N. *Middlesex: Buildings of England,* vol. 3 (Harmondsworth, 1951).

Pittenger, Elizabeth. "'To Serve the Queere': Nicholas Udall, Master of Revels." In Jonathan Goldberg, ed., *Queering the Renaissance* (Durham, N.C., 1994), pp. 162–89.

Plucknett, T. F. T. "The Rise of the English State Trial." *Politica* 2, no. 10 (1937): 542–59.

Pollock, Sir Frederick, and Frederic Maitland. *The History of the English Law before the Time of Edward I* (Cambridge reissue, 1969), 2 vols.

Pollock, Linda. "'Teach Her to Live under Obedience': The Making of Women in the Upper Ranks of Early Modern England." *Continuity and Change* 4, no. 2 (1989): 231–58.

Pollock, Linda. "Living on the Stage of the World: The Concept of Privacy Among the Elite of Early Modern England." In Adrian Wilson, ed., *Rethinking Social History* (1993), pp. 78–95.

Pollock, Linda. "Rethinking Patriarchy and the Family in Seventeenth-Century England." *Journal of Family History* 23, no. 1 (1998): 3–27.

Pollock, Linda. "Domestic Dissidence: Women against Women/Women against Men in the Early Modern Elite Home" (unpublished paper).

Porter, Roy. "Mixed Feelings: The Enlightenment and Sexuality in Eighteenth-Century Britain." In Paul Bouce, ed., *Sexuality in Eighteenth-Century Britain* (Manchester, 1982), pp. 1–27.

Powell, C. L. *English Domestic Relations 1487–1653* (New York, 1917).

Powell, William S. *John Pory: The Life and Letters of a Man of Many Parts* (Chapel Hill, 1977).

Prest, Wilfred. "Hale as Husband." *Journal of Legal History* 14, no. 2 (1993): 142–44.

Quaife, G. R. *Wanton Wenches and Wayward Wives: Peasants and Illicit Sex in Early Seventeenth Century England* (New Brunswick, 1979).

Reeve, L. J. *Charles I and the Road to Personal Rule* (Cambridge, 1989).

Richards, Judith. "'His Nowe Majestie' and the English Monarchy: The Kingship of Charles I before 1640." *Past & Present* 118 (1986): 70–96.

Robinson, Philip. "British Settlement in County Tyrone 1610–1666." *Irish Economic and Social History* 5 (1978): 5–26.

Rogers, Nicholas. "Piggot's Private Eye: Radicalism and Sexual Scandal in Eighteenth-Century England." *Journal of the Canadian Historical Association,* n.s., 4 (1993): 247–63.

Rose, Craig. "Providence, Protestant Union and Godly Reformation in the 1690s." *Transactions of the Royal Historical Society,* 6th ser., 3 (1993): 151–69.

Russell, C. S. *The Fall of the British Monarchies 1637–1642* (Oxford, 1991).

Rutter, John. *Delineations of Fonthill and Its Abbey* (Shaftesbury, 1823).

Schama, Simon. *Dead Certainties (Unwarranted Speculations)* (New York, 1991).

Schochet, Gordon J. *The Authoritarian Family and Political Attitudes in Seventeenth-Century England* (1988).

Shagan, Ethan Howard. "Constructing Discord: Ideology, Propaganda, and English Responses to the Irish Rebellion of 1641." *Journal of British Studies* 36, no. 1 (1997): 4–34.

Shapin, Steven. *A Social History of Truth: Civility and Science in Seventeenth-Century England* (Chicago, 1994).

Sharp, Buchanan. *In Contempt of All Authority* (Berkeley, 1980).

Sharpe, J. A. "Domestic Homicide in Early Modern England." *Historical Journal* 24, no. 1 (1981): 29–48.

Sharpe, J. A. "'Last Dying Speeches': Religion, Ideology and Public Executions in Seventeenth-Century England." *Past & Present* 107 (1985): 144–67.

Sharpe, Kevin. *The Personal Rule of Charles I* (1992).

Sharpe, Kevin. "Private Conscience and Public Duty in the Writings of Charles I." *The Historical Journal* 40, no. 3 (1997): 643–65.

Simpson, Anthony. "Masculinity and Control: The Prosecution of Sex Offenses in Eighteenth-Century London." Unpublished Ph.d. diss. (New York University, 1984).

Smith, Bruce. *Homosexual Desire in Shakespeare's England: A Cultural Poetics* (Chicago, 1991).

Smuts, R. Malcolm. *Court Culture and the Origins of a Royalist Tradition in Early Stuart England* (Philadelphia, 1987).

Somers, Margaret R. "Narrativity, Narrative Identity and Social Action: Rethinking English Working Class Formation." *Social Science History* 16, no. 4 (1992): 591–630.

Somerset, Anne. *Unnatural Murder: Poison at the Court of King James I* (1997).

Spencer, Colin. *Homosexuality: A History* (1995).

Spiegel, Gabrielle. "History, Historicism, and the Social Logic of the Text in the Middle Ages." *Speculum* 65 (1990): 59–86.

Stephen, James Fitzjames. *A History of the Criminal Law of England* (1883; fasc. repr., 1996), 3 vols.

Stephen, Leslie. *Hours in a Library* (New York, 1875), 3 vols.

Stewart, Alan. *Close Readers: Humanism and Sodomy in Early Modern England* (Princeton, 1997).

Stone, Lawrence. *The Crisis of the Aristocracy 1558–1641* (Oxford, 1965).

Stone, Lawrence. *The Family, Sex and Marriage in England 1500–1800* (New York, 1977).

Stone, Lawrence. *Road to Divorce: England 1530–1987* (Oxford, 1990).

Trumbach, Randolph. *Sex and the Gender Revolution: Heterosexuality and the Third Gender in Enlightenment London.* (Chicago, 1998).

Trumbach, Randolph. "The Birth of the Queen: Sodomy and the Emergence of Gender Equality in Modern Culture, 1660–1750." In Martin Bauml Duberman, Martha Vicinus, and George Chauncey Jr., eds., *Hidden from History: Reclaiming the Gay and Lesbian Past* (New York, 1989), pp. 129–40.

Trumbach, Randolph. "Sodomy Transformed: Aristocratic Libertinage, Public Reputation and the Gender Revolution of the Eighteenth Century." *Journal of Homosexuality* 19 (1990): 105–24.

Underdown, David. *Revel, Riot and Rebellion: Popular Politics and Culture in England 1603–1660* (Oxford, 1985).

Underdown, David. "The Taming of the Scold: The Enforcement of Patriarchal Authority in Early Modern England." In A. J. Fletcher and John Stevenson, eds., *Order and Disorder in Early Modern England* (Cambridge, 1985), pp. 116–36.

Underdown, David. *A Freeborn People: Politics and the Nation in Seventeenth-Century England* (Oxford, 1996).

Victoria History of the Counties of England (1900–ongoing).

Wagner, Peter. "The Pornographer in the Courtroom: Trial Reports about Cases of Sexual Crimes and Delinquencies as a Genre of Eighteenth-Century Erotica." In Paul Bouce, ed., *Sexuality in Eighteenth-Century Britain* (Manchester, 1982), pp. 120–40.

Walker, Garthine. "Rereading Rape and Sexual Violence in Early Modern England." *Gender & History* 10, no. 1 (1998): 1–25.

Wall, Alison. "The Wiltshire Commission of the Peace 1590–1620: A Study of its Social Structure." Unpublished master's thesis (University of Melbourne, 1966).

Wall, Alison. "For Love, Money or Politics? A Clandestine Marriage and the Elizabethan Court of Arches." *The Historical Journal* 38, no. 3 (1995): 511–33.

Walsham, Alexandra. *Church Papists: Catholicism, Conformity, and Confessional Polemic in Early Modern England* (Woodbridge, 1993).

Weil, Rachel. "Sometimes a Scepter Is Only a Scepter: Pornography and Politics in Restoration England." In Lynn Hunt, ed., *The Invention of Pornography* (New York, 1993), pp. 125–53.

Weil, Rachel. *Gender, the Family and Political Argument in England 1680–1714* (Manchester, forthcoming).

White, Beatrice. *A Cast of Ravens: The Strange Case of Thomas Overbury* (1965).

White, Hayden. *The Content of the Form: Narrative Discourse and Historical Representation* (Baltimore, 1987).

White, James Boyd. *Heracles' Bow: Essays on the Rhetoric and Poetics of the Law* (Madison, 1985).

Wiles, R. M. *Serial Publication in England before 1750* (Cambridge, 1957).

Wiles, R. M. *Freshest Advices: Early Provincial Newspapers in England* (Columbus, 1965).

Williams, Patricia J. *The Alchemy of Race and Rights* (Cambridge, Mass., 1991).

Wiltenburg, Joy. *Disorderly Women and Female Power in the Street Literature of Early Modern England and Germany* (Charlottesville, 1992).

Woodbridge, Linda. *Women and the English Renaissance: Literature and the Nature of Womenkind 1540–1620* (Urbana, 1986).

Woudhuysen, H. R. *Sir Philip Sidney and the Circulation of Manuscripts 1558–1640* (Oxford, 1996).

Wrigley, E. A., and R. S. Schofield. *The Population History of England 1541–1871* (1981).

Zwicker, Steven. *Lines of Authority: Politics and English Literary Culture 1649–1689* (Ithaca, 1993).

INDEX